Professional Writing
for Social Work Practice

Daniel Weisman, MSW, PhD, is a professor at Rhode Island College School of Social Work and former chair of the Bachelor of Social Work Department. He directs Rhode Island College's Applied Research and Training Project, is co-principal investigator/evaluator, Project Restore, Rhode Island Office of Child Support Services, and evaluates programs for several Rhode Island state departments, as well as private non-profit agencies in several states. He is a certified site visitor for the Council on Social Work Education. Dr. Weisman has co-authored two other books, written chapters in several anthologies, and published articles in social work and labor studies journals.

Joseph L. Zornado, PhD, is a professor of English at Rhode Island College and is the director of the Faculty Center for Teaching and Learning. He teaches Children's Literature, Literature and Film, American Literature, Zen and Literature, and many more. Zornado has published two novels, an academic monograph, numerous scholarly articles, essays, reviews, poetry, blogs, website content, tweets, posts, and other forms of electronic writings. He published his first scholarly book, *Inventing the Child: Culture, Ideology and the Story of Childhood* in 2001 with Routledge. Still in print and critically acclaimed, *Inventing the Child* was issued as a paperback in 2006. A Korean translation appeared in the spring of 2011. His two novels are works of futurist speculation in the spirit of Orwell and Huxley and are published by Iron Diesel Press. The third and final volume of this trilogy will be published in 2014. He lives in Connecticut with his wife and their three children.

Professional Writing for Social Work Practice

DANIEL WEISMAN, MSW, PhD

JOSEPH L. ZORNADO, PhD

SPRINGER PUBLISHING COMPANY

NEW YORK

Springer Publishing Company, LLC
11 West 42nd Street
New York, NY 10036
www.springerpub.com

Acquisitions Editor: Sheri W. Sussman
Production Editor: Michael O'Connor
Composition: Absolute Service, Inc.

ISBN: 978-0-8261-0926-2
E-book ISBN: 978-0-8261-0927-9
Student Workbook ISBN: 978-0-8261-9999-7

The Student Workbook is available for download from www.springerpub.com/weisman-workbook

13 14 15 16 / 5 4

The author and the publisher of this Work have made every effort to use sources believed to be reliable to provide information that is accurate and compatible with the standards generally accepted at the time of publication. The author and publisher shall not be liable for any special, consequential, or exemplary damages resulting, in whole or in part, from the readers' use of, or reliance on, the information contained in this book. The publisher has no responsibility for the persistence or accuracy of URLs for external or third-party Internet websites referred to in this publication and does not guarantee that any content on such websites is, or will remain, accurate or appropriate.

Library of Congress Cataloging-in-Publication Data

Weisman, Daniel.
  Professional writing for social work practice / Daniel Weisman and Joseph L. Zornado.
    p. cm.
  Includes bibliographical references.
  ISBN 978-0-8261-0926-2 — ISBN 978-0-8261-0927-9 (ebook)
  1. Communication in social work. 2. Social case work reporting. 3. Communication in social work—Case studies. 4. Social case work reporting—Case studies. I. Zornado, Joseph L. II. Title.
  HV29.7.W45 2012
  808.06'6361--dc23
                          2012037737

Special discounts on bulk quantities of our books are available to corporations, professional associations, pharmaceutical companies, health care organizations, and other qualifying groups.
If you are interested in a custom book, including chapters from more than one of our titles, we can provide that service as well.

For details, please contact:
Special Sales Department, Springer Publishing Company, LLC
11 West 42nd Street, 15th Floor, New York, NY 10036-8002
Phone: 877-687-7476 or 212-431-4370; Fax: 212-941-7842
Email: sales@springerpub.com

Printed in the United States of America by Gasch Printing.

To our families:
Vivian, Lori, Merith, Debbie, Emily, Clara, and Jack.
To all our students over almost 50 combined years
at Rhode Island College, who inspired this book.

Contents

Preface   ix
Acknowledgments   xvii
To the Reader   xix

PART I: INTRODUCTION   *1*

1. "The Jones Family"—Self-Assessment   *3*

PART II HBSE, SOCIAL WORK PRACTICE, AND SOCIAL POLICY   *11*

2. Human Behavior in the Social Environment (HBSE)   *17*
  Cases
    1   Family Assessment: The Driver Family   *18*
    2   Children at Risk: The Gramme Family   *25*
    3   Medical Social Work Intake: Hospital-Setting Health, Mental Health, and Substance Abuse Issues   *29*
    4   Corrections: Parole-Readiness Report   *34*
    5   Mental Health: Integrated Summary of Care   *40*
    6   School Social Work: Social Assessment   *45*
    7   Organizational Assessment: Tender Mercies Homeless Shelter   *55*
    8   Community Needs Assessment: Deaf and Hard-of-Hearing Residents   *60*

3. Social Work Practice   *67*
  Cases
    9   Individual Social History: James—Mental Health and Substance Involvement   *68*
    10   Family Social History: Adjudicated Family With Multiple Issues   *73*
    11   Emergency Motion: Child Neglect   *80*
    12   Emergency Motion: Family Court   *84*
    13   Crisis Planning: Psychotic Episode   *89*
    14   Annual Treatment Plan: Mental Health Diagnoses   *92*
    15   Disabilities: Client Progress Notes   *97*
    16   Disabilities: Status Notes and Progress Notes   *101*

4. Social Policy   *109*
>   Cases
>   Press Releases and News Coverage   *110*
>   17   Press Release: Public Announcement of a Grant   *114*
>   Letters to (Newspaper) Editors   *117*
>   18   A Letter to the Editor: Daily Newspaper—Giveaways to the Rich Don't Work   *118*
>   19   Weekly Newspaper: State Constitutional Convention   *122*
>   20   Advocacy Letter: Same-Sex Marriage   *126*
>   Written (and Oral) Testimony at Hearings   *129*
>   21   Domestic Partner Health Benefits Bill   *130*

PART III AGENCY-BASED WRITING: WRITING, RESEARCH REPORTS, GRANTS, AND LETTERS   *135*

5. Writing Research Reports   *137*
>   Cases
>   22   Client Report Using Frequency Distributions: Project Restore   *142*
>   23   Survey Report to the State Legislature: Gun Ownership and Domestic Violence   *159*
>   24   Satisfaction Survey of BSW Students at a Social Work Program: Report and Executive Summary   *166*
>   Focus Group Reports   *178*
>   25   Focus Group Report: Parents and Teachers Program   *179*
>   26   Reporting Research Results to Influence Social Policy: The Fredonia Estate Tax   *190*

6. Grant Writing   *199*
>   Cases
>   27   Grant Application: Small Religious or Family Foundations   *203*
>   28   Letter to a Private Foundation   *209*
>   29   Letter Soliciting a Grant From a For-Profit Corporation   *216*
>   30   Application for a New Grant From a State Department ($120,000)   *221*

7. Letters   *231*
>   31   Agency Letter to a Client   *232*
>   32   Thank-You Letter to a State Department   *236*
>   33   E-mail List Call to Action   *238*
>   34   Letter of Agreement   *242*
>   35   Letter From a Private Agency to a State Agency   *246*
>   36   Letter of Support for a Grant Application   *250*
>   37   Thank-You Letter to a Politician   *254*

Appendix A: Glossary of Writing and Writing Errors   *259*
Appendix B: Resumés and Cover Letters   *297*
>   *Cover Letter*   *300*
>   *Resumé*   *301*
Index   *303*

Preface

Why do we need another book on writing for social work practice? In order to answer this question, we will begin with a review of some challenges that arise every day in social work practice, and all human service settings. Then we will explain how this book addresses the need for improved writing skills for the full range of practice settings in which social workers are employed, using an approach that corresponds with the ways most adults learn. We will conclude with some ideas for making best use of this book.

WHY DO WE NEED ANOTHER BOOK ON WRITING FOR SOCIAL WORK PRACTICE?

Picture these true scenarios.

- You are a social worker at a mental health center and you are asked for a letter of support for a grant that would provide expanded evening and weekend programs for your clients.
- You work at a homeless shelter, and a client's application for subsidized housing requires a reference letter.
- The nursing home you work in asks you to compose and mail out a recruitment notice for a new family support group.
- As facilitator of a parenting skills group, your case notes are subpoenaed by family court, which is hearing a petition for the state to take custody of the children of one of your group members.
- At the counseling and family service center where you are a case manager, a client fails to show up for three consecutive appointments. You are worried about his well-being, but he has no home phone. You need to send him a letter.
- The state legislature is considering a bill that would eliminate Medicaid eligibility for children of families with less than five years of residency in your state, including some in your caseload. You know your experiences with immigrants and other recent arrivals could help lawmakers make an informed decision.

- Your supervisor sends you to an interagency coalition about unmet service needs facing low-income people in your city or town, and then asks you to write a brief report of the meeting, for distribution to the full staff.
- You work in an after-school program for children from low-income families, and hear about availability of small grants for recreational equipment. All you have to do is write to the foundation with an explanation of what you would do with the grant, and how it would be helpful.

The last example happened during the lead author's first six months out of social work school. With no guidelines, he wrote a brief letter asking for photographic supplies so his group members could learn photography and develop some positive peer-group skills. About a month later, he received notification that the group had been awarded the grant.

All eight examples, and thousands more like them (and unlike them), occur every day. As you looked at the list, did you experience any concerns about your own ability to rise to the challenge? You should, because these are not easy tasks. You have to gather and sort through the necessary information, decide what to include and omit, put it in logical order, convey it in appropriate language, and get it on paper (or computer screen) in (gulp) error-free writing. We have found that getting what you know down on paper—or into your computer—is more challenging to many of our students than the previous four tasks combined.

This is a book about writing for generalist social work practice. BSWs and MSWs are employed in a wide range of settings, requiring all kinds of writing: case notes, progress notes, assessments, incident reports, case summaries, op-ed essays, press releases, research reports, meeting minutes, grant applications, and letters to various agencies, clients, courts, and newspapers. This is only a partial list. In the lead author's 40-plus-year career as a social worker, he cannot recall a single day that he did not have to write something related to practice that someone else would read at some point, with potential consequences for others.

In spite of how much writing social workers need to do, when students ask for a resource to help with their writing, we are at a loss. There are books about the kinds of writing social workers do to record our work with individuals and families, but there are no books about writing for the broader range of settings, roles, and purposes that we encounter, even if we practice in a small social service system. As the list above illustrates, our need to write competently extends well beyond client files. Further, students' need for writing instruction extends beyond simply learning the "platforms" (outlines agencies use). Nearly all of our students need instruction related to sentence structure, punctuation, word usage, spelling, and general principles about how best to organize information. This book addresses those needs. In it you will find instruction about the basic writing skills required for human service work, with examples from several practice settings with various kinds of client systems.

A member of the Commission on Social Work Practice (CSWE), a career gerontologist, commented about her frequent messages to students doing field work in her agency: "If you cannot write it competently and accurately, it did not happen, either for the client or the agency." Students do not take the message very seriously. When they hear it from their field supervisors, however, students begin to understand the close link between writing skills and professional success. For that reason, we anchored this book in agency settings. Most of the case scenarios presented in this book came from field supervisors and other full-time practitioners. A few came from our own experiences.

According to the National Association of Social Work (NASW) Code of Ethics:

> The primary mission of the social work profession is to enhance human well-being and help meet the basic human needs of all people, with particular attention to the needs and empowerment of people who are vulnerable, oppressed, and living in poverty. A historic and defining feature of social work is the profession's focus on individual well-being in a social context and the well-being of society. Fundamental to social work is attention to the environmental forces that create, contribute to, and address problems in living. (http://www.naswdc.org/pubs/code/code.asp)

Consider the four components of our primary mission:
- Enhance human well-being
- Help meet basic needs
- Empower people who are vulnerable, oppressed, and living in poverty
- Address environmental forces

None of these purposes can occur without keeping written records of our work and communicating our insights to others. In the narrowest sense, we can help "meet basic needs" temporarily, but the purpose of the profession is to enhance the human condition, which requires written communication among social worker practitioners, between practitioners and clients, and between practitioners and society.

Furthermore, the NASW Code of Ethics delineates social workers' ethical responsibility to maintain client records (3.04 Client Records):

1. Social workers should take reasonable steps to ensure that documentation in records are accurate and reflect the services provided.
2. Social workers should include sufficient and timely documentation in records to facilitate the delivery of services and to ensure continuity of services provided to clients in the future.
3. Social workers' documentation should protect clients' privacy to the extent that is possible and appropriate and should include only information that is directly relevant to the delivery of services.
4. Social workers should store records following the termination of services to ensure reasonable future access. Records should be maintained for the number of years required by state statutes or relevant contracts.

Maintaining client records is a component of one ethical standard (#3). There are five additional standards. A look at the full list of six ethical standards comprising the Code confirms the importance of competent written communication:

1. Responsibilities to clients
2. Responsibilities to colleagues
3. Responsibilities in practice settings

4. Responsibilities as professionals
5. Responsibilities to the profession
6. Responsibilities to the broader society

All of these basic responsibilities comprise our identity as a social work professional, and none of them can be performed without adequate written communication skills.

In recent years, documentation as a component of "risk management" has garnered considerable attention (Reamer, 2005). Risk management means protecting clients, agencies, and social workers with regard to potential and actual cases of complaints or litigation. This places a burden on social workers to document our work accurately, competently, and appropriately. What this means is that, as a social work practitioner, you must document your work with the right amount of information, and in a timely manner; you must use appropriate and precise language; and, finally, you must have the basic writing skills in order to demonstrate professional competence and credibility.

The CSWE is responsible for periodic reviews and accreditation for the approximately 700 BSW and MSW programs across the country. Among the ten "core competencies" required of degreed social workers is Educational Policy 2.1.1—*Identify as a professional social worker and conduct oneself accordingly. Social workers serve as representatives of the profession, its mission, and its core values. They know the profession's history. Social workers commit themselves to the profession's enhancement and to their own professional conduct and growth. Social workers:*

- *advocate for client access to the services of social work;*
- *practice personal reflection and self-correction to assure continual professional development;*
- *attend to professional roles and boundaries;*
- *demonstrate professional demeanor in behavior, appearance, and* **communication***;*
- *engage in career-long learning; and*
- *use supervision and consultation.*
  (emphasis added)

"Communication" is reiterated in Educational Policy 2.1.3—*Apply critical thinking to inform and* **communicate** *professional judgments. Social workers are knowledgeable about the principles of logic, scientific inquiry, and reasoned discernment. They use critical thinking augmented by creativity and curiosity. Critical thinking also requires the synthesis and* **communication of relevant information.** *Social workers*

- *distinguish, appraise, and integrate multiple sources of knowledge, including research-based knowledge, and practice wisdom;*
- *analyze models of assessment, prevention, intervention, and evaluation; and*
- ***demonstrate effective oral and written communication in working with individuals, families, groups, organizations, communities, and colleagues.***
  (CSWE, 2011; emphases added)

The social work profession recognizes the importance of writing from both ethical and practical perspectives. But what about employers? A training program for new child welfare workers in several states begins with the following statement:

> *Excellent writing skills are as important to serving children and families as a fleet of county vehicles or good foster homes. Child welfare professionals must be able to express their thoughts in descriptive, concise, and accurate terms. The keys to comprehensive and descriptive writing are good grammar, appropriate punctuation, and correct spelling. Finally, the child welfare professional must know how to construct efficient sentences and cohesive paragraphs.* (Sopko, 2000)

To these reasons, add the reality that much of social work practice must be documented to organizations who fund our efforts as well as organizations responsible for accreditation. A considerable amount of social work intervention is reimbursement-funded, meaning agencies and practitioners are paid by insurance companies and health plans, including Medicaid and/or Medicare, for services provided. Sometimes our work is contract or grant-funded, requiring periodic reports of activities and results to the funder, and sometimes there are applications requesting re-funding. Agencies that provide health, mental health, residential, and/or child care services may be subject to periodic accreditation reviews, requiring so-called "self-studies" that comprise narratives of the work and the outcomes, as well as reviews of client files. In all of these circumstances, written documentation of our work must be complete and well-written.

HOW TO USE THIS BOOK

As a teaching and learning tool, this book works with the five social work curricular sequences, so students can review writing that corresponds to content they are studying at any given time. In this way, writing can be practiced throughout the curriculum, rather than exclusively in one writing-intensive course.

If you are a student, read this book as if a field supervisor is speaking to you. Almost all the material came from social work field instructors who supervise students and employees. The field instructors all responded enthusiastically when invited to provide material because they recognize the need for social workers to write competently.

We designed this book to correspond with the ways most students learn: from the specific to the general (inductively) and in relation to practice. So, each chapter has some brief descriptive information followed by real case studies. In addition, we structured the book to correspond with the way social work education is organized: five sequences. And because "best practice" dictates that we "begin where the client is," in this case, the *client* is you, the *student*, and in the spirit of "best practice" you may begin anywhere you would like.

Those who would start at the beginning will find a self-assessment exercise with some of the most common social work writing errors, complete with corrections. The self-assessment is an actual child welfare case record infused with writing errors that cover the major writing categories. Depending on your results, you might want to consult the Glossary in Appendix A for help with those categories that give you the most trouble.

If you have a specific interest in certain social work settings or populations, you can select case studies that interest you, for example, mental health, from any combination of chapters. If you are the eclectic type, you may want to jump around and choose random case studies.

If you would rather use this book with classes or field work, either on your own or as supplemental work for your courses or placement, regardless of whether you take the self-assessment, open to the chapter that corresponds with the work in question. All of social work education is organized into five sequences:

1. Human behavior—theory and assessment
2. Practice
3. Policy
4. Research
5. Field

We have a chapter for each sequence. Each chapter contains introductory information about documentation and then a selection of case studies, along with actual documents supplied by human service agencies. We changed the names and identifying information and inserted many writing errors, followed by corrections and explanations. Numbers on the right side of the original document tell you the page location of the corresponding content in the corrected document. If you have no preference, we suggest you take the self-assessment and use this book in conjunction with your courses and placement.

As you will see, we had to make appropriate adaptations to accommodate the way social work education sequences overlap. For example, we would be the first to argue that all of social work is about practice, so the practice chapter could contain all the case studies. If we did this, however, the book's content would not correspond to different social work sequences. Instead, we organized the case studies to reflect how the sequences address and support practice:

- human behavior including assessment documents (individual clients, a community, and an organization);
- practice documentation of work done with individuals and families (mostly descriptive);
- policy documents social workers use to influence policies and organizational practices (e.g., advocacy letters);
- research reports using data and surveys, including a needs assessment based on data collected from students in a BSW program;
- organizational work, including writing that occurs in agencies such as meeting announcements and minutes, letters among agencies, or a program report; and
- grant applications for small grants (usually a narrative without a template).

Also, some scenarios cross sequences, such as the data-based report in the organizational chapter. As you review the case studies, keep in mind that most of them will be applicable to other sequences. As we said, everything is about practice.

If you are a faculty member, program director, chairperson, or dean this book can be assigned at any point in a curriculum and used by students in any or every sequence. You may want to poll your field supervisors for copies of forms used for agency documentation, so students can be prepared when they arrive at field placements and job sites. The primary purpose of this book is to help the social work practitioner develop the writing skills he or she needs to do the job as completely as possible. As a supplement to the book there is a supplemental Student Workbook made available for additional practice and study (**The Student Workbook is available for download from www.springerpub.com/weisman-workbook**). To further supplement this book, you might assign Diane Hacker's (2009) writing manual, which covers a wider range of writing issues, albeit not applied to social work, and/or Sidell's (2011) case recording guide, which contains numerous reporting forms and information about documenting work with individuals and families.

METHODOLOGY

We began this project in 2010 with an inquiry on the BSW Listserv about the need for a resource to address and support student writing. We received immediate and consistent encouragement, along with an extensive list of common writing problems. We then consulted with professionals in the field of writing pedagogy, who provided us with more information about writing issues and promising practices. From there, we polled our school's social work field instructors, and a variety of social work education colleagues around the country for examples of best practices in social work documentation. We are indebted to all the contributors and a few colleagues who provided their guidance and consultation. They are all listed in the Acknowledgments section.

REFERENCES

CSWE (2010). Educational policy and accreditation Standards. Alexandria, VA: CSWE. Retrieved from http://www.cswe.org/File.aspx?id=13780

Hacker, D. (2009). *A pocket style manual,* (5th Ed.). Boston: Bedford/St. Martin's.

NASW. (2008). *Code of ethics of the National Association of Social Workers.* Washington, DC: NASW. Retrieved from http://www.naswdc.org/pubs/code/code.asp

Reamer, F.G. (2005). Documentation in social work: Evolving ethical and risk-management standards. *Social Work, 50*(4), 325–334.

Sidell, N.L. (2011). *Social work documentation: A guide to strengthening your case recording.* Washington, DC: NASW.

Sopko, G.P. (2000). *Basic writing skills: A training outline.* Mechanicsburg, PA: The Pennsylvania Child Welfare Training Program.

Acknowledgments

This book is a collaboration between professors of Social Work and English, and numerous colleagues, and countless students who helped us learn how to help them.

Jennifer Perillo and Sheri W. Sussman from Springer Publishing provided resources, insights and encouragement. The result is this volume, based on the premise that adults learn better through inductive than deductive strategies, and that adult writers learn to write best by doing a lot of writing. Our families and colleagues made meaningful contributions, read early drafts, and helped to shape the final product you have in your hands. We are deeply indebted to them.

The following people and organizations made additional substantive contributions to our thinking, and/or contributed the materials from which we adapted the case studies. We are deeply indebted to all of them.

ARC of Southern Bristol County (MA), Michael Andrade, Executive Director
Barrington (RI) *Times*
Becky Caouette
Child Welfare Institute of Rhode Island, Bruce Rollins and Tonya Glantz
Mandy Crandall
Fellowship Human Resources (ME, MA, RI, PA, DE, NC)
Patti Ivry
Christiane Petrin Lambert
Peter Loss
Stephen M. Marson
Diane Martell
Mental Health Association of RI, Vivian G. Weisman, Executive Director
Nicole R. Morin, LICSW, Rhode Island Hospital
National Association of Social Workers, RI Chapter, Richard Harris, Executive Director
Policy Studies, Inc. (Denver, CO), David Price
Poverty Institute (of RI)
Providence Business News
Providence Journal
Rhode Island Coalition for the Homeless, Jim Ryczek

Rhode Island Parent Information Network
Erin Clare Sears
Janice Smith, CWI
Spurwink (RI), Pamela Watson and Felicia Deutsch
Merith Weisman
Debbie Weisman Clasie
Monique Willett, Lifespan

To the Reader

Perhaps one of the most valuable things about this book is that it recognizes that learning to write means learning how to write in different contexts, for different circumstances, and with different purposes and audiences in mind. We begin with the premise that effective writing requires a range of skills if you are to be successful in your professional writing as a social worker. According to most current research, we learn how to write even as we learn about a particular discipline. Each discipline has its own culture, its own ways of communicating, and so as we learn the language of our discipline, we learn to write in that discipline. What we have to say as social workers, and how we have to say it if we are to say it effectively, go hand in hand.

Writing for social work practice is a lot like writing in any discipline or profession—writing is a form of communication that depends on readers as much as writers. When we write we join in on a conversation—sometimes it is informal and casual, other times it is quite formal and serious. These conversations were going on long before we arrived on the scene, and will continue long after we leave. Meanwhile, there are rules of communication at work determined by long practice, and many of these conventions are widely shared while others are limited to the specific discipline of our field. As we join the conversation it is important to learn and respect the communication conventions of our chosen discipline in both content and form.

This book invites you to pay attention to how others have been writing in the field of social work for many years. This book invites you to read and learn by practicing and by becoming aware of the content and form of the writing "conversation" going on all around you in the social work world.

This book will help you to understand both the "what" and the "how" of professional writing for social work practice. And practice you must. People learn to write not by being told about writing, but by digging in and working with writing, and by writing their own work day in and day out. Only through practice can writers improve, grow more confident, and become fluent in the communication conventions of their discipline. Perhaps more than anything else, effective writers feel a profound stake in their work. This means that they believe what they have to say matters; they write with a clear purpose in mind, and how they present their work matters just as much.

Getting the formatting, the grammar, spelling, and punctuation right also matters—the formal elements of a piece of writing are a lot like the icing on the cake, or better yet, like a fine suit of clothes. If you want people to take you seriously, it may not matter how much money you spend on your wardrobe if you choose to sleep in your suit or dress the night before a big job interview. You will be judged by your appearance, just as you will be judged by the appearance of your writing. Figure out what you need to say and be sure you understand why it matters. Then, make sure it follows standard conventions of written English. Dress up your ideas so they look credible, neat, and clear. That way you will have a much better chance of being taken seriously by your reader, and a much better chance of accomplishing what you set out to do with your writing.

This book is special because it was written by a professor of social work and a professor of English. Each knew something of the other's discipline when we began. As we put this book together, we found ourselves increasingly informed by the other's field. The product is a fusion of writing and practice, for practice. We kept the material focused on writing for practice.

We also were guided by the current knowledge about how adults learn: the book moves from specific to general while remaining interest-centered from beginning to end. The 37 cases in each of the seven chapters come from actual social work practice and are based on actual documents produced by social workers. The cases cover a large range of practice situations and populations. Each case offers a learning experience for excellent writing. Each case offers an interactive experience for the reader. We hope you will enjoy this experience of learning by doing in the context of real practice.

Best wishes.

Daniel Weisman
Joseph L. Zornado

I

Introduction

We begin this book with a case study of a family with multiple challenges. A child protective services social worker wrote the case notes. They describe the "Jones Family," their current situation, and plans for follow-up services. This is an actual case note from a state's Child Welfare Department. Here and throughout this book we have changed names and details to protect individual identities. Most importantly, we have inserted a series of writing errors for you to find and correct. These exercises will help you to identify and correct problems with sentence structure, word usage, punctuation, excess verbiage, informal language, spelling, and syntax. At the end of each case you will find explanations of the corrections we recommend, along with examples. Use this chapter—and the chapters that follow—to help you develop your skills as a writer for social work practice.

"The Jones Family"–
Self-Assessment

This is an exercise to test your writing strengths and challenges. The following case notes come from an actual client record. The narrative appears twice: first with 40 writing errors, ranging from word usage to sentence structure, punctuation, unnecessary verbiage, and spelling; the second with the errors corrected and explained. Numbers on the right side of the original document note the page location of the corresponding content in the corrected document. This exercise may help you identify your strengths and challenges as a writer. For full explanations of writing issues, see Appendix A.

Family	Abbreviations
Alice Jones, mother, 23	DCW: Department of Child Welfare (state)
Keith Jones, father, 25	BCI: Bureau of Criminal Investigation
Eli, 3 ½	
Evan, 2 ¾	

Note: the missing articles, "the" and "a," are deliberate, and common omissions in clients' files. Each human service agency has its own protocols.

ORIGINAL VERSION

FAMILY COMPOSITION: (6)

This family is constituted of mother, Alice Jones, age 23, father, Keith Jones, age 25, and there two children, Evan, age 2 ¾ and Eli, age 3 ½. Although, Mother and father have been married for 2 years but lived together for a year before that. The family reside in a one bedroom house in Xtown that they rent from an out of state landlord. Mother and father described no family support other then mothers sister who lives in Ytown (about seven miles away).

BACKGROUND INFORMATION:

A BCI report reveals that father has a history of domestic violence. Previous DCW involvement includes allegations of neglect. Reports indicate that mother has "a long history of psychosis and trauma". The current opening occurred following reports to DCW that mother was not taking her psychiatric medication, not in counseling and "self-medicating with marijuana and other drugs." The caller also stated (7) that father had been violent throwing things and threatening mother in front of the two children. When DCW worker went out to the home they assessed that the children were unsafe. I feel as though the children could not be safely maintained at home. The living conditions in the home presented with multiple hazards, and parents' demonstrate a lack of understanding and limited ability to alleviate these conditions. DCW worker and mother were able to reach maternal aunt by phone, and she agreed to take the children temporarily.

CURRENT SITUATION:

After the children were removed, maternal aunt had 2nd thoughts and asked that DCW place the children elsewhere. Maternal aunt stated that she was sorry but that she "just could not handle two small children". DCW tried to address maternal aunts concerns, but she maintained that she could knot do it. The oldest child, Eli, is currently placed in a non-relative foster home. The youngest child, Evan, is placed in the county childrens' emergency shelter. Mother and father were evicted from their (8) rental apartment when the landlord saw the condition of the home. Mother had a brief stay in the hospital following a psychotic episode. The too are currently together; "staying with friends." Mother has been referred to and recieved a substance abuse and mental health evaluation. She's being scene on an outpatient bases for both. Father was referred for domestic violence treatment and substance abuse treatment. The oldest child, Eli, has been referred for a child development evaluation. The youngest child

is being assessed thru the childrens' shelter. The family was also referred
to a local agency for outreach services specializing in family support,
mental health and substance abuse as well.

NOTES FOR FOLLOW-UP

What I think is that this family has more strengths then the record
reflects, and should be re-evaluated in 6 months. In addition, this family
may benefit from more referrals; nutrition, job training, mental health
assessment, develop their employment potential and improve their literacy
skills. These resources may be of benefit to them.

CORRECTED VERSION

Each number in the corrected version refers to an explanation below.

FAMILY COMPOSITION:

This family includes ① the mother, Alice Jones, age 23, father, Keith Jones, age 25, and their ② two children, Evan, age 2 ¾ and Eli, age 3 ½. ③ Mother and father have been married for two ④ years but lived together for a year before that. The family resides ⑤ in Xtown ⑥, in a one bedroom house that they rent from an out-of-state ⑦ landlord. Mother and father describe no family support other than ⑧ mother's ⑨ sister, ⑩ who lives in Ytown (about seven miles away).

BACKGROUND INFORMATION:

A BCI report reveals that father has a history of domestic violence. Previous DCW involvement includes allegations of neglect. Reports indicate that mother has "a long history of psychosis and trauma." ⑪ The current case ⑫ opening occurred following reports to DCW that mother was not taking her psychiatric medication, not in counseling, ⑬ and

cont.

EXPLANATIONS FOR CORRECTIONS:

1. Incorrect word. Unnecessary verbiage.
2. "Their" is the possessive; "there" refers to a place.
3. "Although," is not followed by comma. Beginning a sentence with "Although" can often lead to an incomplete sentence, as it would here. The sentence stands and is complete without "Although." With this introduction— "Although,"—it is an incomplete sentence.
4. Numerals 1–10 should be spelled out. [This may vary in some agencies.]
5. "Resides" is the verb form for a singular noun (family). The family resides.
6. Misplaced modifier. General rule: a word or phrase that adds information to a noun or noun phrase (words containing the noun), should be as close as possible to the word(s) being modified. In this case, "that they rent. . ." modifies (or elaborates on) the house (noun), not the town (different noun). In other words, the house gets rented, not the town, so "that they rent" should be placed as close to the house as possible.
7. "Out-of-state" should be hyphenated because it is one entity used as a compound modifier.
8. Than (not then). "Than" is for comparisons; "then" refers to time or sequences.
9. Mother's: apostrophe before the "s" because this is the singular possessive case (mother owns something (sister); it is mother's sister.
10. Sister is followed by a comma, not a semicolon. Commas separate phrases from each other, and signify pauses for the reader, so that sentences make sense. Semicolons separate two complete sentences that can stand on their own, or (usually) multi-word items in a list (usually after a colon).
11. Quote marks go after periods and commas in the U.S. In the UK and Commonwealth countries (e.g., Canada), all punctuation goes after the quotation mark.
12. We inserted the word "case" because it was not clear what the sentence was about.
13. We added a comma to indicate the "not" in "not in counseling," did not pertain to the next phrase, "self medicating. . ." In fact, she was not in counseling but was self medicating; the comma helps keep it clear that the "not" does not carry forward.

cont.

"self-medicating with marijuana and other drugs." ⑭ The caller also stated that father had been violent, ⑮ throwing things and threatening mother in front of the two children. When DCW worker went out to the home, she ⑯ assessed that the children were unsafe. It appears that ⑰ the children cannot ⑱ be maintained at home safely. ⑲ The living conditions in the home present ⑳ multiple hazards, and parents ㉑ demonstrate a lack of understanding and limited ability to alleviate these conditions. DCW worker and mother were able to reach maternal aunt by phone, and she agreed to take the children temporarily.

CURRENT SITUATION:

After the children were removed, maternal aunt had second ㉒ thoughts and asked that DCW place the children elsewhere. The maternal aunt stated that she was sorry but that she "just could not handle two small children." ㉓ DCW tried to address maternal aunt's ㉔ concerns, but she maintained that she could not ㉕ do it. The oldest child, Eli, is currently placed in a non-relative foster home. The youngest child, Evan, is placed in the county

cont.

EXPLANATIONS FOR CORRECTIONS:

14. Same as # 10: commas and periods go inside the quotation mark.
15. The comma indicates a pause for the reader. The father was violent, throwing things. . .
16. Verb-noun agreement. In this case the subject of the sentence, the DCW worker (singular) should be a "she" (singular), not a "they" (plural).
17. "I feel as though" is fine for chatting among friends, but the phrase is too informal for professional use. We substituted more professional language that reflects the same content.
18. "Could not" is past tense, but this sentence is written in the present tense ("cannot").
19. "Could not (or cannot) be safely maintained at home" contains a split infinitive phrase (to be maintained).. Better: keep "be maintained" intact, and place the modifier "safely" just before or just after it, for example: "Cannot be maintained at home safely" is better than "cannot be safely maintained at home." Still, splitting infinitives is more a judgment call than a writing error. Strive for clarity.

20. "Presented with" is an incorrect verb form for this statement. Better: "The living conditions present multiple hazards."
21. "Parents' demonstrate" is incorrect because the apostrophe connotes ownership. That doesn't make any sense. The sentence is saying that parents demonstrate a lack of understanding. The word "parents" is a straightforward plural subject—a noun. There is no ownership implied in the sentence, so there is no need for an apostrophe.
22. The informal abbreviation, 2nd, does not belong in this narrative, unless it is accepted convention in the agency.
23. As above, the period goes inside the quotation mark.
24. Singular possessive: the aunt's concerns. A possessive is required here because the concerns belong to the aunt.
25. Knot and not are homophones. They sound the same but mean very different things. "Not" is the correct word here. It is a good idea to proofread for homophones, which seem to sneak into our writing when we least expect it. See Appendix A of this book on homophones and social work writing.

cont.

children's ㉖ emergency shelter. Mother and father were evicted from their
rental apartment when the landlord saw the condition of the home. Mother
had a brief stay in the hospital following a psychotic episode. The two ㉗ are
currently together, ㉘ "staying with friends." ㉙ Mother has been referred to and
received ㉚ a substance abuse and mental health evaluation. She is ㉛ being
seen ㉜ on an outpatient basis for both. Father was referred for domestic
violence treatment and substance abuse treatment. The oldest child
has been referred for a child development evaluation. The youngest child
is being assessed through ㉝ the children's ㉞ shelter. The family was also referred
to a local agency for outreach services. ㉟ The agency specializes in family support,
mental health and substance abuse.

NOTES FOR FOLLOW-UP

I think this family ㊱ has more strengths than ㊲ the record
reflects, and should be re-evaluated in six ㊳ months. In addition, this family
may benefit from more referrals: ㊴ nutrition, job training, mental health
assessment, employment and literacy ㊵ . These resources may be of benefit to them.

EXPLANATIONS FOR CORRECTIONS:

26. "Children's" is the proper way to write the possessive for children. Although it is plural, the apostrophe comes before the 's.' Men's and women's are other examples of this exception.
27. Two (not too): another homophone. Too means "also" or "excessive."
28. We added a comma to separate two thoughts.
29. Period inside the quotation mark.
30. "Received" is spelled incorrectly.
31. "She's" is a conjunction for "she is." Conjunctions should be avoided in professional writing.
32. Another homophone: scene and seen.
33. "Through" is the correct word. "Thru" is informal.
34. See #26: children's is the plural possessive for children.
35. The original sentence contained a misplaced modifier and a redundancy. "Specializing in family support, mental health and substance abuse as well" modified "the agency," not the "outreach services." The agency specialized in those services; outreach is one way they did it. So "specializing in . . . ." should be placed closer to "agency" than "services." The second problem was "and" and "as well." They are redundant; one should be deleted. In order to solve both problems, we revised the sentence into two sentences.
36. Unnecessary verbiage: "I think" is more concise than "what I think is."
37. Homophone: "then" refers to time; "than" is for comparisons.
38. Spell out numbers from one through ten.
39. Colon, not semicolon.
40. Parallelism. The list was: *nutrition, job training, mental health assessment, develop their employment potential and improve their literacy skills.* The first three led with nouns (nutrition, job, and mental health); the last two led with verbs (develop and improve). When items in a sentence are listed or presented as parallel to each other, they should be characterized in similar language.

How many errors did you find? More important, what patterns do you see in the errors you found and the ones you missed? This may tell you how to use this book. In fact, the errors can be grouped into categories, and you can focus on working on those topics that gave you the most trouble.

Punctuation [#s 9, 10, 11, 13, 14, 15, 21, 23, 24, 26, 28, 29, 31, 34, 39] In these examples, commas, semicolons, colons, apostrophes and placement of quotation marks have very specific uses and are not interchangeable. Commas separate words and phrases to make sentences read clearly and precisely. Semicolons separate two complete sentences or multi-word items in a list, usually after a colon, which means "as follows" or "specifically." Apostrophes serve two purposes: to show the possessive or to join two words together (#31). Here are examples of the two uses of apostrophes:

- Contractions: "My brother's feeling badly today." "Brother is" becomes "brother's" with the apostrophe (other examples of contractions: it's, isn't, doesn't, I'll, you'd).
- Possessive: "My brother's grammar book got him through his college writing courses." Here, the apostrophe connotes ownership.

Quotation marks are handled differently in the United States than in United Kingdom countries. In the United States, when a quotation ends, the quotation mark goes outside any commas or periods. On some occasions the quotation is inside another punctuation mark, for example, a question mark or an exclamation point. Semicolons and colons go outside the quote mark [#s 10, 14, 23 and 29].

Misplaced modifiers are words or phrases that get positioned incorrectly in sentences [#s 6, 19 and 35]. The general rule is to place modifying language as close as possible to the objects or actions being modified. Often, misplaced modifiers will be placed at the end of a sentence, several words or phrases away from their targets, or inside a verb phrase. For example, "to be safely maintained at home"—"to be maintained" is the verb phrase; "safely" should go before or after "to be maintained" and not in the middle of the phrase. Since we tend to talk this way, it feels awkward to move modifiers to more appropriate places in sentences, but our narratives represent our professional self and serve our clients with clarity and competence. For more on misplaced modifiers, see page 268 of the Glossary, in Appendix A.

Homophones are words that sound the same but mean different things [#s 8, 25, 27, 32 and 37]. There are dozens that can confound and change the meaning of your writing. See Appendix A for more information on homophones.

Sentence structure [#s 3, 16, 18, 36 and 40] covers a number of writing issues: incomplete and run-on sentences; syntax; redundancies; the passive voice; and parallelism. There is more on this in Appendix A.

Awkward syntax [#36] is a way of saying something indirectly instead of affirmatively: "It was my view that the family was supportive." Try to say more with less: "I believe the family was supportive." Another example: "What happened next was that the family expressed concern about their housing situation"; better: "The family expressed concern about their housing situation."

<u>Parallelism</u> [#40] means items that have the same level of narration should be worded similarly. Here is an example of a parallelism problem: *When I arrived at the family's home, I found the children doing their homework, the parents preparing dinner, newspapers being read by the cousins, and laundry being folded by the brother-in-law.* Correct wording: **When I arrived at the family's home, I found the children doing their homework, the parents preparing dinner, cousins reading newspapers, and the brother-in-law folding the laundry.** [All four phrases are in the active voice in the second example; active and passive voices are mixed in the former case.]

<u>Grammar and spelling</u> (other than punctuation and sentence structure) [#s 4, 20, 30].

<u>Word usage and professional language</u> [#s 1, 2, 5, 7, 17, 22, 33, 38]. Some wording may be grammatically correct but be too informal for professional purposes. One example is contractions: he's, it's, didn't. Contractions are grammatically acceptable but do not belong in professional narratives.

HBSE, Social Work Practice, and Social Policy

The following three chapters address documentation of social work activities with individuals, families, groups, organizations and communities. In Chapter 2, Human Behavior in the Social Environment (HBSE), we included scenarios in which assessment is the primary focus. The case studies are documentation used to assess client, target, action, and change agent systems, as well as communities and organizations involved in change efforts. In Chapter 3, Practice, the focus is descriptive reporting. This separation into HBSE and Practice is not entirely neat, as assessment and descriptive information overlap in many reports. We categorized material based on the predominant information provided in reports: if documentation emphasizes assessment, we placed the case in the HBSE chapter; if the major thrust is periodic reviews, incident reporting or case closing, we included it in the Practice chapter. In Chapter 4, the cases are episodes of social workers using written documents to influence policy.

CASE DOCUMENTATION: OPEN, MONITOR, REPORT, CLOSE

Agencies typically adopt their own styles for documentation of their work with clients. When you begin a field placement or a job, the orientation will include the agency's documentation rules and procedures, including review of client files. So, no book or class can provide the authoritative, one-right-way of writing for all agencies; but we can cover some of the basics, which may help you adapt to the rules you find where you practice.

Case documentation serves several purposes: open new cases; monitor clients' progress in the course of treatment (provision of services); report significant events; close cases. Agencies will have forms and/or procedures for each of these purposes. Some of these forms have categorical check-offs (e.g., demographics), but there are spaces for narratives, so details can (sometimes must) be described. One agency lists eight different forms, but they fall into the four broad categories listed above (open, monitor progress, report events, close): case notes, contact notes, progress notes, communication logs, incident reports, treatment plans, assessments, and quarterly reviews (Fellowship Human Resources, 2011).

You will find that agencies are required to document their work for several reasons, including legal liability, reimbursement for services and continuity of care (the next worker can pick up where the previous worker left off; multi-member treatment team members can coordinate their work). In the course of your career, you may need to write a *court letter* in relation to a client or family. This means your narrative may contribute to a judge's decision. There are several court letters in the practice chapter. This section of the book is about case-level written narratives.

Opening New Cases

Documents that record new case openings (or re-openings), typically include <u>assessments</u> of the client's functioning in relation to the services in question. Check-off information may include the client's diagnoses, family, communication skills, psychosocial history, education, substance use, living situation, environmental risks, finances, legal issues, and psychological functioning.

Narrative fields may include description of presenting issues, client's appearance and affect, problem and treatment history, client's perceptions, and practitioner's impressions.

Monitoring Progress

Some agencies will schedule periodic reviews of their clients' progress. Intervals can vary from a week to a year. Some agencies will use a template, perhaps similar to their intake forms, consisting of check-offs and narrative fields. Others will direct the social worker to specified fields, including diagnostic categories identified in the intake (case opening assessment). Some periodic reviews may be limited to progress on identified issues; other reviews may include all the fields contained in case opening forms. Either way, narratives likely will be included in these reviews.

Reporting Incidents

Agencies typically have procedures for workers to document events or incidents of significance. These can occur routinely, such as after treatment sessions, and/or subsequent to significant events. There may be check-offs, but narratives are likely to be required, so the full import and details of an incident can be reported.

Closing Cases

When client services are terminated by clients, the agency or outside sponsors, a case closing document should be completed by the service provider. Check-offs and narratives will include client status and functioning at the time of closing, progress toward goals, recommended treatment, and reasons for termination.

Court Letters

Social workers write court letters most frequently in the field of child welfare, but the need can arise in almost any practice setting. Court letters become part of formal case records. You may be asked for specific information, or (more likely) to report your experiences, assessments, and recommendations (with reasons) with individuals and/or families under court adjudication.

One state's child welfare department describes seven kinds of court letters (CWI, 2011):

1. **Court Motion:** *Change of Placement, Visitation, Permission to Give Consent (medical, travel, etc.)*
2. **Domestic Court Study**
3. **Involuntary Termination of Parental Rights,** *including agency involvement (current & prior); background history (mother, father & child); visitation; recommendation*
4. **Juvenile Court Study**
5. **Summary of Facts** *to substantiate allegations of abuse, neglect and/or dependency, including cover letter, summary of case, list of witnesses; examples:*
   a. **Straight Petition**—*seeking custody, but not removal of the children*
   b. **Ex-Parte Petition**—*seeking custody and removal of the children*
6. **Review – Adjudicated Cases:** *update on case since last hearing; parents' progress with service plan(s), where children are placed, needs of the family*
7. **Letter for Permanency Hearing**
   a. *All review information and permanency planning recommendation*
   b. *A Service Plan must be submitted with this court letter*

Format

- *Review and permanency letters:*
  - *Introduction*
  - *Progress toward service plan goal/update since last court hearing*
  - *Placement*
  - *Visitation*
  - *Recommendations*
- *All other letters: narratives*
- *Check with the court about expected font size*

Content

- *Factual information*
- *Use objective language*
- *Be clear and concise*
- *Clearly state the source of all information*
- *Addresses safety, risk, permanency, and well-being*

Professional Writing Skills

- *Use of language*
  - *Wordiness*
    - *Be concise*
    - *Eliminate unnecessary information*
    - *Avoid acronyms and jargons*
  - *Active vs. passive voice*
    - *Use active voice*
    - *Use language that is specific, clear, and accurate*

- *Watch for common writing errors*
- *Easily confused word pairs*
- *Changes the meaning of the sentence*

Spell check won't help!

This last section, format, and content, are instructive for all case documentation because any practice scenario can become subject to external review. In all these situations, completeness, accuracy, objectivity, brevity, and competent writing are essential.

Rules for Writers of Client Records

A review of documentation practices leads to a general outline of content included in case notes: What happened/is happening? Why do we think it happened/is happening? What are we going to do about it? If we substitute professional language, it looks like this: Data, Assess, Plan (DAP). A Family Service agency client progress note operationalizes DAP this way (FSRI, 2011):

- *Data: Focus of session, observations, predominant discussions (including significant client comments) and current concerns*
- *Assess: Current functioning, mental status (including mood, affect, etc.), client cooperation, changes in status, clinician's explanation of above data, etc.*
- *Plan: Homework/tasks to complete, significant future meetings, plans for next session*

DAP notes, and variations of them, are in wide use across the spectrum of human service. One variation, for example, is SOAP (Subjective description [client's perspective], Objective description [social worker's version, based on the evidence], Assessment, and Plan. The "SO" in SOAP is an elaboration of the "D" in DAP. The "AP" (assess and plan) is the same.

A hospital social service department uses this guideline for narratives (RIH, n.d.):

The social work assessment is tailored to the unique circumstances of the patient and the reason for referral. It MAY include: the presenting problem or reason for referral; history of presenting problem; baseline functional status; family and social history; prior medical and psychiatric (including substance abuse) treatment; mental status; coping and adjustment skills; school and vocational history; assessment and diagnosis; treatment plan; and follow up plan. Assessment is ongoing and the treatment plan may change as the patient and or family's needs and situation changes.

Specific protocols, as outlined in policies and procedures in the Administrative Manual, guide the clinical social work intervention and treatment plan in circumstances such as child and elder abuse, abuse of a patient in a health care facility, abuse of an adult with developmental disabilities. Continued social work intervention is determined by the presenting problem and plan of care by the physician and multidisciplinary team, within the cultural and ethnic context of the patient's family and community and the patient's right to self-determination. The social worker makes referrals to community services and agencies based upon the identified needs of the patient and family, the clinical assessment and recommends follow-up services if indicated.

A multi-state agency serving clients with mental health and substance issues identifies these criteria for case documentation (Fellowship HR, 2011):

Rules to Follow

"…(A)bide by the basic tenets of proper documentation, as this will become part of the consumer's legal record. It is the responsibility of (the clinical worker) to create a summary that is objective and that accurately paints a picture of the consumer's life situation. The following is a list of what is and is not appropriate when composing the integrated summary:

DO
- *Include the strengths*
- *Include the barriers to treatment*
- *Include the consumer's response to past treatment*
- *Include a professional clinical assessment of the treatment issues*

DO NOT
- *Use biased language*
- *Use personal opinions*
- *Use slang language"*

COURT LETTERS

Court letters straddle the artificial line between HBSE and Practice. On one hand, they report assessments of individuals under court adjudication. On the other hand, court letters may report episodes and events so the court can construct a picture of the person in his or her environment. We included two "Emergency Motion" court letters (Case Studies 11 and 12) in the Practice chapter because they are more descriptive than analytical. The rule for court letters is a good template for most case-based documentation: be brief, accurate, complete, objective, and error-free.

AGENCY- AND COMMUNITY-LEVEL DOCUMENTATION

The HBSE chapter includes two "macro"-level assessments: an agency and a community. The organizational assessment is based on interviews with clients of a homeless shelter; the community analysis is based on a needs assessment for health and mental health services for deaf and hard-of-hearing residents. Both narratives are reports of data collected to assess the respective systems' ability to make adaptations on behalf of their constituencies.

Target systems for agency- and community-level assessments will include a variety of "stakeholders" in those systems. Therefore, writing is as important as it is for case-level documentation. The reader must have respect and confidence in the reporter. The documents must stand on their own as products with integrity.

WRITING FOR ADVOCACY

Chapter 4 contains a press release, letters to editors, testimony, and an advocacy letter. (Case 26 in Chapter 5 also addresses public policy, utilizing data collected by an agency.) The forms and purposes differ from those of assessment and practice reports, but the writing criteria are identical: brevity, clarity, direct writing, no writing errors. The introduction to Chapter 4 explains the "rules" of writing to influence policy and policy makers.

CONCLUSION

In sum, your field placement and, later, employer will provide you with the agency's expectations and procedures for case and cause documentation. You will need to write concisely and competently, regardless of the purpose. You may be expected to use abbreviations, initials, capitals in particular situations and/or other procedures; you always will be expected to write competently.

SOURCES

CWI (2011). Refresher: Case Documentation & Legal Writing for Child Welfare. Providence, RI: Child Welfare Institute.

FSRI (2008). Client Progress Note. Providence, RI: Family Service, Inc.

Fellowship Human Resources (2011). Documentation Guidelines: Clinical and Risk Management Guidelines. Lincoln, RI: Fellowship HR, Inc.

RIH (n.d.). Clinical Social Work Scope of Assessment. Providence, RI: Rhode Island Hospital.

2

Human Behavior in the Social Environment (HBSE)

The next two chapters address Human Behavior in the Social Environment (HBSE) and Social Work Practice. HBSE-informed theories provide social workers with the knowledge base to assess clients, define and target needs, take appropriate actions, and operate effectively as change agents within diverse systems, communities, and organizations involved in change efforts. In the HBSE chapter, we include several documentation scenarios in which assessment is the primary focus. In the practice chapter, descriptive reporting is the focus.

This chapter contains eight cases: cases one and two are assessments in child welfare cases: a family and a child. Cases three through six are assessments of individuals in four different contexts (hospital, prison, mental health treatment, and public school). Cases seven and eight are assessments of organizational capacity and community needs, respectively. Numbers on the right side of the original documents note the page locations of the corresponding content in the corrected documents.

1 – Family Assessment: The Driver Family
2 – Children at Risk: The Gramme Family
3 – Medical Social Work Intake: Hospital Setting (Health, Mental Health and Substance Abuse Issues)
4 – Corrections: Parole-Readiness Report
5 – Mental Health: Integrated Summary of Care
6 – School Social Work: Social Assessment
7 – Organizational Assessment: Tender Mercies Homeless Shelter
8 – Community Needs Assessment: Deaf and Hard of Hearing Residents

HUMAN BEHAVIOR IN THE SOCIAL ENVIRONMENT

CASE 1: FAMILY ASSESSMENT: THE DRIVER FAMILY

The following case document is about the Driver family: Danni (adolescent), Danielle and Jarrod (parents), and Jimmy (infant). This family case study, which helps Child Protective Service (CPS) clinicians and case managers assess the family's level of functioning, determine service plan goals, and monitor progress over time, contains seventy-eight writing errors.

STATE OF FREDONIA
DEPARTMENT OF CHILD PROTECTIVE SERVICES
FAMILY CENTERED RISK, AND PROTECTIVE CAPACITY
ASSESSSMENT AND SERVICE PLAN

Family members mentioned in the document	Abbreviations used in the document
Jarrod Driver, father, 33 Danielle, mother, 33 Danni, female, 14 Jimmy, male, 8 months	CPS: Child Protective Services CPI: Child Protective Investigator

ORIGINAL VERSION

Family's Story

Jarrod and Danielle, met in high school. Jarrod was drawn to the shy Danielle that seemed in some ways kind of lost. As they dated he began to see her strong spirit and her committment to making something of herself. Danielles mother, passed away, when she was a senior in High School. She lived with a girlfriend after her mother had passed away and she recalls this time of her live as "extremely difficult, stressful and when she was at her worst". She stated what happened next was she turned to smoking pot and alcohol use as a way to cope but reports she did not need any formal intervention to stop. Danielle reports she was not close to her dad as he and her mother divorced when she was ten years old. She does not currently know his whereabouts. (20)

Danielle and Jarrod married in September following there graduating high school—both were just 18 years old. Jarrod worked in many jobs and Danielle worked as a secretary at the community elementary school. In retrospect Danielle thinks that she was to young to get married. Danni was born just ten months after Danielle and Jarrod were married.

It seems to Danielle that life has taken on many turns that she never would have expected. Danni needed emergency surgery when she was eleven (a kidney problem). Because this ocurred at a time when Jarrod was just starting a new job, it was not covered by insurance and this put the family (21) under tremendous financial strain. They have been paying off the medical bills for the passed three years. The financial strain caused stress in there marriage. "Jarrod doesn't really like to talk about things", says Danielle. Danielle is worried that the family "is one paycheck away from being on the streets". Jarrod indicates that she is over dramatizing there financial situation—it appears to me that this is an ongoing discussion. "He is just so darn positive that everything will work out. . .he calls me his little worrywart".

Just when they where starting to climb out of debt and Danielle thought that it might be "her chance", she found out she was pregnant with Jimmy. She blames Jarrod as they had talked about having another child but Danielle didn't want too. Although, she had initially considered it because she thought that it might bring them closer, but she decided not to because "she really did not want to start all over with diapers, middle of the night feedings, and etc." Jarrod appeared to take a "don't worry about it" approach and looking back, Danielle feels as though she was pressured into it. (22)

CPS was called because the neighbors were concerned about the baby crying on a daily basis for extended periods of time, what was reported as loud screaming between mom and her oldest child and the allegation of mother leaving the children alone. In reviewing state database for history this family has had several calls made in the past over similar allegations. CPS went out on a routine call and threw the investigation process indicated the mother on the eight-month old for lack of supervision.

The family home present in disarray and somewhat chaotic; food is all over the place, dirty dishes all over the kitchen and what appeared to be animal feces on the floor. The parents are, for the most part, uninvolved in their eldest daughters life (Danni 14yr's old) and they either do not or are unable to adequately supervise her and manage her behavior. The youngest child (Jimmy 8months old) appears unkempt and dirty personal hygiene and clothing. All interactions thus far between CPS and the family Jimmy has been in clothes that were not appropriate (for the season or his size. (23)

Safety Decision: It seems to me that do to lack of supervision, neglectful care and potential substance abuse of mother, the children are not safe in the home wile Jarrod is on the road. (24)

Safety Plan: Jarrod is very upset by the involvement of the child protection agency and has agreed to take two weeks' of vacation to take care of the children and also to try to put things in place to make it safe for him to leave again. He seems to have developed more insite that all is not "OK" with his family." His mother is also willing to come and help him during these two weeks and potentially a bit longer as well. While she cannot care for the children she can help to teach him how to care for the children. She can also help Danielle to better understand how to feed and care for Jimmy. A potential downfall of this plan is that Jarrod could become dependant on his mother, we will have to keep an eye on that.

CASE 1: CORRECTED VERSION

Each number in the corrected version refers to an explanation below.

Jarrod and Danielle ① met in high school. Jarrod was drawn to the shy
Danielle who ② seemed in some ways kind of lost. As they dated he began
to see her strong spirit and her commitment ③ to making something of
herself. Danielle's ④ mother passed away ⑤ when Danielle ⑥ was a senior in high
school ⑦. She lived with a girlfriend after her mother ⑧ passed away and
she recalls this time of her life ⑨ as "extremely difficult, stressful and when
I was at my worst." ⑩ She stated that ⑪ she turned
to smoking pot and alcohol use as a way to cope, ⑫ but ⑬ did not
need any formal intervention to stop. Danielle reports she was not close to
her dad as he and her mother divorced when she was 10 years old. She
does not ⑭ know his whereabouts.

Danielle and Jarrod married in September, ⑮ following their ⑯ graduation from ⑰ high
school—both were ⑱ 18 years old. Jarrod worked in many jobs and
Danielle worked as a secretary at the community elementary school.
In retrospect, ⑲ Danielle thinks that she was too ⑳ young to get married.
Danni was born just ten months after Danielle and Jarrod were married.

cont.

EXPLANATIONS OF CORRECTIONS

1. No comma needed because there is no pause required.
2. "Who" is the correct pronoun for people.
3. Spelling error.
4. Apostrophe required to indicate possession.
5. No commas before or after "passed away" because no pauses are needed.
6. "She" could be confusing – refer specifically to Danielle or her mother for clarity.
7. The "high school" is not named, so it is not a proper noun, therefore do not capitalize it.
8. Simple past tense for clarity and brevity.
9. Word usage: life and live—"life" is a noun; "live" is a verb or adjective.
10. Two errors in this sentence: the quote is Danielle's words about herself, so it should be in the first person (I and me). Also, the period should go inside the close-quote mark.
11. "What happened next" is unnecessary and passive wording.
12. Insert comma between independent clause and phrase.
13. Delete "Reports she" because it is redundant with "She stated that" (and changes tenses).
14. "Currently" is unnecessary.
15. Insert comma between independent clause and phrase.
16. Homophone error: insert *their* and delete *there* to indicate the possessive.
17. Correct wording: graduate "from" high school.
18. "Just" is the author's opinion.
19. Comma after introductory phrase. Write out numbers from one through ten.
20. Homophone error: too and to—"too" means also or excessive.

cont.

Danielle believes ㉑ that life has taken on many turns that she never ㉒ expected. Danni needed emergency surgery when she was eleven (a kidney problem). Because this occurred ㉓ at a time when Jarrod was just starting a new job, it was not covered by insurance. ㉔ This put the family under tremendous financial strain. They have been paying ㉕ the medical bills for the past ㉖ three years. The financial strain caused stress in their ㉗ marriage. "Jarrod doesn't really like to talk about things," ㉘ says Danielle. Danielle is worried that the family "is one paycheck away from being on the streets." ㉙ Jarrod indicates that she is over-dramatizing ㉚ their ㉛ financial situation— this appears to be ㉜ an ongoing discussion. "He is just so darn positive that everything will work out. . .he calls me his little worrywart." ㉝

Just when they were ㉞ starting to climb out of debt and Danielle thought that it might be "my chance," ㉟ she learned that ㊱ she was pregnant with Jimmy. She blames Jarrod as they had talked about having another child but Danielle did not want to ㊲. ㊳ She had considered it initially ㊴ because she

cont.

EXPLANATIONS OF CORRECTIONS

21. Correct passive constructions and activate key verb by avoiding unnecessary words.
22. Use simple past tense.
23. Spelling error.
24. Beware of unnecessarily long sentences. Separated into two sentences for clarity.
25. "Paying off" is redundant. Make your point as economically as possible.
26. Homophone error: past and passed—past means "ago"; passed means "went by."
27. Homophone error: their and there (see #16).
28. Comma location: comma belongs inside close-quotation mark.
29. Period location: period belongs inside close-quotation mark.
30. Hyphenate when two adjectives follow one another: "over-dramatizing."
31. Homophone error: their and there (see #16).
32. Delete unnecessary authorial intrusion.

33. Period location: period belongs inside close-quotation mark.
34. Word choice: were and where—were is past tense for "to be"; where refers to a place.
35. Two errors: the quote should be in the first person because it is Danielle's words about herself ("my" not "her"), and the comma belongs inside the close-quotation mark.
36. Professional writing vocabulary: "learned that" is more professional than "found out."
37. Homophone error: to and too (see #20). "Did not" is preferable to "didn't."
38. Beginning a sentence with the word "although" often leads to an incomplete sentence, as in this example; either place the comma after the complete introductory phrase ("although she had considered it,") and then complete the sentence, or drop "although."
39. Misplaced modifier: the modifier "initially" split the verb form, "had considered."

cont.

thought that it might bring them closer but she decided not to ④⓪ because "I ④①
really did not want to start all over with diapers, middle of the night feedings,
④② etc." Jarrod appeared to take a "don't worry about it" approach and
looking back, Danielle feels that ④③ she was pressured into it.

CPS was called because the neighbors were concerned about: 1) the baby crying
on a daily basis for extended periods of time, 2) loud screaming between mom and
her oldest child, and 3) mother leaving the children alone ④④. The ④⑤ state database
indicates ④⑥ that this family has had several calls in the past over similar allegations ④⑦.
CPS went ④⑧ on a routine call and, ④⑨ through ⑤⓪ the investigation process,
⑤① indicated the mother on the eight-month-old (Jimmy) ⑤② for lack of supervision.

The family's home presents ⑤③ in disarray and is somewhat chaotic: ⑤④ food and
dirty dishes cover most surfaces in the kitchen; apparent animal

cont.

EXPLANATIONS OF CORRECTIONS

40. Use commas sparingly for clarity. In this case they are not required because connecting conjunctions make the sentence clear and link the two independent clauses.
41. Use the first person (I) because Danielle is talking about herself.
42. "And" "etc." are redundant; here, it was Danielle's quote, but there is no point in repeating her grammatical error.
43. Use "that" rather than "as though" because "that" is more active and direct.
44. This sentence had multiple problems: it was a run-on sentence, it lacked parallel construction, and it used passive language. We rewrote it for consistency, clarity and active language.
45. Corrections 45–47 are about one poorly-worded sentence. 45: Article (the) was missing.
46. The subject phrase of this sentence had two problems: passive construction and a lack of parallel construction. We rewrote the sentence so that the language is direct and the verb ("indicates") is in the same tense and conjugation as the noun ("database").
47. We then corrected the predicate portion of the sentence so that the noun and verb agree ("this family has had several calls in the

past"); We also eliminated two redundancies: "in the past" and "history"; "calls" and "made."
48. 48–52 are about one sentence. 48: "went" and "out" are redundant.
49. Insert comma before and after a non-essential phrase.
50. Homophone error: through and threw ("threw" means hurled or propelled; "through" means completed or transgressed).
51. Insert comma, with #49 bracketing a phrase that could be removed without changing the meaning of the sentence.
52. Eight-month-old should be spelled out and hyphenated; We added "Jimmy" in parentheses for clarity.
53. "The family home present" is incorrect. "The family's home presents" is clearer, especially the conjugation of "presents" to match the singular noun (home). We used the possessive (family's), an optional change.
54. A colon is preferable to semicolon because the next information is an elaboration (a list of sorts) of "disarray and somewhat chaotic." The food, dirty dishes and possible feces are presented as the evidence of "disarray and chaos."

cont.

feces are on the floor ⑤⑤. The parents are, for the most part, uninvolved in their eldest daughter's ⑤⑥ life (Danni, 14 years old ⑤⑦) and they either do not (possibly cannot) adequately supervise her or ⑤⑧ manage her behavior. The youngest child (Jimmy, 8 months ⑤⑨) appears unkempt and dirty (i.e., personal hygiene and clothing) ⑥⓪. In all interactions to date, the CPS worker has reported Jimmy as wearing clothes that were not appropriate (for the season or his size) ⑥①.

cont.

EXPLANATIONS OF CORRECTIONS

55. This sentence had two other problems: "all over the place" and "all over the kitchen" are imprecise and judgmental; the separate phrases describing the home's appearance were not parallel in structure. Here is the sentence as written: *"The family home present in disarray and somewhat chaotic; food is all over the place, dirty dishes all over the kitchen and what appeared to be animal feces on the floor."* The underlined phrases are three ways the home was "in disarray and chaotic." "Food is all over the place" is a complete sentence. "Dirty dishes all over the kitchen" has no verb so it is not a sentence. "What appeared to be animal feces on the floor" is not a sentence (no verb). So the three statements are not parallel. Our correction eliminates the unhelpful language ("all over the place" and "all over the kitchen") and makes the three descriptions parallel. Alternatively, the sentence could be broken into shorter sentences: *The home was chaotic and messy. For example, food and dirty dishes covered most surfaces, and what appeared to be animal feces was on the floor.*

56. Use the singular possessive: "Danielle's."

57. "Danni, 14 years old" is more professional than "Danni 14 yrs old."

58. *". . .they either do not or are unable to adequately supervise her"* has the parallelism problem of "do not" (negative wording)

and "are unable" (positive wording). While grammatically acceptable, this switch in voices is confusing, so we reworded the language. In addition, "adequately" is an adverb that modifies both "supervise" and "manage" (verbs), but was placed inside the infinitive form, "to supervise." "Adequately" should be placed somewhere else, perhaps after "behavior," but that raises the problem of misplacing the modifier, "adequately." This is one of those exceptions to the rule about not splitting infinitives. We left "adequately" where it was because any "fix" made the sentence worse.

59. See # 57: "Jimmy, 8-months" is more appropriate.

60. Semicolon is incorrect because the next phrase is not a full sentence. We used "i.e.," meaning "that is" or "specifically," to show that hygiene and clothing are the meaning of "unkempt and dirty." A colon would work too.

61. The original sentence had a few problems, notably the sentence's subject—"interactions"—did not have a verb, so this was not a complete sentence. Also, "thus far" is less professional than "to date," and a preposition or some wording is needed to link "interactions" with "Jimmy." We used the proposition "in" as a way of connecting the two elements of the sentence.

cont.

Safety Decision: ⑥② Due ⑥③ to lack of supervision, neglectful
care and potential substance abuse of mother, the children are not safe in
the home while ⑥④ Jarrod is on the road.

Safety Plan: Jarrod is very upset by the involvement of the child
protection agency, ⑥⑤ and has agreed to take two weeks ⑥⑥ of vacation to take
care of the children and ⑥⑦ to try to put things in place to make it safe
for him to leave again. He seems to have developed more insight ⑥⑧ that all
is not "OK" with his family. ⑥⑨ His mother is ⑦⑩ willing to come and help
him during these two weeks, ⑦① and potentially a bit longer ⑦②. While she
cannot care for the children, ⑦③ she can help to teach him how to care for them ⑦④.
For example, she can help Danielle to better understand how to feed and
care for Jimmy ⑦⑤. A potential disadvantage ⑦⑥ of this plan is that Jarrod could
become dependent ⑦⑦ on his mother. ⑦⑧ We will have to keep an eye on that.

EXPLANATIONS OF CORRECTIONS

62. "It seems to me" is unnecessary" and passive wording.
63. Homophone error: Due and do—"due" refers to a deadline; "do" is an action.
64. Homophone error: while and wile—"while" means during; "wile" means cunning or trickery.
65. Insert comma between independent clause and phrase.
66. No possessive required.
67. "And" and "also" are redundant.
68. "Insite" is not a word.
69. Delete unnecessary close-quotation mark.
70. Split verb form error: "also" does not belong inside "is willing"; We eliminated "also" as unnecessary.
71. Insert comma between independent clause and phrase.
72. "As well" and "and" are redundant.
73. Insert comma after an introductory phrase.
74. No need to repeat the word "children"; "them" is clear.

75. "Also" does not fit the thought here. Jarrod's mother can help; one way is to improve Danielle's parenting skills. We used "for example" instead of "also." Also, we left the split infinitive ("to better understand") because we could not think of a better place to put "better." We might have reworded the sentence entirely: *For example, she can help improve Danielle's parenting skills.*
76. Word choice: "disadvantage" refers to a barrier while "downfall" means a loss of status or position.
77. Spelling error.
78. Run-on sentence. We split it into two separate sentences. A comma cannot be used to connect two complete sentences. Either a semicolon (if the two thoughts are closely related) or a conjunction (e.g., but, and, however, therefore) can be used, or two separate sentences are needed.

CASE 2: CHILDREN AT RISK: THE GRAMME FAMILY

This document is taken from the case file of a family that receives services from a state child welfare department. There are 40 writing errors in this document.

Family members mentioned in the document	Abbreviations used in the document
Anna Gramme, 23 (mother) Ben, male, 4 Isabel, female, 18 mos Kevin, male, 4 mos Johnetta, 41 (MGM)	CPI = Child Protective Investigator CPS = Child Protective Services (state child welfare department) MGM = maternal grandmother (Johnetta) FSCI = Fredonia State Correction Institution (state prison) FCH = Fredonia Children's Hospital; mos = months

ORIGINAL VERSION

Anna is 23. She is a single mother with 3 children (Ben 4, Isabel 18 mos, Kevin 4 mos). CPI investigated Isabel falling down from the 3rd floor landing to the second. Anna was inside, changing Kevin. Isabel broke her left leg. Although, no prior history as a parent. Anna was at Fredonia house child shelter for 9 months when she was 17 due to wayward behavior. In addition, she was also a victim of neglect when she was 7 do to her mothers' (Johnetta) alcohol abuse. Fortunately, Johnetta cooperated with CPS during both openings and reported that she's been sober since Anna was 11. The childrens father is at the FSCI. CPI indicated [confirmed] the case for lack of supervision and the case was opened to CPS. (27)

6 Weeks after the first opening, Isabel is taken to FCH again. This time with 3rd degree burns. She was in the tub, with the drain open waiting for Anna to give her a bath, Kevin started to cry and Anna went into the next room. Ben came into the bathroom and turned on the hot water to "help". The water temperature being 120 degrees. Kevin sustained burns consistent with the explanation. (28)

Safety Decision:
Children are conditionally safe.

Safety Plan:
Anna realizes that she has become overwhelmed caring for 3 small children. Anna asks MGM to come and stay with them for 2 weeks as Isabel will need additional care when she is released from the hospital. At that point MGM has stated that she could continue to support Anna by visiting several times per week and assisting with families night time

routine (dinner, bath, bedtime). CPS has spoken with MGM and confirmed that MGM is both able and willing to assist; and that MGM understands and agrees with her role in the safety plan. In addition, Anna has also notified the Landlord whom will lower the temperature on the water heater. MGM states that she will purchase a safety gate this week to put at the top of the staircase. Anna will also go through the home and identify additional safety hazards and develop a specific plan to address each hazard.

CASE 2: CORRECTED VERSION

Each number in the corrected version refers to an explanation below.

Anna is 23. She is a single mother with three ① children (Ben, 4, Isabel, 18 months, Kevin, four-months). CPI investigated Isabel falling down from the third floor landing to the second. Anna was inside the apartment ② at the time ③, changing Kevin's diaper ④. Isabel broke her left leg. Although ⑤ Anna has no ⑥ history of neglect ⑦ as a parent, ⑧ she was at Fredonia House Child Shelter ⑨ for nine ⑩ months when she was 17 years old, ⑪ due to wayward behavior. ⑫ She was also a victim of neglect when she was 7, ⑬ due ⑭ to her mother's ⑮ (Johnetta) alcohol abuse. ⑯ Johnetta has ⑰ cooperated with CPS during both openings and reports ⑱ that she has ⑲ been sober since Anna was 11. The children's ⑳ father is at the FSCI. CPI indicated (confirmed) the case for lack of supervision, ㉑ and the case was opened to CPS.

Six ㉒ weeks ㉓ after the first opening, Isabel was ㉔ taken to FCH again. This time, she had third-degree burns ㉕. She was in the tub, with the drain open, ㉖ waiting for Anna to give her a bath ㉗. Kevin started to cry and Anna went into the

cont.

EXPLANATIONS OF CORRECTIONS

1. Spell out numbers one through ten, except ages.
2. "The apartment" added for clarity.
3. "At the time" added for clarity.
4. "Diaper" added for clarity.
5. There is no comma required after one-word introductory conjunction.
6. "Prior" is redundant with "history."
7. "Of neglect" added for clarity.
8. Insert comma between subordinate and independent clauses.
9. Capitalize proper noun: the agency's title.
10. Spell out numbers one through ten, except ages.
11. Insert comma between independent clause and phrase.
12. Delete "In addition" because it is redundant with "also."
13. Insert comma between independent clause and phrase.
14. Homophone error: do and due—"do" is an action; "due" refers to a deadline.
15. Use singular possessive: mother's ("mothers'" is plural possessive) – several mothers' alcohol abuse.
16. Delete "fortunately" because it is the writer's opinion, not a professional observation.
17. Use "has cooperated" because it is proper tense, as it took place over time in the past, and continues in the present.
18. The verb "reports" could be present tense because it is happening now, or past tense, because it happened at one time before. Here the proper verb tense is an option.
19. Spell out "she has"; contractions should be avoided in professional writing.
20. Plural possessive of children is children's—more than one child possess the noun "father".
21. Insert comma before a connecting conjunction (two independent clauses).
22. Spell out numbers at beginning of sentences.
23. The word "weeks" should not be capitalized because it does not begin a sentence.
24. Incorrect verb tense; events occurred in the past.
25. Incomplete sentence: "This time with 3rd degree burns" lacks a verb. We rewrote the sentence with a verb (had), and corrected "3rd degree" as "third-degree."
26. Commas should bracket a phrase that may be removed without substantially changing the sentence's meaning.
27. Run-on sentence error. Use a period to replace the comma and create two complete sentences.

cont.

next room. Ben came into the bathroom and turned on the hot water to
"help." ㉘ The water temperature was 120 degrees, and the child sustained burns
consistent with the explanation.

Safety Decision:
Children are conditionally safe.

Safety Plan:
Anna realizes that caring for three ㉙ small
children overwhelms her. Anna asked ㉚ MGM to stay ㉛ for two ㉜ weeks, ㉝ as
Isabel will need additional care when she is released from the hospital.
MGM states that she could continue to support Anna
after Isabel returns home, by visiting several times per week and assisting with the family's nighttime
routine (dinner, bath, bedtime) ㉞. CPS has spoken with MGM and confirmed
that MGM is both able and willing to assist ㉟ and that MGM understands
and agrees with her role in the safety plan. In addition, Anna has ㊱
notified the landlord ㊲, ㊳ who ㊴ will lower the temperature on the water heater.
MGM states that she will purchase a safety gate this week to put at the
top of the staircase. Anna will also go through the home, ㊵ identify
additional safety hazards, ㊶ and develop a specific plan to address each hazard.

EXPLANATIONS OF CORRECTIONS

28. Period location: period goes inside close-quotation mark.

29. We reorganized the sentence for active writing and clarity. Spell out numbers from one through ten, except ages.

30. Past tense should be used: "Anna asked."

31. Avoid redundant language: "come and" is redundant with "stay."

32. Spell out numbers from one through ten, except ages.

33. Insert comma before a connecting conjunction and to link two independent clauses. Also, the word "as" is not an "official" connecting conjunction, but suffices for documentation purposes.

34. The original sentence, "At that point MGM has stated that she could continue to support Anna by visiting several times per week and assisting with families night time routine (dinner, bath, bed-time)" had several errors: "at this point" is unnecessary verbiage and there is verb tense disagreement with "has stated"; the word "could" should replace "can" (present tense); the word "families'

should be "family's" to indicate the singular possessive; nighttime should be a closed compound; we inserted "after Isabel returns home" for clarity. Here is the corrected sentence: "MGM states that she can continue to support Anna after Isabel returns home by visiting several times per week and assisting with the family's nighttime routine (dinner, bath, and bedtime)."

35. Semicolon was incorrectly used because the subsequent phrase is not a complete sentence. Semicolons separate two complete sentences or items in a list.

36. Delete "also" because it is redundant with "in addition."

37. The word "landlord" should not be capitalized because it is a common noun.

38. Insert comma to separate an independent clause from phrase.

39. "Who" is correct; "whom" is used if it does not take a verb. In this case, "who" takes the verb "will lower."

40 & 41. Insert commas to separate independent clause from phrases.

CASE 3: MEDICAL SOCIAL WORK INTAKE: HOSPITAL-SETTING HEALTH, MENTAL HEALTH, AND SUBSTANCE ABUSE ISSUES

This is a hospital-based social worker's intake note about a patient who was referred to the social work department by a medical doctor. This social worker wrote two versions of the intake: brief and briefer, both using many abbreviations. In some social work settings, abbreviations are a must, as the social worker explains (in the box, below). The extent and nature of abbreviations in use will vary across human service settings. Learn and adapt to the conventions of any organization in which you practice. In this case, the social worker provided us with a list of commonly-used abbreviations.

We inserted twenty-one punctuation, word usage, and sentence structure errors. Deliberate shorthand, such as the absence of articles "the," " a," "an" and use of numerals, is accepted practice in this setting, so we did not correct these "errors." Again, you would check with your agency to be clear about writing expectations. Note the difference between the two narratives. How much important information is missing from the very brief "EMR" version? Abbreviations save some space, no doubt, but tight, precise, and focused writing saves much more.

"In the medical setting we use a lot of abbreviations, especially now that our space to convey information has been limited. Hospitals generally use military time." — Medical social worker

Patient and family mentioned in the document	Abbreviations used in the document
Male 53 y.o. Caucasian Family: wife and two sons (15 & 13)	SI/HI = suicidal/homicidal ideation A/VH = auditory/visual hallucinations X's = times Y = year/s w/ = with SOB = shortness of breath Hx = history h/o = history of p.r.n = as needed etoh = alcohol + = positive f/u = follow up Pt = patient PCP = primary care physician SW/Sw = social worker or social work department

cont.

Patient and family mentioned in the document	Abbreviations used in the document
	MD = physician Labs = laboratory tests Dept = department Lb = pound ED = Emergency Dept Avai = available Svcs = services SOB = shortness of breath

Patient Name
Patient Identification Number
Patient Date of Birth

ORIGINAL VERSION

0943 (military time): SW received referral from MD for depression/anxiety. (32)
Pt is a pleasant, 53 yo, Caucasian, male who lives with his wife of 14 years
and two teenage sons, Adam 13 and Brian 15. Pt is accompanied
by his wife whom pt identifies is also his primary support and caregiver.
Pt presents in the Emergency Room with symptoms of depression and
anxiety but denies any SI/HI or A/VH. Pt's wife verbalizes her concern as
pt does carry a h/o suicide attempts x's 3 which resulted in hospitalization.
Last hospitalization/attempt was 4 years ago. Pt presents with a flat affect
and depressed mood, decreased appetite with 15 lb weight loss in one
month, deceased ability to concentrate, decreased energy and irritability.
Pt also reports poor sleep at 2–4 hours of broken sleep per night.
Pt reports panic attacks upon waking; noting racing heartbeat, dry mouth
and SOB. Current medications include paxil 40mg, lorazepam .5mg p.r.n
Pt reports his current stressors' include recent job loss, an ailing parent
and issues with his eldest son at school. Pt denies any legal issues or legal
hx. Pt does report a family h/o depression and anxiety on his maternal side
and h/o etoh dependence with his father and older brother. Pt denies drug
or etoh use tho admits to cigarette use w/ a pack per day hx x's 15 years.
Pt completed his GED and vocational training and has worked as an
electrician for 35 years. Pt states he lost his job when the company he (33)
loyally worked for went bankrupt. Pt verbalizes his concern about paying
bills, supporting his family and finding knew employment at his age. Pt is
currently uninsured and is receiving unemployment at $650.00 per week.
Pt states his PCP has been proscribing his medications and he does not
see a therapist or psychiatrist presently. SW offered emotional support
to patient and his wife as well as discussed resources available through
the Dept of Human Services. Additionally, SW also provided resources
for mental health services with sliding scale fees for continuual support
and assistance in dealing with grief issues regarding his mother who is

terminally ill. Of note, pt's labs came back + for cocaine and marijuana. MD has cleared pt medically and pt does not feel he needs inpatient hospitalization for his depression or anxiety. Pt to f/u with mental health agency's and community resources for support. Sw to remain available for support and services as needed. [Signature of SW with credentials and pager number]

Condensed format for Electronic Medical Record (EMR) computer dates/ times note

Clinical Social Work Note: SW received referral from MD for depression/ anxiety. Pt is a pleasant, 53yo, Caucasian male accompanied to the Ed by his wife of 14years. Pt lives with his wife and two teenage sons. Pt presents with a flat affect and depressed mood, complaining of SOB, panic attacks, 15lb weight loss x's 1 mo., poor sleep, irritability, decreased concentration. Pt carries a h/o suicide attempts x's 3 with hospitalization. Last hospitalization 4 y ago. Pt denies SI, HI or A/VH. Pt reports recent job loss, ailing mother and issues with oldest son. Pt denies drug or etoh use, despite labs, +cocaine and marijuana. Pt receives unemployment. Sw provided emotional support, community resources and mental health resource information. Sw to remain avai. for support/svcs as needed.

[Name, credentials and pager]

CASE 3: CORRECTED VERSION

Each number in the corrected version refers to an explanation below.

0943 (military time): SW received referral from MD for depression/anxiety.
Pt is a ① 53 yo, Caucasian, male who lives with his wife of 14 years
and two teenage sons, Adam 13 and Brian 15. Pt is accompanied
by his wife who ② pt identifies ③ his primary support and caregiver.
Pt presents in the Emergency Room with symptoms of depression and
anxiety, ④ but denies any SI/HI or A/VH. Pt's wife verbalizes her concern as
pt carries ⑤ a h/o suicide attempts x's 3, which resulted in hospitalization.
Last hospitalization/attempt was 4 years ago. Pt presents with a flat affect
and depressed mood, decreased appetite with 15 lb weight loss in one
month, deceased ability to concentrate, decreased energy, and irritability.
Pt ⑥ reports ⑦ 2–4 hours of broken sleep per night.
Pt reports panic attacks upon waking, ⑧ noting racing heartbeat, dry mouth
and SOB. Current medications include paxil 40mg, lorazepam .5mg p.r.n
Pt reports his current stressors ⑨ include recent job loss, an ailing parent
and issues with his eldest son at school. Pt denies any legal issues or legal
hx. Pt reports ⑩ a family h/o depression and anxiety on his maternal
side, ⑪ and h/o etoh dependence with his father and older brother. Pt denies
drug or etoh use though ⑫ admits to cigarette use w/ a pack per day hx x's 15 years.
Pt completed his GED and vocational training, ⑬ and has worked as

cont.

EXPLANATIONS OF CORRECTIONS

1. Delete "pleasant." It is opinion and adds no helpful information.
2. "Whom" is incorrect because it takes a verb: "who patient identifies is also his primary support and caregiver." "Who is" is a noun and verb, so who is correct. Otherwise stated, "is" gives action to the "who/whom" pronoun, so who is correct.
3. Delete "is also." It is unnecessary.
4. Insert comma to separate independent clause and phrase.
5. "Carries" is briefer than "does carry."
6. Delete "also." It is unnecessary.
7. "Poor sleep" is unnecessary, as the specific information follows in the next phrase.
8. Semicolon is incorrectly used, as there are not two independent clauses being connected.
9. Delete apostrophe because no possessive required.
10. "Reports" is briefer than "does report."
11. Insert comma to separate independent clause and phrase.
12. "Tho" is not an acceptable abbreviation.
13. Insert comma to separate independent clause and phrase.

cont.

an electrician for 35 years. Pt states he lost his job when the company he ⑭
worked for went bankrupt. Pt verbalizes his concern about paying
bills, supporting his family and finding new ⑮ employment at his age. Pt is
currently uninsured and is receiving unemployment at $650.00 per week.
Pt states his PCP has been prescribing ⑯ his medications, ⑰ and he does not
see a therapist or psychiatrist presently. SW offered emotional support
to patient and his wife as well as discussed resources available through
the Dept of Human Services. Additionally, SW ⑱ provided resources
for mental health services with sliding scale fees for continual support
and assistance in dealing with grief issues regarding his mother, ⑲ who is
terminally ill. Of note, pt's labs came back + for cocaine and marijuana.
MD has cleared pt medically and pt does not feel he needs inpatient
hospitalization for his depression or anxiety. Pt to f/u with mental health
agency's and community resources for support. Sw to remain available
for support and services as needed. [Signature of SW with credentials and
pager number]

Condensed format for Electronic Medical Record (EMR) computer dates/
times note

Clinical Social Work Note: SW received referral from MD for depression/
anxiety. Pt is a ⑳ 53yo, Caucasian male, ㉑ accompanied to the Ed
by his wife of 14years. Pt lives with his wife and two teenage sons.
Pt presents with a flat affect and depressed mood, complaining of SOB,
panic attacks, 15lb weight loss x's 1 mo., poor sleep, irritability, decreased
concentration. Pt carries a h/o suicide attempts x's 3 with hospitalization.
Last hospitalization 4 y ago. Pt denies SI, HI or A/VH. Pt reports recent
job loss, ailing mother and issues with oldest son. Pt denies drug or etoh
use, despite labs, +cocaine and marijuana. Pt receives unemployment.
Sw provided emotional support, community resources and mental health
resource information. Sw to remain avai. for support/svcs as needed.

[Name, credentials and pager]

EXPLANATIONS OF CORRECTIONS

14. "Loyally" is opinion. If patient used the
term, it would be ok to include it in quotes if
the writer thinks it is important information.

15. Homophone error: new and knew—"knew"
means was aware of; "new" means not used.

16. Incorrect word choice: "prescribe" medications; "proscribe" means to rule out or
forbid.

17. Insert comma before a connecting conjunction (two independent clauses).

18. "Also" is redundant with "additionally."

19. Insert comma to separate independent
clause and phrase.

20. "Pleasant" is opinion (see #1).

21. Insert comma to separate independent
clause and phrase.

CASE 4: CORRECTIONS: PAROLE-READINESS REPORT

In the Fredonia Adult Corrections Center (ACC), a prisoner in the sexual offender treatment unit is assessed for his readiness for parole. The writer is the unit director, an MSW practitioner.

Review this assessment for writing errors and unnecessary verbiage. We inserted 40 writing errors, including one entire convoluted (i.e., confusing) sentence, which we rewrote in the corrected version.

REDONIA DEPARTMENT OF CORRECTIONS
SEX OFFENDER TREATMENT PROGRAM
P.L., ACSW, Director
March 2009 PAROLE REPORT

Individual mentioned in the document	Abbreviations used in the document
Ira Amici, male, 32	SOTP: Sexual Offender Treatment Program CPI: Child Protective Investigator CPS: Child Protective Services (state child welfare department) MGM/F/P: maternal grandmother/ father/parent FSJCC: Fredonia State Juvenile Corrections Center FCH: Fredonia Children's Hospital Mos: months

This is the first review on a nine-year sentence for Mr. Amici. He has participated in the SOTP for 2 years.

ORIGINAL VERSION

Original Report

It seems to me that Mr. Amici's initial attitude was wildly mixed. He openly admitted his crimes, a past history/record of sexual assaults, and was willing to take responsibility for feelings of attraction towards other inmates. He reveals a complicated history of child neglect, sexual abuse, placement in custody, child residential centers, and foster homes at an early age. He readily discussed a troubling and tangled business and romantic relationship with another convicted sex offender who he met in prison in 2005. On the other hand, Mr. Amici was controlling, demanding, and arrogant. He verbally violated another inmate's personal boundaries, and insisted on a transfer to Kentucky; his home state. He regularly

(37)

fluctuated between overreacting and expressing regret. To say Mr. Amici was a volatile and difficult person would be a tremendous understatement.

Mr. Amici was suspended from the Program for two months in December, 2007, for making a threat towards another SOTP inmate, after overpersonalizing a criticism made by the other inmate. In fact, he was advised at the time of suspension that despite his arrogance, he had shown promise in his forthright disclosures about himself, and could be permitted to return early. Since, he diligently completed suspension homework assignments, and assumed complete responsibility for his poor judgment he was returned in January, 2008.

(38)

Since that time, Mr. Amici's attitude has seen remarkable changes. He continues to demonstrate over personalization, impatients, and attention seeking behaviors, however, he has ceased controlling others, making dramatic demands, and has considerably calmed and matured. He visibly waits to respond, resisting impulses to act immediately and impulsively. He continues to participate actively in his core groups, and has moved forward on a coarse of self-analysis and personnel accountability. He is consistently open about his deficits, relationships, personal and family history, current deviant fantasy level, and emotions across the board. He is willing to express anger and other emotions in an appropriate manor, and is unafraid of admitting that he struggles with deviant fantasies, as should be expected with offenders' who sexually abuse children. He excepts criticism and modifies accordingly, without previous drama. He has formed a healthy relationship with his cellmate and has taken the opportunity to seek support from other SOTP participants. Mr. Amici has come along whey in a short 2 years.

Mr. Amici has demonstrated a fairly good grasp of the contributing factors involved in his offenses, paralleling his earlier performance in treatment – self-absorption and unmitigated rage. Presently, he speaks of these issues rather then acting on them. Ironically, while he openly accepts responsibility for his crimes, he has clinically and historically stalled at that important point. He needs to redouble his efforts to explore the depthful issues and traumas which "feed" his impulses, such as in the area of his recent romantic entanglement, the void between he and his father, and his past abandonment by his family.

(39)

On a whim, I recently asked Mr. Amici to work for the Program as a clerk, to which he agreed, and has been responsible and diligent in his duties. I have also asked him to prepare, for a future date, some type of block class to share his ability to make honest disclosures despite his own resistance, a critical skill that perhaps can be discussed with inmates new to the Program. I am thrilled that Mr. Amici has accepted the challenge.

It is my opinion that Mr. Amici is not yet ready to handle parole release. However, despite past difficulties, he has shown a clear determination to prevail over his sexual aggression and rage. He deserves credit for weathering the upheaval inherent in the recovery process, some of which was self-imposed. Overall, I believe an 18 month review is a realistic time frame for him to make a sustained change in the factors in this report. Since Mr. Amici is an offender whom will ultimately need the strongest support and accountability from parole supervision, 18 months will allow a reasonable time to consider those options.

CASE 4: CORRECTED VERSION

Each number in the corrected version refers to an explanation below.

① Mr. Amici's initial attitude was considerably ② mixed. He openly admitted his crimes, a past history/record of sexual assaults, and was willing to take responsibility for feelings of attraction towards other inmates. He revealed ③ a complicated history of child neglect, sexual abuse, and ④ placement in custody, child residential centers, and foster homes, ⑤ at an early age. He readily discussed a troubling and tangled business and romantic relationship with another convicted sex offender whom ⑥ he met in prison in 2005. On the other hand, Mr. Amici is ⑦ controlling, demanding, and arrogant. He verbally violated another inmate's personal boundaries, and insisted on a transfer to Kentucky, ⑧ his home state. He regularly fluctuates ⑨ between overreacting and expressing regret. To say Mr. Amici is ⑩ a volatile and difficult person would be an ⑪ understatement.

Mr. Amici was suspended from the Program for two months in December, 2007, for making a threat toward another SOTP inmate,

cont.

EXPLANATIONS OF CORRECTIONS

1. "It seems to me" is passive construction and wordy.
2. Word choice: "Considerably" expresses depth without overly editorializing.
3. "Revealed" is descriptive; "openly admitted" is more editorial and judgmental.
4. Parallelism. The list begins with "a complicated history of child neglect, sexual abuse, [and] placement. . ."; after that, the list shifts to the kinds of placements, breaking the pattern created in the first listed items. The solution is insertion of "and" before "placement," indicating that the "complicated history" list is ending. The next list elaborates on "placements," not "complicated history."
5. We inserted a comma before "at an early age" to indicate that "at an early age" applies to all the placements on the list, not just the last one, "foster homes." "At an early age" comes close to being a misplaced modifier because it modifies "placements," not "foster homes." We could not figure out a reasonable way to move "at an early age" closer to "placements," so we used a comma, which indicates "at an early age"

is not singularly modifying "foster homes." This is an example of a complex sentence that runs the risk of becoming convoluted or run-on. The comma and the parallelism correction help the sentence maintain its meaning. Another option is to rewrite the sentence as separate, simpler sentences.
6. "Whom" is correct because this is the predicate portion of the sentence, and the pronoun (who or whom) does not take a verb.
7. Here we encounter syntax errors. The narrative is written entirely in the past, which avoids shifting tenses. But those actions that are still ongoing should be written in the present tense. Rule: if it happened in the past, write it in the past tense; if it is a permanent or current situation, write it in the present tense.
8. Insert a comma here not semicolon, because there are not two complete sentences.
9. Syntax problem, see #7.
10. Syntax problem, see #7.
11. Avoid editorializing: "tremendous" adds the writer's non-clinical opinion.

cont.

after over-personalizing ⑫ a criticism made by the other inmate. ⑬ He was advised at the time of suspension that despite his arrogance, he had shown promise in his forthright disclosures about himself, and could be permitted to return early. Since ⑭ he diligently completed suspension homework assignments, and assumed complete responsibility for his poor judgment, ⑮ he was returned in January, 2008.

Since that time, Mr. Amici's attitude has seen remarkable changes. He continues to demonstrate over-personalization ⑯, impatience ⑰, and attention-seeking ⑱ behaviors, however, he has ceased controlling others and making dramatic demands, and has considerably calmed and matured. He visibly waits to respond, resisting impulses to act immediately and impulsively. He continues to participate actively in his core groups, and has moved forward on a course ⑲ of self-analysis and personal ⑳ accountability. He is consistently open about his deficits, relationships, personal and family history, current deviant fantasy level, and emotions, ㉑ across the board. He is willing to express anger and other emotions in an appropriate manner ㉒, and is unafraid of admitting that he struggles with deviant fantasies, as should be expected with offenders who sexually abuse children. He accepts ㉓ criticism and modifies accordingly, without previous drama. He has formed a healthy relationship with his cellmate and has taken the opportunity to seek support from other SOTP participants. Mr. Amici has come a long way ㉔ in a short two years.

Mr. Amici demonstrates ㉕ a fairly good grasp of the contributing factors involved in his offenses, paralleling his earlier performance in treatment – self-absorption and unmitigated rage. ㉖ He speaks of these

cont.

EXPLANATIONS OF CORRECTIONS

12. Compound word needs a hyphen.
13. "In fact" is excess verbiage; it adds nothing to the sentence.
14. Introductory conjunctions do not require a comma.
15. The phrase "and assumed complete responsibility for his poor judgment" should be bracketed with commas because the sentence can stand if the phrase is removed.
16. Hyphen required. See #12.
17. "Impatients" is not a word.
18. Be sure to hyphenate some compound noun adjective phrases when the two words are of equal value.
19. Homophone error: course and coarse— "coarse" means rough, uneven or vulgar.
20. Homophone error: personal and personnel—"personal" means private or

individual; "personnel" refers to people, usually employees.
21. This is a convoluted sentence. Insert comma between independent clause and phrase.
22. Homophone error: manner and manor— "manner" means self-comportment or style; "manor" is a castle or mansion.
23. Homophone error: accepts and excepts— "accepts" means agrees to or takes ownership; "excepts" means sets aside or avoids.
24. Homophone error: way and whey—"whey" is milk powder.
25. Verb tense error. Mr. ____ still demonstrates a grasp of the contributing factors, so this sentence should be written in the present tense.
26. Delete "presently" because it is redundant with the verb form, "speaks."

cont.

issues rather than ㉗ acting on them. Ironically, while he openly accepts responsibility for his crimes, he has clinically and historically stalled at that important point. He needs to redouble his efforts to explore the fundamental ㉘ issues and traumas which "feed" his impulses, such as ㉙ his recent romantic entanglement, the void between him ㉚ and his father, and his past abandonment by his family.

㉛ I recently asked Mr. Amici to work for the Program as a clerk, to which he agreed. ㉜ He has been responsible and diligent in his duties. I have also asked him to prepare, for a future date, a presentation for inmates, to share his ability to make honest disclosures despite his own resistance, a critical skill that may help others who are new to the Program ㉝. ㉞ Mr. Amici has accepted the challenge.

I believe ㉟ that Mr. Amici is not ㊱ ready to handle parole release. However, despite past difficulties, he has shown a clear determination to prevail over his sexual aggression and rage. He deserves credit for weathering the upheaval inherent in the recovery process, some of which was self-imposed. Overall, I believe an 18-month ㊲ review is a realistic time frame for him to make a sustained change in the factors identified ㊳ in this report. Since Mr. Amici is an offender who ㊴ ultimately ㊵ will need the strongest support and accountability from parole supervision, 18 months will allow a reasonable time to consider those options.

EXPLANATIONS OF CORRECTIONS

27. Homophone error: than vs. then—"than" is for comparisons; "then" refers to time.
28. "Depthful" is not a word; "fundamental" conveys the same concept. This is a vocabulary issue.
29. "In the arena of" is unnecessary wordiness.
30. "He" is incorrect because this is the predicate portion of the sentence.
31. We deleted "on a whim" because it is about the writer, not the client, and adds nothing to the sentence; it is unnecessary.
32. We separated one sentence with a parallelism problem into separate sentences.
33. This is the sentence we rewrote for clarity. The original was very difficult to follow. Notice that we did not change the meaning of the sentence.

34. "I am thrilled that" is excess verbiage and opinion. See #31.
35. Unnecessary verbiage.
36. "Yet" is unnecessary. He is not ready.
37. Hyphenate double-digit numbers combined with nouns to modify other words.
38. Missing words created ambiguity.
39. Subjective portion of a sentence: use who, not whom.
40. We moved "ultimately" out of the verb form "will need." Ideally, verb forms should not be split by modifiers, but this was one of the few places in this report that we could avoid split verb forms without creating a very awkward sentence.

CASE 5: MENTAL HEALTH: INTEGRATED SUMMARY OF CARE

*This document combines diagnostic and behavioral/cognitive information
for a program participant with mental health diagnoses. We inserted
51 writing errors.*

ORIGINAL VERSION

Sara, also known as "Rudi", is a 25 year old single, African-American   (42)
female who resides independently in the community. She is very
personable and pleasant. Sara was referred from the State Clinic due
to multiple hospitalizations (suicidal ideations/attempts). Sara has been
hospitalized 5 times in the last 6 months and a higher level of service
is required to assist her in maintaining community tenure. Prior to her
admission Sara was diagnosed with the following:

Axis I: Bipolar I Disorder, most recent episode mixed without psychotic
features
Axis II: Borderline Personality Disorder
Axis III: None
Axis IV: Unemployed, temporarily lost custody of two children, limited
support network
Axis V: 55

Saras' symptoms include, but are not limited to: depressed mood,
suicidal ideations/ attempts, self-injurious behaviors, anxiety, low self-
esteem, impulsivity, and rage attacks, ect. Feelings of low self-esteem/
selfimage, feelings of abandonment, and chronic feelings of emptiness.
Currently taking Paxil 20 mg daily, Depakote 500 mg BID, and Klonopin
1mg TID/PRN, drug allergies are not known at this time. As prescribed,
Sara reports that she takes her medications; however, records indicate
times of non-compliance and abuse (i.e., drug overdose). Sara denies any
current or passed problems with substance abuse, though does admit
to having consumed alcohol socially with no significant personal or legal   (43)
consequences. Sara, also reports that she has no current or past legal
issues, outside of a custody case in Family Court currently.

Sara reports that she has no significant health issues; however, she
appears to be slightly overweight. Her medical care is currently being
provided by Dr. Simon Sais.

Sara graduated high school and shares that she would like to go back to
college to pursue a degree in Psychology. Sara is currently unemployed;
however, she states that she would like to find a part-time job working or
volunteering at a daycare because she "misses" her children so much.
Sara reports that she really does not have any hobbies outside of watching
television. Sara identifies herself as a Baptist; however, she has not been

to a religious service in several years and has no intentions of attending such services in the near future. Though, Sara would like to pursue school and employment. She states that the main focus at this time is regaining custody of her two children (four-year old daughter and two-year old son), whom were removed from the home by the Division of Family Services ten months ago do to reported neglect/mistreatment in the home.

Sara currently resides in a two-bedroom apartment, which is subsidized by state assistance and is currently her own guardian. She has applied for disability, but has not yet been approved; her only source of income being welfare.

Sara's family (mother and two sisters) live in the local community. Her two children currently reside with Sara's mother, whom she blames for the removal of her children. Sara currently has bi-weekly supervised visitation with her children. Overall, she describes her relationship with her entire family as estrained.

(44)

During the initial interview, Sara demonstrated limited insite into her mental illness and wasn't sure why she was referred to the Continuous Treatment Team Program. Sara stated that she'd rather continue receiving services from the State Clinic. Sara lacks a strong support network and her limited insite may present as an obstacle to treatment.

Areas of Need to be identified in the Plan:
1. Maintain community tenure
2. Regain custody of her 2 children
3. Pursue higher education
4. Obtain part-time employment or volunteer position

Discharge Criteria:
To transition to a less restrictive setting, Sara will be able to demonstrate the following for at least twelve consecutive months:

- Maintain community tenure
- Regain custody of her 2 children
- Obtain information by local colleges regarding pursing a degree in Psychology
- Participate in the CTT supported employment program or local vocational rehabilitation program to pursue employment

CASE 5: CORRECTED VERSION

Each number in the corrected version refers to an explanation below.

Sara, also known as "Rudi," ① is a 25-year-old ② single ③ African-American female who resides independently in the community. ④ Sara was referred by ⑤ the State Clinic due ⑥ to multiple hospitalizations (suicidal ideations/attempts). Sara has been hospitalized five ⑦ times in the last six ⑧ months, therefore ⑨ a higher level of service is required to assist her in maintaining community tenure. Prior to her admission, ⑩ Sara was diagnosed with the following:

Axis I: Bipolar I Disorder, most recent episode mixed without psychotic features
Axis II: Borderline Personality Disorder
Axis III: None
Axis IV: Unemployed, temporarily lost custody of two children, limited support network
Axis V: 55

Sara's ⑪ symptoms include, but are not limited to: depressed mood, suicidal ideations/attempts, self-injurious behaviors, anxiety, low self-esteem, impulsivity, and rage attacks ⑫. Sara reports feelings of low self-esteem/self image, feelings of abandonment, and chronic feelings of emptiness ⑬.
With no known drug allergies, Sara is taking Paxil 20 mg daily, Depakote 500 mg BID, and Klonopin 1mg TID/PRN ⑭. Sara reports that she takes her medications as prescribed ⑮, ⑯ but records indicate times of non-compliance and abuse (i.e., drug overdose). Sara denies any

cont.

EXPLANATIONS OF CORRECTIONS

1. Insert comma inside the close-quotation mark.
2. Hyphenate "25-year".
3. Delete comma to avoid interrupting a clear thought.
4. Author's opinion, unnecessary information.
5. Referred <u>by</u> not <u>from</u>.
6. Homophone error: due and do—"due" refers to deadline; "do" is an action.
7. Spell out numbers from one through ten.
8. Spell out numbers from one through ten.
9. Incorrect conjunction: "and" connects equal thoughts; in this case the second thought is a consequence of the first, not an equal. Also, notice the spelling of "therefore."
10. Insert comma after the introductory phrase.
11. Use singular possessive.
12. "Ect" is incorrect; "etc." is the correct spelling, but since the list begins with "include," "etc." should not be used.
13. This is not a sentence; we added a subject and verb to complete the sentence.
14. The sentence was written in the passive voice with a misplaced modifier. The replacement sentence is affirmative and active.
15. Misplaced modifier: "as prescribed" should be as close as possible to "taking medication."
16. The semicolon and "however" are unnecessary; "but" is an acceptable connecting conjunction between two independent clauses.

cont.

current or past ⑰ problems with substance abuse, but ⑱ she admits ⑲ to having consumed alcohol socially, ⑳ with no significant personal or legal consequences. Sara ㉑ also reports that she has no current or past legal issues, outside of a custody case in Family Court ㉒.

Sara reports that she has no significant health issues, but ㉓ she appears to be slightly overweight. Her medical care is currently being provided by Dr. Simon Sais.

Sara graduated from ㉔ high school and shares that she would like to go back to college to pursue a degree in psychology ㉕. Sara is currently unemployed, however ㉖ she states that she would like to find a part-time job working or volunteering at a daycare program ㉗ because she "misses" her children so much. Sara reports that she ㉘ does not have any hobbies outside of watching television. Sara identifies herself as a Baptist, however ㉙ she has not been to a religious service in several years and has no intentions of attending such services in the near future. Though ㉚ Sara would like to pursue school and employment, ㉛ she states that the main focus at this time is regaining custody of her two children (four-year old daughter and two-year old son), who ㉜ were removed from the home by the Division of Family Services ten months ago, ㉝ due to reported neglect/mistreatment in the home.

Sara ㉞ resides in a two-bedroom apartment, which is subsidized by state assistance ㉟, and she ㊱ is currently her own guardian. She has applied for disability, but has not yet been approved; her only source of income is ㊲ welfare.

cont.

EXPLANATIONS OF CORRECTIONS

17. Homophone error: past and passed—"past" means "ago"; "passed" means "went by."
18. "But" is an allowable connecting conjunction between two independent clauses.
19. "She admits" is more direct and clearer than "does admit," which is a phrase missing a noun.
20. Insert comma between independent clause and phrase.
21. Delete comma after "Sara" because no pause is needed.
22. "Currently" is redundant with the rest of the sentence.
23. Insert comma before a connecting conjunction. Use "but " not "however" between two independent clauses.
24. "Graduated from" is correct.
25. Psychology should not be capitalized because it is a common noun.

26. See #22.
27. "Daycare" is an adjective, so it needs a noun; we added "program."
28. "Really" is excess verbiage.
29. See #22.
30. Delete comma after the introductory conjunction, "though."
31. This is an incomplete sentence we corrected by linking it with the next sentence.
32. "Who" takes the verb, "were."
33. Insert comma between independent clause and phrase.
34. "Currently" is unnecessary verbiage.
35. Parallelism in listing programs: you have the choice to capitalize or not, but be consistent.
36. "She" inserted for clarity.
37. "Being" is the incorrect form of the "to be" verb.

cont.

Sara's family (mother and two sisters) lives ⊛ in the local community. Her two children ㊴ reside with Sara's mother, whom she blames for the removal of her children. Sara ㊵ has bi-weekly supervised visitation with her children. Overall, she describes her relationship with her entire family as estranged ㊶.

During the initial interview, Sara demonstrated limited insight ㊷ into her mental illness and was not ㊸ sure why she was referred to the Continuous Treatment Team Program. Sara stated that she would ㊹ rather continue receiving services from the State Clinic. Sara lacks a strong support network, but ㊺ her limited insight ㊻ may present as an obstacle to treatment.

Areas of Need to be identified in the Plan:
1. Maintain community tenure
2. Regain custody of her two ㊼ children
3. Pursue higher education
4. Obtain part-time employment or volunteer position

Discharge Criteria:
To transition to a less restrictive setting, Sara will be able to demonstrate the following for at least twelve consecutive months:

- Maintain community tenure
- Regain custody of her two ㊽ children
- Obtain information from ㊾ local colleges regarding pursing a degree in psychology ㊿
- Participate in the CTT-supported ㋕ employment program or local vocational rehabilitation program to pursue employment

EXPLANATIONS OF CORRECTIONS

38. Verb-noun agreement error: the subject, "family," is singular, so the verb must be singular ("lives").

39. "Currently" is excess verbiage.

40. Unnecessary verbiage.

41. "Estrained" is not a word.

42. "Insite" is not a word.

43. Spell out contractions unless approved by the agency.

44. Spell out contractions unless approved by the agency.

45. "But" is more appropriate than "and" because the second half of the sentence is a counterpoint to the first; "and" connects equals.

46. "Insite" is not a word.

47. Spell out numbers from one through ten.

48. Spell out numbers from one through ten.

49. "From" is the correct preposition: information comes <u>from</u>, not <u>by</u>, sources.

50. "Psychology" is not a proper noun and should not be capitalized.

51. "CTT-supported" is hyphenated because it is a compound adjective.

CASE 6: SCHOOL SOCIAL WORK: SOCIAL ASSESSMENT

This is a social assessment written by a school social worker in a public high school. The assessment follows a template used by the district, but is typical of such narratives that school social workers must complete. We inserted 34 writing errors.

Participants mentioned in the document	Abbreviations used in the document
<u>Family members</u> Cathy, 44 (mother) Dominic, 46 (father) Jane, female, 17 Josh, male, 24 <u>Professionals (not teachers)</u> Dr. Albright (PCP) Dr. Harkness (neurologist) Dr. Depp (psychiatrist) Iris Flowers (LICSW) Ms. Rathbone (counselor)	CPS: Child Protective Services (state child welfare department) SFPH: South Fredonia Psychiatric Hospital FHHS: Fredonia Heights High School PCP: primary care physician

ORIGINAL VERSION

SCHOOL DEPARTMENT
PUPIL PERSONNEL SERVICES
Social Assessment

SUMMARY OF SOCIAL ASSESSMENT: (50)

Reason for Referral:
Jane is a 17 year-old female, currently hospitalized at South Fredonia Psychiatric Hospital (SFPH) and has been since 9-8-2010. Jane is considered a senior at Fredonia Heights High School, (FHHS). A social history was requested as part of the initial evaluation process - to determine eligibility for special education. Ms. Doe says she has been concerned with Jane's condition for the last 8 months, and believes that Jane needs to be in a therapeutic school where she can receive the proper care. Information reported here was received through a review of school records, interviews with faculty, and an interview, including a social history assessment, with Ms. Doe. Jane was not part of this social history, due to her current hospitalization.

Birth, Developmental, & Medical History:
Ms. Doe reports having taken insulin during her pregnancy with Jane, due to gestational diabetes. Jane was born a week early, weighing 9 lbs. 12 oz.

at birth. Ms. Doe reports Jane reached developmental milestones earlier than most children, crawling at 3 months, walking at 10 months, talking at about a year, and completing toilet training by 14 months. Ms. Doe reports Jane is allergic to peanuts and is in good health, however in 1995 (at age two) her tonsils were removed and tubes were inserted into her ears. Ms. Doe reports a family medical history of high blood pressure, diabetes and skin cancer.

Jane receives primary medical care through Dr. Albright, who she last visited in May 2009, for migraines. Ms. Doe reports Jane was also seen for migraines by neurologist, Dr. Harkness, who prescribed Depakote, which did not seem to help. Ms. Doe reports migraines may have been the cause of Jane's hallucinations throughout the summer of 2009. In December of that year, Ms. Doe first noticed differences in Janes personality. However Jane did not disclose hallucinations to anyone until March 2010, during her first hospitalization, which followed her disclosure to Dr. Albright that she wanted too kill herself. Dr. Albright attributes Janes health issues to migraines.

(51)

Ms. Doe reports after her first hospitalization, (March 2010), Jane began seeing psychiatrist, Dr. Depp., who prescribed Prozac, which seemed to help. However, Jane was still hallucinating and not disclosing. In May 2010, Dr. D. added Ativan, which made Jane very sleepy. Ms. Doe reports that Jane had three hospitalization episodes over five months in 2010 (March [SF Psychiatric Hospital for suicide ideation], June [Fredonia City General Hospital for cutting]), and July [SF Psychiatric Hospital, again, for hearing voices which told her to harm her family]). Mrs. Doe reports that in July 2010, Jane tried treatment in the SFPH's partial hospitalization program, which was not successful. Ms. Doe reports Jane was readmitted at SF Psychiatric Hospital one more time, on 9/8/10, due to hallucinations, and to try a new course of medication. Ms. Doe reports that after she left Jane on 9/8/2010, she felt something was wrong and was later told that Jane was placed on 1:1 due to cutting.

To summarize, Jane has been hospitalized on four separate occasions in the last 6 months, (3/1/10-3/9/10; 6/17/10-8/19/10; 8/27/10-9/2/10; 9/8/10 through present) all but the second episode at SF Psychiatric Hospital, due to suicidal ideation and psychotic symptoms (auditory / visual hallucinations). According to reports from SF Psychiatric Hospital and Ms. Doe, Jane is currently under the care of psychiatrist (Dr. S.), at SF Psychiatric Hospital, and is diagnosed with Psychotic Disorder NOS and Depressive Disorder NOS, and prescribed Abilify (7.5mg / 2x daily), Prozac (30mg / am), Ativan (1mg / 3x daily) Zyprexa (2.5mg / am/pm) to help treat related symptoms of psychosis, depression and anxiety.

Family Data: (52)

Prior to hospitalization, Jane was living with her mother and father, Cathy and Dominic Doe, who have been married for 25 years. Mr. Doe works for Comprehensive Care Clinic (CCC) and Ms. Doe works for Bean Town Chiropractics, Inc. Jane also has a brother, Josh (24), who is no longer living at home, as he got married in June 2010, and moved out of state. Jane has lived in her current home for the last 5 years; and has moved approximately 5 times throughout her life. State Child Protective Services (CPS) became involved in February 2010, due to Jane's allegation that Ms. Doe hit her on three different occasions in December 2009. Ms. Doe reports the allegations were determined to be unfounded; while being interviewed Jane changed the dates of when mom was physical with her. CPS closed the case in June 2010.

Ms. Doe reports herself and Jane being involved in a car accident about ten years ago, when their car was hit by a drunk driver. Ms. Doe reports Jane has been "vehemently" against drinking since this accident, which is the reason she and Mr. Doe stopped going out with friends for drinks a few nights a week. Ms. Doe also asserts that she and Mr. Doe do not engage in drug use.

Ms. Doe reports Jane having a close relationship with both parents and her brother, however, Jane appears to be closest to her dad.

Social/Emotional & Behavioral Functioning:

Ms. Doe describes Jane as outgoing, caring, funny, needing to be around family, not liking to be alone, and a perfectionist, never thinking her work is good enough. Ms. Doe reports that both parents are involved with discipline when it is warranted, and typical punishment for Jane includes losing privileges, however Jane does not require alot of discipline. Ms. Doe thinks Jane has never been grounded. She believes Jane's delusions and hallucinations dictate her behavior.

Ms. Doe reports prior to hospitalization Jane was very school-driven: she (53) was class president for 3 years, spent much of her free time planning events, being involved with school activities and volunteering in the community, particularly with Big Sisters. Ms. Doe reports Jane was an all-star in softball until eighth grade, when she broke both ankles in two unrelated accidents, and was told she could no longer participate in sports.

Ms. Doe reports Jane started to see clinician, Iris Flowers, LICSW, once or twice a week, for outpatient counseling after her release from SF Psychiatric Hospital in March, until she was rehospitalized in June, and has not been back to see her. Ms. Doe reports Jane will not continue with this clinician after she is released from SF Psychiatric Hospital, as they did not seem to build a therapeutic relationship. Jane may continue with another councilor.

Ms. Doe reports Jane has formed some lasting friendships while in High School. Prior to hospitalizations, she was very involved with her friends and "hung out" like typical teenagers. After hospitalizations, some of them still visit when she is home, but they have been unsure how to handle Jane's recent behaviors. In addition, a few of them have had difficulty maintaining relationships with Jane, as she is unable to have anyone visit at the hospital, accept family.

School History:

Ms. Doe reports Jane has been attending school in the local School District since Kindergarten, and is currently enrolled in 12th grade at FC High School; Jane's hallucinations, which began in 11th grade, caused her to miss many days of school.

As of July 22, 2010, Jane had enough academic credits to put her on track to graduate in June 2011. Ms. Rathbone, guidance counselor, reports Jane needs the following credits in order to graduate: English 12, PE, ½ credit fine arts and 2.5 elective credits. Jane's teachers are consistent in reporting that she is a very brite student, hard worker, motivated to do good and complete work, is not a behavior issue in class, was periodically absent last year, and appeared to become unmotivated in the second semester. 3 teachers gave more detailed reports about Jane and their interaction with her last year and years' prior. Mr. Abel (Contemporary Issues) reported having Jane as a student in her freshman year. He said that she began much the same as this year, was very smart, well spoken, and pleasant. He recalled that after first semester she had a high absentee rate and appeared less motivated. He believes she may not have been as challenged with his class, which could be the reason she did not appear as motivated. Ms. Beta (two writing classes) reported Jane was motivated and completed her work in tenth and eleventh grades, until the second semester last year, when she did not appear as motivated and did not complete work she missed wile out of school. Mr. Charlie (Pre Calculus) reported Jane started off well at the beginning of last year, but in the second semester she did not appear to be as attentive, did not complete as much homework and did not do as well on tests.

(54)

Summary:
Jane is a 17 year-old female currently hospitalized at SF Psychiatric Hospital. A social history was requested as part of the initial evaluation process to determine eligibility for special education. Since hospitalizations began in March, Jane has spent most of her time in SF Psychiatric Hospital; her parents try to visit her on a daily basis. SF Psychiatric Hospital is trying to stabilize Jane's medication and has tried numerous medications that have not been helpful to this point. SF Psychiatric Hospital staff recommends that Jane transition to a therapeutic day school environment, as she needs a low student-to-teacher ratio and a program with significant experience educating psychotic adolescents. Recommendations will be reviewed when all special education evaluations are completed.

CASE 6: CORRECTED VERSION

Each number in the corrected version refers to an explanation below.

SUMMARY OF SOCIAL ASSESSMENT:

Reason for Referral:
Jane, a 17-year-old female, has been hospitalized at South Fredonia
Psychiatric Hospital (SFPH) since 9/8/2010 ①. Jane is
considered a senior at Fredonia Heights High School (FHHS) ②. A social
history was requested as part of the initial evaluation process to
determine eligibility for special education. Ms. Doe says she has been
concerned with Jane's condition for the last eight ③ months, and believes that
Jane needs to be in a therapeutic school where she can receive the proper
care. Information reported here was received through a review of school
records, interviews with faculty, and an interview, including a social history
assessment ④ with Ms. Doe. Jane was not part of this social history, due to
her current hospitalization.

Birth, Developmental, & Medical History:
Ms. Doe reports having taken insulin during her pregnancy with Jane, due
to gestational diabetes. Jane was born a week early, weighing 9 lbs. 12 oz.
at birth. Ms. Doe reports Jane reached developmental milestones earlier
than most children, crawling at 3 months, walking at 10 months, talking at
about a year, and completing toilet training by 14 months. Ms. Doe reports
Jane is allergic to peanuts and is in good health, however in 1995 (at age
2) her tonsils were removed and tubes were inserted into her ears.
Ms. Doe reports a family medical history of high blood pressure, diabetes and
skin cancer.

Jane receives primary medical care through Dr. Albright, whom ⑤ she last
visited in May 2009, for migraines. Ms. Doe reports Jane was also seen for
migraines by neurologist, Dr. Harkness, who prescribed Depakote, which
did not seem to help. Ms. Doe reports migraines may have been the cause
of Jane's hallucinations throughout the summer of 2009. In December of
that year, Ms. Doe first noticed differences in Jane's ⑥ personality. However
Jane did not disclose hallucinations to anyone until March 2010, during

cont.

EXPLANATIONS OF CORRECTIONS

1. Combine relevant information in fewer words for clarity and brevity.
2. Delete comma before parenthesis.
3. Spell out numbers from one through ten.
4. Delete comma because there is no need for a pause.
5. In the phrase, "whom she last visited," the verb "visit" describes "she," not "who." "Who" takes no verb, so the proper form must be "whom."
6. Use a singular possessive apostrophe.
7. Homophone error: to and too—"too" means also or excessive.

cont.

her first hospitalization, which followed her disclosure to Dr. Albright that she wanted to ⑦ kill herself. Dr. Albright attributes Jane's ⑧ health issues to migraines.

Ms. Doe reports after her first hospitalization ⑨ (March 2010), Jane began seeing psychiatrist, Dr. D., who prescribed Prozac, which seemed to help. However, Jane was still hallucinating and not disclosing. In May 2010, Dr. D. added Ativan, which made Jane very sleepy. Ms. Doe reports that Jane had three hospitalization episodes over five months in 2010 (March [SF Psychiatric Hospital for suicide ideation], June [Fredonia City General Hospital for cutting]), and July [SF Psychiatric Hospital, again, for hearing voices which told her to harm her family]). Mrs. Doe reports that in July 2010, Jane tried treatment in the SFPH's partial hospitalization program, which was not successful. Ms. Doe reports Jane was readmitted at SF Psychiatric Hospital ⑩, on 9/8/10, due to hallucinations, and to try a new course of medication. Ms. Doe reports that after she left Jane on 9/8/2010, she felt something was wrong and was later told that Jane was placed on 1:1 due to cutting.

To summarize, Jane has been hospitalized on four separate occasions in the last six ⑪ months ⑫ (3/1/10-3/9/10; 6/17/10-8/19/10; 8/27/10-9/2/10; 9/8/10 through present), ⑬ all but the second episode at SF Psychiatric Hospital, due to suicidal ideation and psychotic symptoms (auditory / visual hallucinations). According to reports from SF Psychiatric Hospital and Ms. Doe, Jane is currently under the care of psychiatrist (Dr. S.), at SF Psychiatric Hospital. ⑭ Jane is diagnosed with Psychotic Disorder NOS and Depressive Disorder NOS, and prescribed Abilify (7.5mg / 2x daily), Prozac (30mg / am), Ativan (1mg / 3x daily), and Zyprexa (2.5mg / am/pm) to help treat related symptoms of psychosis, depression and anxiety.

cont.

EXPLANATIONS OF CORRECTIONS

8. Use a singular possessive apostrophe.

9. Delete comma before parenthesis.

10. "One more time" is redundant with "readmitted."

11. Spell out numbers one through ten.

12. Delete comma before parenthesis.

13. The comma placed before the opening parenthesis belongs after the closing parenthesis.

14. We separated one long, involved sentence into two simpler sentences. The previous sentence could have been rewritten this way too.

15. Spell out numbers from one through ten.

cont.

Family Data:
Prior to hospitalization, Jane was living with her mother and father, Cathy and Dominic Doe, who have been married for 25 years. Mr. Doe works for Comprehensive Care Clinic (CCC) and Ms. Doe works for Bean Town Chiropractics, Inc. Jane also has a brother, Josh (24), who is no longer living at home, as he got married in June 2010, and moved out of state. Jane has lived in her current home for the last five ⑮ years; and has moved approximately five ⑯ times throughout her life. State Child Protective Services (CPS) became involved in February 2010, due to Jane's allegation that Ms. Doe hit her on three different occasions in December 2009. Ms. Doe reports the allegations were determined to be unfounded; while being interviewed Jane changed the dates of when mom was physical with her. CPS closed the case in June 2010.

Ms. Doe reports herself and Jane being involved in a car accident about ten ⑰ years ago, when their car was hit by a drunk driver. Ms. Doe reports Jane has been "vehemently" against drinking since this accident, which is the reason she and Mr. Doe stopped going out with friends for drinks a few nights a week. Ms. Doe also asserts that she and Mr. Doe do not engage in drug use.

Ms. Doe reports Jane having a close relationship with both parents and her brother, however ⑱ Jane appears to be closest to her dad.

Social/Emotional & Behavioral Functioning:
Ms. Doe describes Jane as outgoing, caring, funny, needing to be around family, not liking to be alone, and a perfectionist, never thinking her work is good enough. Ms. Doe reports that both parents are involved with discipline when it is warranted. ⑲ Typical punishment for Jane includes losing privileges, however Jane does not require a lot ⑳ of discipline. Ms. Doe thinks Jane has never been grounded. She believes Jane's delusions and hallucinations dictate her behavior.

cont.

EXPLANATIONS OF CORRECTIONS

16. Spell out numbers from one through ten.
17. Spell out numbers from one through ten.
18. Insert comma before, but not after, conjunction.

19. Two sentences are preferable to one sentence with phrases connected by "and," because the connected phrases are not parallel and equal to each other.
20. "Alot" is not a word. "A lot" is two words.

cont.

Ms. Doe reports prior to hospitalization Jane was very school-driven: she was class president for three ㉑ years. ㉒ She spent much of her free time planning events, being involved with school activities and volunteering in the community, particularly with Big Sisters. Ms. Doe reports Jane was an all-star in softball until eighth grade, when she broke both ankles in two unrelated accidents, and was told she could no longer participate in sports.

Ms. Doe reports Jane started to see clinician, Iris Flowers, LICSW, once or twice a week, for outpatient counseling after her release from SF Psychiatric Hospital in March, until she was re-hospitalized in June, and has not been back to see her. Ms. Doe reports Jane will not continue with this clinician after she is released from SF Psychiatric Hospital, as they did not seem to build a therapeutic relationship. Jane may continue with another counselor ㉓.

Ms. Doe reports Jane has formed some lasting friendships while in high school ㉔. Prior to hospitalizations, she was very involved with her friends and "hung out" like a typical teenager ㉕. After hospitalizations, some of them still visit when she is home, but they have been unsure how to handle Jane's recent behaviors. In addition, a few of them have had difficulty maintaining relationships with Jane, as she is unable to have anyone visit at the hospital, except ㉖ family.

School History:
Ms. Doe reports Jane has been attending school in the local school district since kindergarten ㉗, and is currently enrolled in 12th grade at FC High School. ㉘ Jane's hallucinations, which began in 11th grade, caused her to miss many days of school.

As of July 22, 2010, Jane had enough academic credits to put her on track to graduate in June 2011. Ms. Rathbone, guidance counselor, reports

cont.

EXPLANATIONS OF CORRECTIONS

21. Spell out numbers from one through ten.
22. Similar to #19, this wording requires two separate sentences for parallel construction.
23. Homophone error: counselor and councilor— "counselor" provides guidance; "councilor" is a member of a council.
24. "High school" in this sentence is not a proper noun; no specific school is named. Do not capitalize.
25. This sentence is about Jane, and should be singular.

26. Homophone error: accept and except— "accept" refers to agreement; "except" means preclude.
27. "School district" and "kindergarten" should not be capitalized because they are common nouns.
28. Delete semicolon. Use a period and make two separate sentences because the thoughts are not closely connected.

cont.

Jane needs the following credits in order to graduate: English 12, PE, ½ credit fine arts and 2.5 elective credits. Jane's teachers are consistent in reporting that she is a very bright ㉙ student, a hard worker who is motivated to do well ㉚ and complete work. Jane was periodically absent last year, and appeared to become unmotivated in the second semester, but she is not a behavior issue in class ㉛.
Three ㉜ teachers gave more detailed reports about Jane and their interaction with her last year and years ㉝ prior. Mr. Abel (Contemporary Issues) reported having Jane as a student in her freshman year. He said that she began much the same as this year, was very smart, well spoken, and pleasant. He recalled that after the first semester she had a high absentee rate and appeared less motivated. He believes she may not have been as challenged with his class, which could be the reason she did not appear as motivated. Ms. Beta (two writing classes) reported Jane was motivated and completed her work in tenth and eleventh grades, until the second semester last year, when she did not appear as motivated and did not complete work she missed wile out of school. Mr. Charlie (Pre Calculus) reported Jane started off well at the beginning of last year, but in the second semester she did not appear to be as attentive, did not complete as much homework and did not do as well on tests.

Summary:

Jane is a 17-year-old female currently hospitalized at SF Psychiatric Hospital. A social history was requested as part of the initial evaluation process to determine eligibility for special education. Since hospitalizations began in March, Jane has spent most of her time in SF Psychiatric Hospital; her parents try to visit her on a daily basis. SF Psychiatric Hospital is trying to stabilize Jane's medication and has tried numerous medications that have not been helpful to this point. SF Psychiatric Hospital staff recommends that Jane transition to a therapeutic day school environment, as she needs a low student-to-teacher ratio and a program with significant experience educating adolescents diagnosed with psychiatric illnesses �34. Recommendations will be reviewed when all special education evaluations are completed.

EXPLANATIONS OF CORRECTIONS

29. "Brite" is not a word.
30. One sentence had items in a list that were not parallel to each other. We broke it into two separate sentences. We changed "good" to "well" because the modified word is "do," a verb. "Good" is an adjective; "well" is an adverb.
31. The original sentence combined positives and negatives; we split it into two separate sentences: one listing Jane's strengths and the other listing her challenges.

32. Spell out numbers from one through ten, and all numbers that begin sentences.
33. No possessive apostrophe required here.
34. "Psychotic students" labels people by their diagnosis, defining them as conditions rather than human beings. "Students diagnosed with psychiatric illnesses" retains the intended meaning without defining people by their conditions or challenges.

CASE 7: ORGANIZATIONAL ASSESSMENT: TENDER MERCIES HOMELESS SHELTER

Assessment of organizational capacity and function is a good way to monitor how well programs meet their objectives (both outcomes and methods). In this case, an organization wanted to know how its clients perceive its work. This is different from a satisfaction survey because the research question was focused on the organization's work, rather than clients' happiness. Following is the brief version of the report, with 34 writing errors.

ORIGINAL VERSION

Introduction and Methodology   (57)

Tender Mercies Homeless Shelter conducts client-based needs assessments' every 5 years, as part of it's ongoing self-evaluation process. For the 2008–2009 iteration, TMHS clients' were invited to participate in confidential interviews, held at TMHS's uptown shelter on 4 consecutive Tuesday's in November and December, 2008. The interviews were conducted by faculty and students from Fredonia State College (FSC). All clients were invited to participate, 74 volunteered and completed the 15-minute interviews, a response rate of about 48%. Volunteers were given $5 donut shop debit cards. The procedure was approved by FSC's Institutional Review Board (IRB).

The competed interviews consisting of mostly qualitative data were transcribed and analyzed by Prof. Vera Bright, Ph.D., director of this project.

For the most part, the data is qualitative; client's own words in response to general questions' about there experiences within the agency. The results are most powerful when larger numbers of respondents make similar statements. My view is that when 10% or more of all the respondents make the same comment in response to an open-ended question, that message is reliable. Such was the case here in several messages from clients to the staff of TMHS.

Summary of Findings   (58)

The majority of findings were mostly positive. Clients voiced more appreciation than criticism across the interviewing topics. Using a significance threshold of 10% of respondents (at least eight respondents mentioning the same item) as a criterion, areas of strengths identified by clients were, in order of frequency: shelter and housing, response to emergencies, provision of resources, and being helped. Topics receiving respondents' criticism, in order of frequency, were: thefts, treatment by security staff, conditions of some faculties in the shelter, behaviors of other clients, and some rules and policies.

Other strengths mentioned frequently but less than 10% of the time were personnel interventions (e.g., counseling, etc.) and job preparation. Other weakness's were the food (amount, quantity and quality), not enough heat in the winter, and lack of privacy.

When asked to make specific recomendations, the most-frequently-mentioned-topic was job training, followed by less rules and more security for personal property.

There were some threats to valid data, including the underrepresentation of women in the sample, the interview settings and possible inconsistent data recording by interviewers. The interviewers received training before conducting interviews, but it is possible that they conducted interviews and/or recorded data inconsistently. The reactive effect (face-to-face interviews) is another threat. Data reliability and validity was not tested.

In sum, the results indicate that TMHS's is appreciated by clients, (59) especially it's role in responding to their immediate needs. Criticisms made by respondents are focused on safety, conditions in the shelter and behaviors of residents. What many residents said was that TMHS should provide job training services.

I find it interesting that spirituality, one of TMHS's top guiding principals, was not mentioned as a strength or criticism by any interviewees.

Respectively Submitted,
Vera Bright, Ph.D.
Professor, FSC

CASE 7: CORRECTED VERSION

Each number in the corrected version refers to an explanation below.

Introduction and Methodology

Tender Mercies Homeless Shelter conducts client-based needs assessments ① every five ② years, as part of its ③ ongoing self evaluation process. For the 2008–2009 iteration, TMHS clients ④ were invited to participate in confidential interviews, held at TMHS's uptown shelter on four ⑤ consecutive Tuesdays ⑥ in November and December, 2008. The interviews were conducted by faculty and students from Fredonia State College (FSC). All clients were invited to participate; ⑦ 74 volunteered and completed the 15-minute interviews, a response rate of about 48%. Volunteers were given $5 donut shop debit cards. The procedure was approved by FSC's Institutional Review Board (IRB).

The competed interviews, consisting of mostly qualitative data, ⑧ were transcribed and analyzed by Prof. Vera Bright, ⑨ director of this project.

For the most part, the data are ⑩ qualitative; clients' ⑪ own words in response to general questions ⑫ about their ⑬ experiences in ⑭ the agency. The results are most powerful when larger numbers of respondents make similar statements. I believe ⑮ that when 10% or more of ⑯ respondents make the same comment in response to an open-ended question, that message is reliable. Such was the case here in several messages from clients to the staff of TMHS.

cont.

EXPLANATIONS OF CORRECTIONS

1. Delete apostrophe. No possessive required.
2. Spell out numbers from one through ten.
3. Homophone error: its and it's—"its" is possessive while "it's" is a contraction of "it is." This is one example where possession is indicated by *omitting* the apostrophe.
4. Delete apostrophe. No possessive required.
5. Spell out numbers from one through ten.
6. "Tuesdays" is plural (four Tuesdays), no possessive apostrophe required.
7. Insert semicolon because there are two independent clauses linked.
8. The phrase, "consisting of mostly qualitative data," can be removed without

changing the sentence's meaning, so it should be bracketed with commas.
9. One title per person: either Prof. or Ph.D., but not both.
10. The word "data" is plural, e.g., "the data *are* very interesting."
11. "Clients" is plural.
12. No possessive required.
13. Homophone error: their and there—"their" is used to indicate possession.
14. No need to specify "inside" the agency.
15. Unnecessary verbiage.
16. "All the" is unnecessary.

cont.

Summary of Findings

The majority of findings was ⑰ mostly positive. Clients voiced more appreciation than criticism across the interviewing topics. Using a significance threshold of 10% of respondents (at least eight respondents mentioning the same item) as a criterion, areas of strengths identified by clients were, in order of frequency: shelter and housing, response to emergencies, provision of resources, and being helped. Topics receiving respondents' criticisms ⑱, in order of frequency, were: thefts, treatment by security staff, conditions of some faculties ⑲ in the shelter, behaviors of other clients, and some rules and policies.

Other strengths mentioned frequently but less than 10% of the time were personnel interventions (e.g., counseling ⑳) and job preparation. Other weaknesses ㉑ were the food (amount ㉒ and quality), not enough heat in the winter, and lack of privacy.

When asked to make specific recommendations ㉓, the most frequently mentioned topic ㉔ was job training, followed by fewer ㉕ rules and more security for personal property.

There were some threats to valid data, including ㉖ underrepresentation of women in the sample, the interview settings and possible inconsistent data recording by interviewers. The interviewers received training before conducting interviews, but it is possible that they conducted interviews and/or recorded data inconsistently. The reactive effect (face-to-face interviews) is another threat. Data reliability and validity were ㉗ not tested.

cont.

EXPLANATIONS OF CORRECTIONS

17. The subject, "majority," is singular.
18. "Criticisms" should be plural because there are more than one.
19. Word choice: facilities and faculties—"facilities" are places or resources; "faculties" are abilities or teaching staff.
20. "I.E.," does not take "etc."
21. This is a plural, not a possessive case.
22. "Amount" and "quantity" are redundant.

23. Spelling error.
24. Delete hyphens.
25. Word choice: fewer and less—"fewer" is used when there are countable units of one; "less" is used when describing concepts.
26. Article (the) not needed.
27. Plural: there are two items—validity and reliability.

cont.

In sum, the results indicate that clients appreciate TMHS ㉘,
especially its ㉙ role in responding to their immediate needs. Respondents'
criticisms ㉚ focused on safety, conditions in the shelter and
behaviors of residents. Many residents say ㉛ that TMHS should
provide job training services.

I find it interesting that spirituality, one of TMHS's ㉜ guiding principles ㉝,
was not mentioned as a strength or criticism by any interviewees.

Respectfully ㉞ Submitted,
Vera Bright, Ph.D.
Professor, FSC

EXPLANATIONS OF CORRECTIONS

28. In the original, TMHS is singular, not possessive; also, the sentence was in the passive voice. Use active construction.

29. Singular possessive: no apostrophe for the third person singular pronoun (it).

30. Past tense because the criticisms were made a few months before the report was written, and are not necessarily made in the present.

31. Unnecessary verbiage.

32. "Top" is unnecessary with "guiding"

33. Homophone error: principle and principal—"principle" is a guiding value; "principal" is a noun, in this case, a person in charge or an adjective meaning primary or central.

34. Word choice: respectfully and respectively—"respectfully" conveys respect; "respectively" refers to the order of things in a list.

CASE 8: COMMUNITY NEEDS ASSESSMENT: DEAF AND HARD-OF-HEARING RESIDENTS

Just as social workers engage in assessments with individuals and families, social workers conduct needs assessments at the community and organizational levels in order to diagnose issues and design appropriate interventions. The following case is a report of a committee that conducted a community needs assessment about services for people with hearing impairments. Throughout the document, "Deaf" was capitalized but "hard of hearing" was not. The author explained that "'Deaf' refers to a cultural identity while 'deaf' refers to a lack of hearing ability. The Deaf community typically does not use the term 'hearing impairment.' The audience for the needs assessment was the Deaf community, versus a professional journal, so we used their communication style. Your audience and the values of your audience's culture impact the writing we do as professionals.

ORIGINAL VERSION

Improving Health and Mental Health Services to Fredonia's Deaf and Hard of Hearing Residents:

(63)

NEEDS ASSESSMENT SUMMARY
July 2008

I. Research Review

The 2008 consumer study found that although, many members of the Deaf and hard of hearing communities are satisfied with the medical and mental health services available to them, there are still significant problems in existence. The findings are similar to previous research in Fredonia and throughout other states. The study's identify 5 barriers' for quality care for Deaf and hard of hearing persons;

1. Communication difficulties in making appointments
2. Communication difficulties with health care professionals (including access to interpreters)
3. Health care staff members whom do not understand Deaf and hard of hearing communication and cultural issues.
4. Lack of accessible and culturally appropriate health education programs
5. Lack of mental health interventions designed to meet the needs of the Deaf

II. Models of Change

Illinois Deaf Services 2000 and the Sinai/Advocate Health Project are two examples of how changes in health and mental health care for the Deaf and hard of hearing can occur.

The Illinois Deaf Services 2000 Project was a twenty year effort to
improve the ability of community mental health agencies to provide
services to Deaf consumers. An advocacy group partnered together   (64)
with the Illinois Department of Mental Health to create standards
of care for the Deaf and hard of hearing (Illinois Standard Of Care -
ISOC). A coordinator of Deaf Services than asked the Administrators of
all community mental health agencies in the state to complete a survey
based on ISOC. They found that most of the agencies were not able
to provide culturally appropriate care. The coordinator then met with
the director of each agency to discuss agency needs and obligations,
and offer training, technical support, and resources et al. Annually,
the coordinator tracked there progress toward accessibility. Results
were very positive. Each agency increased in service accessibility and
there was also a 60% increase in the # of Deaf and hard of hearing
consumers' identified by the agencies.

In the **Sinai/Advocate Health Project**, Chicago's two major providers
of medical and mental health care for the Deaf, joined together to learn
more about the health care barriers experienced by the Deaf. First, a
project team of Deaf and hearing individuals asked Deaf consumers
to complete a survey to asking about excess to health care, quality
of care, health knowledge, and health behavior. The team found that
more than one third of the Deaf consumers' did not have access to
an interpreter when they went to the hospital. Also, most of the Deaf
consumers lacked knowledge about important health topics. So, the
project team created two health education programs; one for Deaf
adults with heart disease and the other to help Deaf people with
depression. Each program was six-weeks long. They were taught
by a Deaf health educator fluent in ASL. After participating, the Deaf
consumer's knowledge increased in both programs. Also, the people   (65)
in the depression program reported that they had less symptoms of
depression.

III. Next Steps: Developing an Intervention Strategy

The consumer study is nearly completed so the committee can
move on to it's next project, a study of service providers. Since the
committee wants to change how health and mental health services
are offered, a study of provider agencies, versus individual providers,
would be most useful. A study of the services provided by agencies,
and the problems they face in offering services to the Deaf and hard of
hearing, would be more effective in improving services then a survey
of individual practitioners. The Committee for the Deaf and Hard of
Hearing (CDHH) could first gather information from agencies, and then
return to agencies to help them address solve offer technical expertise,
resources, and etc.

There are several ways to engage in a study of provider agencies. The CDHH could partner with a state agency; either the Department of Health or the Department of Mental Health, Retardation and Hospitals. Alternatively, the CDHH could choose to collaborate with the Fredonia Health Center Association or the State Council of Community Mental Health Organizations. Working with either the state (the big fish) or a nonprofit association (the little fish) allows the CDHH to access Provider Agencies. Provider Agencies will be more responsive to a CDHH survey if it comes to them with the stamp of approval from the State or an provider association.

The committee needs to make several decisions. You're input is needed in order for the group to come to an agreement as to how to proceed at this point.

CASE 8: CORRECTED VERSION

Improving Health and Mental Health Services
to Fredonia's Deaf and Hard of Hearing Residents:

NEEDS ASSESSMENT SUMMARY
July 2008

I. Research Review

The 2008 consumer study found that although ① many members of the Deaf and hard of hearing community ② are satisfied with the medical and mental health services available to them, there are still significant problems ③. The findings are similar to previous research in Fredonia and ④ other states. The studies ⑤ identify five ⑥ barriers ⑦ to ⑧ quality care for Deaf and hard of hearing persons: ⑨

1. Communication difficulties in making appointments
2. Communication difficulties with health care professionals (including access to interpreters)
3. Health care staff members who ⑩ do not understand Deaf and hard of hearing communication and cultural issues.
4. Lack of accessible and culturally appropriate health education programs
5. Lack of mental health interventions designed to meet the needs of the Deaf

II. Models of Change

Illinois Deaf Services 2000 and the Sinai/Advocate Health Project are two examples of how changes in health and mental health care for the Deaf and hard of hearing can occur.

The Illinois Deaf Services 2000 Project was a twenty-year effort to improve the ability of community mental health agencies to provide

cont.

EXPLANATIONS OF CORRECTIONS

1. Delete comma because the sentence structure requires no pause.
2. The document treats the Deaf and hard of hearing population as one entity, so "community" should be singular. If these are two distinct communities, the report should say as much.
3. Unnecessary verbiage.
4. "Throughout" is unnecessary.
5. No possessive required. Plural because multiple studies are discussed.
6. Spell out numbers from one through ten.
7. No possessive required.
8. Corrected preposition.
9. Use a colon here because a list follows.
10. "Who" takes the verb, "to understand" and refers to "health care professionals."

cont.

services to Deaf consumers. An advocacy group partnered ⑪
with the Illinois Department of Mental Health to create standards
of care for the Deaf and hard of hearing (Illinois Standard Of Care -
ISOC). A coordinator of Deaf Services then ⑫ asked the administrators ⑬ of
all community mental health agencies in the state to complete a survey
based on ISOC. They found that most of the agencies were not able
to provide culturally appropriate care. The coordinator then met with
the director of each agency to discuss agency needs and obligations,
and to ⑭ offer training, technical support, and resources ⑮. Annually,
the coordinator tracked their ⑯ progress toward accessibility. Results
were very positive. Each agency increased its ⑰ service accessibility and
there was ⑱ a 60% increase in the number ⑲ of Deaf and hard of hearing
consumers ⑳ identified by the agencies.

In the **Sinai/Advocate Health Project**, Chicago's two major providers
of medical and mental health care for the Deaf, joined together to learn
more about ㉑ health care barriers experienced by the Deaf. First, a
project team of Deaf and hearing individuals asked Deaf consumers
to complete a survey ㉒ asking about access ㉓ to health care, quality
of care, health knowledge, and health behavior. The team found that
more than one-third ㉔ of the Deaf consumers ㉕ did not have access to
an interpreter when they went to the hospital. Also, most of the Deaf
consumers lacked knowledge about important health topics. So, the
project team created two health education programs, ㉖ one for Deaf
adults with heart disease and the other to help Deaf people with
depression. Each program was six ㉗ weeks long. They were taught
by a Deaf health educator fluent in ASL. After participating, the Deaf

cont.

EXPLANATIONS OF CORRECTIONS

11. Delete "together" because it is redundant when used with "partnered."
12. Homophone error: then and than—"then" refers to time; "than" is for comparisons.
13. Do not capitalize "administrators" because it is not a proper noun.
14. "To offer" provides clarity as to the action of the verb—the coordinator offers, not the agency.
15. "Et. Al" means "and the others," and refers to people. "Etc." is incorrect because "and" is already in the sentence and makes "etc." redundant.
16. Homophone error: their and there—"their" is possessive; "there" is a preposition.
17. Word choice: "its" makes more sense than "in."

18. Redundancy: there is no need for both "and" and "also."
19. In this case, write out "number" and avoid abbreviation.
20. No possessive required.
21. "The" is unnecessary.
22. "To" is unnecessary.
23. Homophone error: access and excess— "access" is availability; "excess" is too much.
24. Write-out and hyphenate fractions.
25. Delete apostrophe. No possessive required.
26. Delete semicolon; use a comma between independent and subordinate clauses.
27. Delete hyphen here because "six weeks" is not a compound noun or adjective in this sentence.

cont.

consumers' ㉘ knowledge increased in both programs. Also, the people in the depression program reported that they had fewer ㉙ symptoms of depression.

III. Next Steps: Developing an Intervention Strategy

The consumer study is nearly completed so the committee can move on to its ㉚ next project, a study of service providers. Since the committee wants to change how health and mental health services are offered, a study of provider agencies, versus individual providers, would be most useful. A study of the services provided by agencies, and the problems they face in offering services to the Deaf and hard of hearing, would be more effective in improving services than ㉛ a survey of individual practitioners. The Committee for the Deaf and Hard of Hearing (CDHH) could first gather information from agencies, and then return to agencies to help them address ㉜ technical expertise, resources, ㉝ etc.

There are several ways to engage in a study of provider agencies. The CDHH could partner with a state agency, ㉞ either the Department of Health or the Department of Mental Health, Retardation and Hospitals. Alternatively, the CDHH could choose to collaborate with the Fredonia Health Center Association or the State Council of Community Mental Health Organizations. Working with either the state (the big fish) or a nonprofit association (the little fish) allows the CDHH to access Provider Agencies. Provider Agencies will be more responsive to a CDHH survey if it comes to them with the stamp of approval from the State or a ㉟ provider association.

The committee needs to make several decisions. Your ㊱ input is needed in order for the group to come to an agreement as to how to proceed at this point. Attached is a survey for each committee member ㊲ to complete.

EXPLANATIONS OF CORRECTIONS

28. Use apostrophe to indicate the plural possessive.
29. Word choice: fewer and less—fewer is correct because symptoms can be counted in units of one, e.g., one symptom; had the noun been "pain," less would be correct, because there is no countable unit of pain.
30. "Its" is the correct pronoun for the singular possessive.
31. Homophone error: than and then. (see #12)

32. Avoid unnecessary verbiage.
33. "And" and "etc." are redundant.
34. Use a comma between independent clause and phrase.
35. "An" is used only if the next word begins with a vowel, e.g, "An owl . . ."
36. Homophone error: your and you're— "your" is possessive; "you're" is a contraction of you are.
37. "Each" signifies the singular.

3

Social Work Practice

In the previous chapter, we provided eight cases in which assessment was the primary focus. In this chapter, there are eight more cases, all involving individuals.

The next eight cases represent examples of descriptive writing social workers do routinely. Each is as brief as possible, given the information reported. Ideally, readers will understand the pertinent information within the context of working with clients. Cases nine and ten are social history cases; eleven and twelve are court letter cases. Cases thirteen through sixteen occur in the fields of mental health and disabilities, respectively. Each is primarily a descriptive rather than analytical report. There may be some explicit connection to diagnoses, but the primary purpose of the reports in this section is documentation of events and client functioning. Numbers on the right side of the original documents note the page locations of the corresponding content in the corrected documents.

 9 – Individual Social History: James—Mental Health and Substance Involvement
10 – Family Social History: Adjudicated Family with Multiple Issues
11 – Emergency Motion: Child Neglect
12 – Emergency Motion: Family Court
13 – Crisis Planning: Psychotic Episode
14 – Annual Treatment Plan: Mental Health Diagnoses
15 – Disabilities: Client Progress Notes
16 – Disabilities: Status Notes and Progress Notes

CASE 9: INDIVIDUAL SOCIAL HISTORY: JAMES—MENTAL HEALTH AND SUBSTANCE INVOLVEMENT

In this client case record, there are 53 writing errors, 16 of which are sentence structure mistakes.

Individual mentioned in the document	Abbreviations used in the document
James, male, 36	ADL: Activities of daily living TP: Treatment plan

ORIGINAL VERSION

- 36-year old Caucasian male
- Axis I Alcohol Abuse
- Axis I Schizoaffective Disorder
- Axis II No Diagnosis
- Axis III Hypertension, Acid Reflux
- Axis IV Social Environment, Legal, Primary Support Group, Housing, Economic, Health Care Services, Legal System

JAMES' CLINICAL PROFILE   (70)

- Living in apartment (1 year) 7 miles from town center; prior situation: homeless; continued problems with present housing (bothers neighbors for money and cigarettes); 3 meetings with landlord in the last 10 months; landlord truly likes James and wants to help; but he's worried about loosing other tenants
- See's mother twice per month; estranged from father (do to his refusal to admit infliction of severe physical abuse of James throughout childhood)
- Has relationship with one neighbor (eat dinner together and watch TV occasionally [e.g., twice per month]); walks to coffee shop about three times per week
- Legal involvement (court pending; assaulted police officer when confronted about disruptive behavior at bar; James relapsed after fight with father, drank three beers, subsequent disruptive behavior)
- Desire to work; last job 3 years ago lasting 2 months; fired for sporadic attendence   (71)
- Had 4 months' sobriety last year; what happens now is he drinks about twice times per month, often too intoxication
- Smoke's one pack of cigarettes per day; no desire to decrease; continually asks others' for cigarettes
- View's medications as "poison" and is monitored daily, with continued education/redirection as needed
- Refuses medical appointments, with significant support and direct help needed to convince James to attend and to accompany him through the appointment

- Very limited Activities of Daily Living (ADL) skills; frequent cueing needed for self-care; 1-1 assistance needed for apartment chores, laundry, shopping, budgeting, etc.

BASELINE ASSESSMENT (72)

Strengths

James possesses numerous strengths. He has lived in his current apartment independently for one year. James also enjoys a consistent support system that includes his mother, neighbor, landlord, and the coffee shop he frequents. He possesses familiarity with his manic episodes and the likelihood for substance relapse during such episodes. He also has some work history as well. His last job was 3 years ago. Finally, and not leastly, he has achieved sobriety for 4 consecutive months in the past year.

Barriers

There are several barriers that may impede James progress towards his goal achievement. For example, his limited understanding of the importance of medication. He struggles to maintain motivation, particularly related to Adult Daily Living skills. He has a high risk of alcohol relapse during manic episodes; and recently engaged in substance abuse following a disagreement with his father. James sporadically complies with medication orders, leading to increased symptomatic behavior. Finally, he was recently arrested for assaulting a police officer. These identified barriers are documented within the TP and discussed during the process.

CASE 9: CORRECTED VERSION:

Each number in the corrected version refers to an explanation below.

JAMES' CLINICAL PROFILE

- James has been living ① in an apartment for one ② year.
  His apartment is seven ③ miles from the ④ town center; his prior situation
  is difficult ⑤: homeless; continued problems with present housing (bothers
  neighbors for money and cigarettes); three ⑥ meetings with his ⑦ landlord in the
  last ten ⑧ months. ⑨ James' landlord ⑩ likes James and wants to help; but he's
  worried about losing ⑪ other tenants.
- He sees his ⑫ mother twice per month; he is ⑬ estranged from father (due ⑭ to father's
  ⑮ refusal to admit to ⑯ physical abuse of James throughout childhood).
- He has a relationship ⑰ with one neighbor (occasionally eat dinner and/or watch TV ⑱
  [e.g., twice per month]). He walks to a ⑲ coffee shop about three
  times per week.
- James has some legal involvement pending in court: he assaulted a police officer when
  confronted about disruptive behavior at a bar; he relapsed after a fight
  with father; he drank three beers with subsequent disruptive behavior. ⑳

cont.

EXPLANATIONS OF CORRECTIONS

1. Sentence structure error. The original sentence contained no subject. "James" is the subject of the sentence.
2. Spell out numbers from one through ten.
3. Spell out numbers from one through ten.
4. The direct article (the) was needed for sentence structure.
5. Incomplete sentence: the original sentence contained no subject. "He" is the subject of the sentence.
6. Spell out numbers from one through ten.
7. "Is difficult" is the verb of the sentence, allowing the addition of the colon, followed by the list of challenges James faces.
8. Spell out numbers from one through ten.
9. Punctuate to create a new sentence in order to avoid sentence structure problem and to keep the focus of the sentence clear.
10. Delete "truly" because it is unnecessary.
11. Homophone error: lose and loose. "Lose" means misplace or lack of success; "loose" means unrestrained.
12. Subject and possessive pronoun added for sentence structure; no apostrophe in "see's" because "see" does not possess anything.
13. We added a subject and verb to complete the sentence and keep the semicolon so that is now connects two complete sentences.
14. Homophone: do and due—"do" is a verb; "due" refers to a deadline.
15. We inserted "Father" instead of "his" for clarity.
16. Unnecessary verbiage.
17. We added a subject and article to complete proper sentence structure.
18. When possible, simplify and shorten sentences. Say more with less.
19. We added a subject and article to complete the sentence structure; we replaced the semicolon with a period because the two sentences were not closely related.
20. The first version was not a sentence. We added a subject and verb—"James has"— and treated the items in parentheses as items in a list after a colon. We had to link "subsequent disruptive behavior" with the "three beers," using the conjunction "with," for parallel structure in the list.

cont.

- James wants ㉑ to work. His last job, three years ago, lasted two months ㉒; he was ㉓ fired for sporadic attendance.
- He had ㉔ four ㉕ months of ㉖ sobriety last year; he now drinks about twice ㉗ per month, often to ㉘ intoxication.
- He Smokes ㉙ one pack of cigarettes per day, expresses ㉚ no desire to cut back ㉛, and ㉜ continually asks others ㉝ for cigarettes.
- He views ㉞ medications as "poison" and is monitored daily, with continued education/redirection as needed.
- He refuses ㉟ medical appointments. He needs significant support and direct help (e.g, accompaniment) to be convinced to attend appointments. ㊱
- He demonstrates ㊲ very limited Activities of Daily Living (ADL) skills: ㊳ frequent cueing needed for self-care; 1-1 assistance needed for apartment chores, e.g., ㊴ laundry, shopping, budgeting. ㊵

cont.

EXPLANATIONS OF CORRECTIONS

21. We separated the simple declarative sentence, "James wants to work" from the rest of the information, for clarity and simplicity.
22. We restructured the wording to create a complete sentence, placing commas around a phrase that could be removed without changing the meaning of the sentence.
23. We added a subject and verb—"he was."
24. We added a subject and verb.
25. Spell out numbers from one through ten.
26. "Months of," not "months'" because there is no possessive.
27. Delete "times" because it is redundant with "twice."
28. Homophone error: to and too—"too" means excessive or also.
29. The sentence needed a subject: "He." "Smokes" does not take an apostrophe because it does not possess anything.
30. For sentence structure, we replaced the semicolon with a comma, and created a phrase—"expresses no need to cut back." The semicolon requires two independent clauses; the comma separates the independent clause and a phrase.

31. Word choice: we changed "reduce" to "cut back" for clarity.
32. We linked the sentence by including a comma, the conjunction "and," so that the sentence fragment becomes joins the rest and becomes one complete sentence.
33. We added "others," a noun, for clarity.
34. See #29. The sentence needed a subject: "He." "Views" does not take an apostrophe because it does not possess anything.
35. See #29. The sentence needed a subject: "He." "Refuses" does not take an apostrophe because it does not possess anything.
36. Passive wording corrected to active voice.
37. See #29. The sentence needed a subject and verb: "He demonstrates."
38. Semicolon should be a colon because it initiates a list, which is correctly separated with semicolons.
39. E.g., replaces the comma because the list is examples of chores; it is not parallel with the "limited activities."
40. No "etc." after e.g. or i.e.

cont.

BASELINE ASSESSMENT

Strengths

James possesses numerous strengths. He has lived independently ㊶ in his current apartment for one year. James also enjoys a consistent support system that includes his mother, neighbor, landlord, and friends whom he sees at ㊷ the coffee shop he frequents. He understands ㊸ his manic episodes and the likelihood of ㊹ substance relapse during such episodes. He also has some work history ㊺. His last job was three ㊻ years ago. ㊼ He has achieved sobriety for four ㊽ consecutive months in the past year.

Barriers

There are several barriers that may impede James' ㊾ progress towards his goal achievement. His understanding of the importance of medication is limited. ㊿ He struggles to maintain motivation, particularly related to Adult Daily Living skills. He has a high risk of alcohol relapse during manic episodes, (51) and recently engaged in substance abuse following a disagreement with his father. James sporadically complies with medication orders, leading to increased symptomatic behavior. (52) He was recently arrested for assaulting a police officer. These identified barriers are documented within the TP and discussed during the process.

EXPLANATIONS OF CORRECTIONS

41. Misplaced modifier: "independently" modifies "lived," not "apartment."
42. A coffee shop is inanimate, and cannot offer support, but people there can. Note "whom," not "who," because "friends" does not take a verb.
43. Excess verbiage simplified with one word.
44. Incorrect preposition.
45. "As well" is redundant with "also."
46. Spell out numbers from one through ten.
47. "Finally, and not leastly" is incorrect for several reasons: The wording as it was adds no information. If "finally" was acceptable, "not leastly" would be an unnecessary authorial opinion. Finally, "leastly" is not a word.
48. Spell out numbers from one through ten.
49. Singular possessive for name ending in "s."
50. The original was not a sentence because it lacked a verb.
51. Do not use a semicolon when words do not form an independent clause.
52. "Finally" adds no information.
53. In the "clinical profile," I added periods to sentences that did not have them.

CASE 10: FAMILY SOCIAL HISTORY: ADJUDICATED FAMILY WITH MULTIPLE ISSUES

This is taken from the case file of a family that receives services from the state child welfare department. The case record was written by the primary social worker. There are 62 errors in this document, including omission of relevant information in places. The occasional omission of the direct article (the) appears permissible to the agency and is not corrected.

CPS language: The word "indicated" means the allegations were confirmed by an investigation.

Family members mentioned in the document	Abbreviations used in the document
Allison, 36 (mother) Thomas, 39 (father) James, male, 16 Ryan, male, 10 Rebecca, female, 8	CPI = Child Protective Investigator CPS = Child Protective Services (state child welfare department) MGM/F/P = maternal grandmother/father/ parent FSJCC = Fredonia State Juvenile Corrections Center FCH = Fredonia Children's Hospital; mos = months

ORIGINAL VERSION

This family opened to CPS, following a call to the Child Abuse and Neglect Hotline. The reporter is a neighbor. She reported that Ryan, age 10, and Rebecca, age 8, had run to her house because they were afraid of their mother. They went on to say that the mother, Allison, had hit and punched Ryan and that he had a bruise under his eye, scratches and a cut swollen lip. The sister, Rebecca, reportedly tried to stop her mother, and her mother pulled Rebecca's hair and poked her. No injuries as to Rebecca were reported, thank goodness. The reporter said that mother had a history of violent behavior. Reporter said that the children called their MGM who picked up the children from the reporter's home. MGM informed the mother she and MGF would be keeping the children for the night with them. They also said they were going to contact the childrens' father, Thomas, whom was at work, as well.

(76)

The family has had prior involvement with CPS. Previously in March of 2006 mother was Indicated for Neglect as to all three children, for an allegation of Physical Abuse- Drug /Alcohol Abuse. Family was open to services with no legal status; according to records it appears that mother cooperated with treatment services, and the case was closed in January 2007.

During the current CPS Investigation, the MGPs reported that they were   (77)
called by Ryan and Rebecca at the neighbors' house because they were
afraid of their mother, and to please pick them up. The MGPs reported that
mother had stopped by the house earlier, and that she became very upset
and emotional; that she was saying angry things to MGM. They went on
to explain that this behavior was not the norm for their daughter, Allison.
They suggested that mother has been very stressed over the families'
plan to move so they can be closer to Thomas's work. The grandparents'
reported that they had taken Ryan to the local hospital where he was
examined by Dr. Averson. MGPs said they were willing to keep the children
as long as needed, including the older sibling James, who was not at home
during the time of the incident. Being he was at his friend's house.

When the CPI met with Ryan he provided further details, saying that his
mother saw him on the phone with his grandmother. She had "got mad",
slapped him and took the phone and hung up. Ryan said that he grabbed
his jacket and ran out the back door to his friend's house. Ryan explained
that he came back later thinking that his mother would have calmed
down, but what happened next was that she started to hit him, slammed
him against the wall and hit him all over his body, causing the bruises.
CPI observed Ryan who had a bruise under his eye, a cut/swollen lip,
a scratch on his neck and another on his arm.

The report from the emergency room doctor confirms that the injuries were
consistent with Ryan's explanation. The CPI also interviewed Rebecca.
She said that when her brother came home, there mother started hitting
him. She said that she grabbed her brother to help pull him away from
their mother. Although, Rebecca said that once he got free, they both
ran outside to the neighbor's house to call their grandparents. Rebecca
said that this is the first time their mother has been that angry and hit her   (78)
brother so many times, Allison's a good mother, just tense about things.

When the CPI interviewed mother, Allison, she said that she did not hit
Ryan. Not that hard anyway. She said Ryan has been "acting up" and
that he left the house without permission. She said he has been skipping
school and told her he wanted to go live with his grandparents. Allison
said when Ryan came home she tried to talk to him but he "gave her an
attitude". She said that she wanted him to stop and listen so she grabbed
him by the arms but he ran out the door and fell causing him to hurt his
eye and lip.

The CPI met with the oldest child, James, at the familes' home.
He reported that he was not home at the time of the alleged incident.
He reported that he felt safe at home, that he did not wish to go to his
grandparents and wished to remain at home. He reported he had never

witnessed his mother being physical with his brother or sister. A review of the state CPS data base revealed that James has several pending juvenile charges which include possession of cocaine, breaking and entering, and possession of a stolen motor vehicle. James does not attend school as his mother signed him out when he turned 16. He sometimes works for a relative doing landscaping.

The CPI spoke with father, Thomas, outside his place of employment. Thomas said he was aware of the situation because the MGPs had called him. He said he was glad the children were with their grandparents and that he wanted them to stay there as he works full time. He states that he works 12 hour days on the weekends and is not home much.

The CPS Investigation has been completed and mother, Allison was Indicated for Physical Abuse- Excessive/Inappropriate Discipline and for Physical Abuse- Cut, Bruise and Welt with her son, Ryan, as the victim. She was also indicated for Neglect-Other Neglect with her daughter, Rebecca, as the victim.

(79)

CPS filed a straight petition with family court. The oldest child, James remained at home with his mother and father continuing to take pick-up jobs as they come his way. The two younger siblings, Ryan and Rebecca, continue to stay with their grandparents' through an agreed upon family arrangement.

Since opening, the hotline received several reports that mother was allowing James to have parties in the home and that mother and James were drinking alcohol together. The report was designated as an I/R (information referral). Being only 16, CPS can file charges against Allison for giving him alcohol, as he is legally a miner.

James has been adjudicated on his pending juvenile charges. At the pretrial court hearing he admitted sufficient facts to the three charges: breaking & entering, possession of a stolen motor vehicle and possession of cocaine. James was sentenced to the FSJCC for 12 months; 6 months to serve and 6 months probation and he was also ordered to pay reasonable restitution and he must perform 50 hours of community service too. After one month at the JCC, the court approved a Temporary Community Placement and James was transferred to the ____ Residential Substance Abuse Treatment Program.

The family currently remains open to CPS through both the Family Services Unit and the Juvenile Correction Services.

CASE 10: CORRECTED VERSION

Each number in the corrected version refers to an explanation below.

This family opened to CPS ① following a call to the Child Abuse and
Neglect Hotline. The reporter is a neighbor. She reported that Ryan,
age 10, and Rebecca, age 8, had run to her house because they were
afraid of their mother. They said ② that the mother, Allison, had
hit and punched Ryan, ③ and that he had a bruise under his eye, scratches
and a cut and ④ swollen lip. The sister, Rebecca, reportedly tried to stop her
mother, but ⑤ her mother pulled Rebecca's hair and poked her.
Rebecca did not have any reported injuries ⑥ ⑦. The reporter said that mother
had a history of violent behavior. Reporter said that the children
called their MGM who picked up the children from the reporter's home.
MGM informed the mother she and MGF would keep ⑧ the children
for the night ⑨. They also said they were going to contact the
children's ⑩ father, Thomas, who ⑪ was at work ⑫.

The family has ⑬ prior involvement with CPS. ⑭ In March of
2006, ⑮ mother was Indicated for Neglect as to all three children:
Physical Abuse- Drug/Alcohol Abuse ⑯. Family
was open to services with no legal status; according to records it
appears that mother cooperated with treatment services, and the case
was closed in January 2007.

cont.

EXPLANATIONS OF CORRECTIONS

1. We deleted the comma because it interrupts a clear thought and is unnecessary.
2. "Went on to say" is wordy and unnecessary. "They said" is more precise.
3. We inserted a comma for clarity; without the comma, it appears Allison hit Ryan and someone else; the comma separates the action so that readers knows they are no longer reading about Allison's hitting.
4. He had both a cut and a swollen lip.
5. "And" is not appropriate because the two thoughts are not parallel or equal. "But" is appropriate because the second idea is a counterpoint to the first.
6. Passive voice. Use active voice so that it is clear who is doing what to whom.
7. Avoid authorial opinions.
8. Passive voice. Use active voice so that it is clear who is doing what to whom.
9. We deleted "with them" because it is redundant with "keep."
10. "Children's" is the possessive for "children."
11. "Whom" is incorrect because there is a verb—"was"; "who" takes a verb; "whom" does not.
12. We deleted "as well" because it is redundant with "also."
13. We changed "has had" to "has" because the sentence is present tense.
14. "Previously" is redundant with the earlier date, March, 2006. A better way to write this sentence: The family was involved with CPS in the past.
15. We inserted a comma for clarity. It is customary to include a brief pause after a date.
16. Convoluted sentence. The colon introduces a list of information clarifying the sentence.

cont.

During the current CPS Investigation, the MGPs reported that they were
called by Ryan and Rebecca at the neighbor's ⑰ house because they were
afraid of their mother. The children asked to be picked up ⑱. The MGPs reported that
mother had stopped by the house earlier, that she became very upset
and emotional, ⑲ and that she had said angry things to MGM. They
explained ⑳ that this behavior was not the norm for their daughter, Allison.
They suggested that mother had been ㉑ very stressed over the family's ㉒
plan to move so they could ㉓ be closer to Thomas's work. The grandparents ㉔
reported that they had taken Ryan to the local hospital where he was
examined by Dr. Averson. MGPs said they were willing to keep the children
as long as needed, including the older sibling, ㉕ James, who was not at home
during the time of the incident. James was at his friend's house at the time. ㉖

When the CPI met with Ryan, ㉗ he provided further details, saying that his
mother saw him on the phone with his grandmother. She had "got mad," ㉘
slapped him and took the phone and hung up. Ryan said that he grabbed
his jacket and ran out through ㉙ the back door to his friend's house. Ryan explained
that he came back later, ㉚ thinking that his mother would have calmed
down, but ㉛ she slammed him against the wall and hit him all over his body,
causing bruises. CPI observed Ryan who had a bruise under his eye,
a cut/swollen lip, a scratch on his neck and another on his arm.

The report from the emergency room doctor confirms that the injuries were
consistent with Ryan's explanation. The CPI also interviewed Rebecca.
She said that when her brother came home, their ㉜ mother started hitting
him. She said that she grabbed her brother to help pull him away from
their mother. ㉝ Rebecca said that once he got free, they both
ran outside to the neighbor's house to call their grandparents. Rebecca

cont.

EXPLANATIONS OF CORRECTIONS

17. We inserted the singular possessive – an apostrophe belongs before the "s."
18. We corrected the parallelism error by creating two different sentences.
19. We deleted the semicolon because there are not two independent clauses.
20. Wordy: "explained" replaces "went on to explain." Say more with less.
21. Verb tense error: we inserted the "compound past tense" rather than "simple past tense."
22. We inserted the singular possessive.
23. Verb tense error. We inserted the correct tense: "conditional past tense."
24. We deleted the apostrophe because there is no possessive required.
25. Surround "James" with commas because the word, "James," can be removed from the sentence without changing its meaning.
26. The original was not a sentence—"being" does not work as a main verb.
27. We placed a comma after introductory phrase.
28. We located the comma inside the close-quotation mark.
29. We added "through" for clarity.
30. We added a comma for clarity. The comma indicates a pause to indicate that "thinking" does not relate to "later," but to Ryan.
31. Unnecessary verbiage.
32. Homophone error: their and there. "Their" indicates the possessive, as in "their car."
33. We deleted "although" as unnecessary language.

cont.

said that this is the first time their mother has been that angry and hit her brother so many times. ㉞ Allison is ㉟ a good mother, just tense about things.

When the CPI interviewed mother, Allison ㊱ said that she did not hit Ryan, ㊲ not that hard anyway. She said Ryan has been "acting up" and that he left the house without permission. She said he had ㊳ been skipping school and told her he wanted to go live with his grandparents. Allison said when Ryan came home, ㊴ she tried to talk to him but he "gave her an attitude." ㊵ She said that she wanted him to stop and listen, ㊶ so she grabbed him by the arms, but he ran out, ㊷ and fell, ㊸ causing him to hurt his eye and lip.

The CPI met with the oldest child, James, at the family's ㊹ home. He reported that he was not home at the time of the alleged incident. He reported that he felt safe at home, ㊺ did not wish to go to his grandparents, ㊻ and wished to remain at home. He reported he had never witnessed his mother being physical with his brother or sister. A review of the state CPS data base revealed that James has several pending juvenile charges which include possession of cocaine, breaking and entering, and possession of a stolen motor vehicle. James does not attend school, ㊼ as his mother signed him out when he turned 16. He sometimes works for a relative, ㊽ doing landscaping.

The CPI spoke with father, Thomas, outside his place of employment. Thomas said he was aware of the situation because the MGPs had called him. He said he was glad the children were with their grandparents and that he wanted them to stay there as he works full time. He states that he works 12-hour ㊾ days on the weekends and is not home much.

cont.

EXPLANATIONS OF CORRECTIONS

34. Run-on sentence. Correct with proper punctuation.

35. Avoid using contractions.

36. Deleted "she" because it was confusing.

37. We linked the incomplete sentence to the previous sentence with a comma, separating independent clause and phrase while correcting sentence structure.

38. We corrected the verb tense.

39. We inserted a comma for clarity because "she" refers to Allison, not Ryan.

40. We placed the comma inside the close-quotation mark.

41. We inserted a comma for clarity before the conjunction, "so."

42. "The door" is unnecessary; we inserted a comma for clarity, though in this example a comma is optional.

43. We inserted a comma between the independent clause and the following phrase.

44. We inserted an apostrophe to indicate the singular possessive.

45. Unnecessary words. Say more with less.

46. We inserted a comma between the independent clause and following phrase.

47. We inserted a comma before the conjunction linking two independent clauses.

48. We inserted a comma between the independent clause and the following phrase.

49. Always hyphenate two-digit numbers in compound adjectives.

cont.

The CPS Investigation has been completed and mother, Allison, ⑤⓪ was Indicated for Physical Abuse (Excessive/Inappropriate Discipline and Cut, Bruise and Welt) with her son, Ryan, as the victim.
She was also indicated for Neglect (Other Neglect) with her daughter, Rebecca, as the victim. ⑤①

CPS filed a petition with family court. The oldest child, James remained at home with his mother and father, ⑤② continuing to take pick up jobs ⑤③. The two younger siblings, Ryan and Rebecca, continued ⑤④ to stay with their grandparents ⑤⑤ through an agreed-upon family arrangement.

Since opening, the hotline received several reports that mother was allowing James to have parties in the home and that mother and James were drinking alcohol together. The report was designated as an I/R (information referral). ⑤⑥ CPS can file charges against Allison for giving him alcohol, as he is legally a minor. ⑤⑦

James has been adjudicated on his pending juvenile charges. At the pretrial court hearing, ⑤⑧ he admitted sufficient facts to the three charges: breaking & entering, possession of a stolen motor vehicle and possession of cocaine. James was sentenced to the FSJCC for 12 months, ⑤⑨ six months to serve and six ⑥⓪ months probation. ⑥① He was also ordered to pay reasonable restitution and he must perform 50 hours of community service ⑥②. After one month at the JCC, the court approved a Temporary Community Placement and James was transferred to the ____ Residential Substance Abuse Treatment Program.

The family currently remains open to CPS through both the Family Services Unit and the Juvenile Correction Services.

EXPLANATIONS OF CORRECTIONS

50. Use commas to set off words that can be removed without changing a sentence's meaning.

51. The original sentence was difficult to understand; parentheses separate details of the charges and help to clarify the sentence. An alternative way to convey this information is: The CPS Investigation has been completed. Allison was Indicated for: 1) Physical Abuse towards Ryan (Excessive/Inappropriate Discipline); 2) Physical Abuse towards Ryan (Cut, Bruise and Welt); and 3) Neglect of Rebecca (Other Neglect).

52. We inserted a comma between the independent clause and following phrase.

53. Wordy. Say more with less.

54. Verb tense agreement. If Ryan continued (past tense), the girls remained (past tense).

55. We deleted the apostrophe because there was no possessive required.

56. The introductory phrase is about James, yet the following subject is CPS.

57. Homophone error: minor and miner— "minor" means lesser or under the age of consent; "miner" refers to mining.

58. We inserted a comma after the introductory phrase.

59. We inserted a comma and deleted the semicolon because a comma is required between an independent clause and a phrase.

60. Spell out numbers between one and ten.

61. Run-on sentence. Correct with proper punctuation.

62. We deleted "and" because "and" and "too" are redundant.

CASE 11: EMERGENCY MOTION–CHILD NEGLECT

The following is an emergency motion, filed with the family court by Child Protective Services (CPS), requesting immediate temporary state custody and placement of two children, because their single mom was found to be incapacitated. There are 26 writing errors.

Participants mentioned in the document	Abbreviations used in the document
<u>Family</u> Janice, mother, no age given Ernie, father, no age given Michelle, female, newborn <u>Professionals</u> Dr. Headon Wright, psychiatrist Pauline Baker, CPI Carol Holmes, LICSW, hospital social worker Dr. Healey Wells, physician at FGH Judge Woodley Gavel	CPS: Child Protective Services (state) CPI: Child Protection Investigator FGH: Fenwick General Hospital Tox: toxicology

ORIGINAL VERSION

Summary of Facts to Substantiate Allegations of Abuse, Neglect and/or Dependency

On April 10, a report was made to the child abuse hot line reguarding mother, Janice. The reporter stated that Janice gave birth to a baby girl on April 7. Unfortunately, tox screens completed at birth were positive for cocaine. The reporter stated that Dr. Wright filed a 72 hour hold on child, Michelle. The reporter also stated that mother admitted to using Vicodin during the pregnancy. Medical records indicate that mother had only 1 prenatal visit during this pregnancy.

(82)

On April 11 this investigation was assigned to Child Protective Investigator Pauline Baker. CPI Baker spoke with Carol Holmes, social worker at Fenwick General Hospital (FGH). Hospital Social Worker told CPI Baker that mother refused to give a urine tox screen at delivery but that the baby's urine screen came back positive for cocaine. CPI Baker obtained the Physician's Report of Examination, filed by Dr. Wells, M.D. The PRE states "+ urine tox screen for cocaine -newborn-1 prenatal visit (three weeks prior to delivery)".

CPI Baker spoke with Janice, mother, on April 12. Janice told CPI Baker that she 'experimented heavily' with drugs in the passed, but has not used drugs in years. She stated that after the death of her friend she began

using again. She said she started using crack cocaine to "cope", and
has used as recently as last week. She also stated that she used Vicodin
early on in her pregnancy. She learned she was pregnant but said she just
couldn't handle everything without the drugs.

Janice told CPI Baker that the baby's father, Ernie, also used crack (83)
cocaine with her during her pregnancy. On April 12 CPI Baker met with
father, Ernie at his sisters' home were the couple has been staying. Father,
Ernie admitted to smoking crack cocaine with mother, Janice, several
times during her pregnancy. Father told CPI Baker that when he was
younger he had a problem with heroin but had been clean for three years.

On April 12 a verbal ExParte was granted by Judge Gavel.

In order to insure the safety and welfare of newborn, Michelle, the
Department of Child Protective Services respectively requests that an
ExParte, Order of Detention be granted on the above-named child.

_____   _____
Child Protective Investigator   Child Protective Investigator Supervisor

CASE 11: CORRECTED VERSION

Each number in the corrected version refers to an explanation below.

On April 10, a report was made to the child abuse hotline regarding ①
mother, Janice. The reporter stated that Janice gave birth to a baby girl
on April 7. ② Tox screens completed at birth were positive for
cocaine. The reporter stated that Dr. Wright filed a 72-hour ③ hold on child,
Michelle. The reporter also stated that mother admitted to using Vicodin
during the pregnancy. Medical records indicate that mother had only one ④
prenatal visit during this pregnancy.

On April 11, ⑤ this investigation was assigned to Child Protective Investigator
Pauline Baker. CPI Baker spoke with Carol Holmes, social worker at Fenwick
General Hospital (FGH). Hospital Social Worker told CPI Baker that mother
refused to give a urine tox screen at delivery, ⑥ but ⑦ the baby's urine screen
came back positive for cocaine. CPI Baker obtained the Physician's Report of
Examination, filed by Dr. Wells ⑧. The PRE states "+ urine tox screen for
cocaine -newborn-1 prenatal visit (three weeks prior to delivery)." ⑨

CPI Baker spoke with Janice, mother, on April 12. Janice told CPI Baker
that she 'experimented heavily' with drugs in the past ⑩, but had ⑪ not used
drugs in years. She stated that after the death of her friend she began
using again. She said she started using crack cocaine to "cope," ⑫ and ⑬
used as recently as last week. She stated that she also ⑭ used Vicodin
early ⑮ in her pregnancy. She said ⑯ she knew ⑰ she was pregnant but
couldn't handle everything without the drugs.

cont.

EXPLANATIONS OF CORRECTIONS

1. We corrected the spelling error: "regarding."
2. "Unfortunately" is opinion. Avoid including your opinion.
3. Two-digit numbers as adjectives get hyphenated.
4. Spell out numbers from one through ten.
5. We included a comma after introductory phrase (optional because this phrase states a date).
6. We inserted a comma before conjunction between two independent clauses.
7. We deleted the second "that" in this sentence because it is unnecessary.
8. Use only one title per person, either Dr. or M.D.
9. We placed the period before close-quotation mark.

10. Homophone error: past and passed—"past" means ago; "passed" means went by.
11. We fixed the incorrect verb tense.
12. We placed the comma before close-quotation mark.
13. We used the simple past tense.
14. "Also" should modify "used," not "stated" (she also used Vicodin).
15. Avoid informal and unnecessary verbiage.
16. "She said" belongs at the beginning of the sentence because it describes both messages: "<u>she said</u> she knew she was pregnant, and <u>she said</u> she couldn't cope without drugs."
17. Word choice: "Knew" makes more sense than "learned."

cont.

Janice told CPI Baker that the baby's father, Ernie, ⑱ used crack cocaine with Janice ⑲ during her pregnancy. On April 12, ⑳ CPI Baker met with father, Ernie, at his sister's ㉑ home where ㉒ the couple has been staying. Father, Ernie, ㉓ admitted to smoking crack cocaine with mother, Janice, several times during her pregnancy. Father told CPI Baker that when he was younger he had a problem with heroin, ㉔ but had been clean for three years.

On April 12, ㉕ a verbal ExParte was granted by Judge Gavel.

In order to ensure ㉖ the safety and welfare of newborn, Michelle, the Department of Child Protective Services respectively requests that an ExParte, Order of Detention be granted on the above-named child.

_____ _____
Child Protective Investigator   Child Protective Investigator Supervisor

EXPLANATIONS OF CORRECTIONS

18. "Also" and "with her" are redundant.
19. The pronoun, "her," could apply to either Janice or Pauline. Be specific.
20. We inserted a comma after the introductory phrase (optional), see #5.
21. We inserted a comma after Ernie because his name could be removed without changing the meaning of the sentence, and an apostrophe to indicate the singular possessive.
22. Word choice: where and were—"where" refers to a place; "were" is past tense for "to be."

23. We inserted a comma to set off Ernie because "Ernie" can be removed without changing the sentence's meaning.
24. We inserted a comma between the independent clause and the following phrase.
25. We inserted a comma after introductory phrase (optional), see #5 and #20.
26. Word choice: ensure and insure: "ensure" means guarantee; "insure" refers to insurance.

CASE 12: EMERGENCY MOTION: FAMILY COURT

The following is an emergency motion, filed with the family court by Child Protective Services (CPS), requesting immediate temporary state custody and placement of two children, because their single mom was found to be incapacitated.

There are 23 <u>punctuation</u> errors in the narrative, including errors of omission (missing punctuation) and commission (incorrect punctuation).

Participants	Abbreviations
Shelly, mother, no age given Ima, female, 8 Ura, female, 6 Professionals Carrie Moore, CPI Harvey Loade, FSU worker	CPS: Child Protective Services (state department) CPI: Child Protective Investigator FSU: Family Service Unit (of CPS) EMT: Emergency Medical Technician MRI: Magnetic Resonance Imaging ER: Emergency Room FGH: Fenwick General Hospital

ORIGINAL VERSION

<u>CONFIDENTIAL</u>

{PRIVATE}

Dear Judge, (86)

This matter; is before the Court today—for an emergency motion; and to inform the Court of recent changes in the situation of the above named family members'.

On October 2 CPS was informed by a community provider that they had been to the home and found mother to be confused, and incoherent. This individual was concerned about the safety of the children and the mother. CPS contacted Police Dispatch and a rescue was sent to the home. EMT and Police found that mother was incapacitated the entire family was transported to Fenwick General Hospital (FGH) for medical evaluations'.

CPI Carrie Moore and FSU worker Harvey Loade, responded to the hospital. After initial ER examinations mother was admitted pending further examination and both children were placed on 72-hour hold and admitted for observation.

Subsequent to admission it had been determined that mother has a (87)
serious medical condition. Preliminary tests disclosed a cancerous

tumor. An MRI is scheduled. Mother's current condition remains unstable, she is experiencing periods of diminished lucidity. She is not likely to be released from the hospital, in the near future. She is unlikely to be able to provide care for either herself or her children in the near future.

Medical examinations revealed that the children are in good health, all vital signs are normal, but understandably upset about the condition of their mother's. Both children have significant developmental disabilities and, according to their medical records at FGH, "require ongoing support and services at home; and in school".

The Department respectfully requests that, this Court grant the Department temporary custody of Ima, age 8, and Ura age 6 in order that they may be placed outside of the home, in an environment which can meet their extensive special needs. The Department will continue to monitor the medical condition of Shelly [mother] and will work to develop a service plan with her, to assist her in regaining her ability to safely parent her two children. Given her current medical diagnosis, this process may be long and complicated. The Department will seek to insure that the children are involved with their mother during her treatment and recovery, and that particular attention will be paid to the provision of services that will assess and enhance mothers parenting ability throughout this period of time.

(88)

Respectfully Submitted,

_____

Social Caseworker II

Approved by: _____

LIST OF WITNESSES

CASE 12: CORRECTED VERSION

Each number in the corrected version refers to an explanation below.

Dear Judge,

This matter ① is before the Court today ② for an emergency motion, ③ and to inform the Court of recent changes in the situation of the above-named family members. ④

On Oct 2, ⑤ CPS was informed by a community provider that they had been to the home and found mother to be confused ⑥ and incoherent. This individual was concerned about the safety of the children and the mother. CPS contacted Police Dispatch, ⑦ and a rescue was sent to the home. EMT and Police found that mother was incapacitated; ⑧ the entire family was transported to Fenwick General Hospital (FGH) for medical evaluations. ⑨

CPI Carrie Moore and FSU worker Harvey Loade ⑩ responded to the hospital. After initial ER examinations, ⑪ mother was admitted pending further examination, ⑫ and both children were placed on 72-hour hold and admitted for observation.

cont.

EXPLANATIONS OF CORRECTIONS

Every error was either a misuse or an omission of correct punctuation.

#1 & #2: No punctuation required. We deleted the semicolon and the dash.

3. Semicolon improperly used. Commas are used to separate independent and subordinate clauses.

4. We deleted the apostrophe because the possessive is not required; it is a simple plural noun.

5. We inserted a comma after the complete introductory phrase, though this is optional because the phrase is a date.

6. We deleted the comma because it is redundant with "and."

7. We inserted a comma because it is necessary to break two non-parallel phrases.

8. This is a run-on sentence because the appropriate punctuation is missing. Either insert a semicolon or period to create two sentences.

9. We deleted the apostrophe because there is no possessive; it is a simple plural noun.

10. We deleted the comma because there is nothing to break up—it is a simple declarative sentence.

11. We inserted a comma in order to separate the introductory phrase from the independent clause.

12. We inserted a comma for clarity and to separate "further examination" from "both children."

cont.

Subsequent to admission, ⑬ it had been determined that mother has a serious medical condition. Preliminary tests disclosed a cancerous tumor. An MRI is scheduled. Mother's current condition remains unstable; ⑭ she is experiencing periods of diminished lucidity. She is not likely to be released from the hospital in the near future. She is unlikely to be able to provide care for either herself or her children in the near future.

Medical examinations revealed that the children are in good health: ⑮ all vital signs are normal.⑯ But understandably both children are upset about the condition of their mother.⑰ Both children have significant developmental disabilities and, according to their medical records at FGH, "require ongoing support and services at home ⑱ and in school." ⑲

The Department respectfully requests that ⑳ this Court grant the Department temporary custody of Ima, age 8, and Ura, age 6, ㉑ in order that they may be placed outside of the home, in an environment which can meet their extensive special needs. The Department will continue to

cont.

EXPLANATIONS OF CORRECTIONS

13. We inserted a comma in order to separate the introductory phrase from the independent clause.
14. We inserted a semicolon and deleted the comma in order to separate two independent clauses. As an alternative, a period and two separate sentences could be used.
15. We inserted a colon instead of a comma because "all vital signs are normal" is a definition of "in good health." If "all vital signs are normal" does not mean the same thing as "in good health," a semicolon would replace the comma to separate two independent clauses. The comma is incorrect in both interpretations of the sentence, "all vital signs are normal."
16. We ended the sentence here instead of allowing it to become run-on, and incoherent.
17. We created a new declarative sentence from the sentence fragment that makes the

original sentence difficult to comprehend. Also, "mothers" should be singular and not possessive—no apostrophe required.
18. We deleted the semicolon because there is no list; nor are there two independent clauses to join.
19. The period goes inside the close-quotation mark. This is true for commas also. Other punctuation marks go outside the close-quotation mark unless they are part of the quote. For example, if a quote ends in a question mark because it was originally a question, the question mark is placed inside the close-quotation mark.
20. We deleted the comma because it is unnecessary
21. We inserted commas to bracket Ura's age.

cont.

monitor the medical condition of Shelly [mother], ㉒ and will work to develop a service plan with her, to assist her in regaining her ability to safely parent her two children. Given her current medical diagnosis, this process may be long and complicated. The Department will seek to insure that the children are involved with their mother during her treatment and recovery, and that particular attention will be paid to the provision of services that will assess and enhance mother's ㉓ parenting ability throughout this period of time.

Respectfully Submitted,

_____

Social Caseworker II

Approved by: _____

LIST OF WITNESSES

EXPLANATIONS OF CORRECTIONS

22. We inserted a comma in order to provide clarity: the department will both monitor and work with the mother.

23. We inserted the apostrophe indicating the possessive: "parenting ability" belongs to the mother, as in "the mother's . . ."

Note: Look at your correct and incorrect answers. We included eleven sentences with comma errors, including omissions of commas to separate introductory phrases from complete sentences, or to separate two non-parallel phrases. There were several errors in usage of semicolons, apostrophes, and placement of close-quote marks. On two occasions, we use punctuation to avoid run-on or convoluted sentences. In one case, #15, we included an error involving the colon. Check the Glossary section for additional explanations and examples.

CASE 13: CRISIS PLANNING: PSYCHOTIC EPISODE

The following is a case record about Tom, who suffered from a severe psychotic episode. The narrative describes the episode and the subsequent events, concluding with the discovery of the trigger. There are 23 writing errors in the document.

Documentation of crises requires comprehensive but dispassionate reporting of events. Details and chronological order are important, but the writer's feelings are irrelevant.

Family members mentioned in the document	Abbreviation used in the document
Tom, male, 20 Jodi, mother, no age given	ER: Emergency Room

ORIGINAL VERSION

- Tom is a 20 year old schizophrenic male, paranoid type. He has been living in community residential facilities for 5 years. During a recent outing with 2 of his housemates and 2 staffs Tom appeared to "lose it" for no obvious reason. As the group was riding down a busy street, Tom suddenly began yelling "No, No". He began hitting himself in the head, removed his seatbelt and lied upon the floor of the van crying. Staff members attempted to assist Tom by trying to remove him from the vehicle, after pulling over and parking. Making physical contact with Tom appeared to escalate him further. He began kicking and yelling. He was incontinent and was visibly shaking. With a loss for how to respond, the staff called 911 for help.

  (90)

- The arrival of the police and an ambulance prompted Tom, to try to run away, from his providers. He was stopped by the police and than transported to the emergency department for an evaluation. After administering a dose of Ativan and performing a psychiatric evaluation, Tom was diagnosed by emergency department personnel as suffering from a psychotic episode. 6 hours after arriving at the ER, Tom was discharged back to the residential program.

- Following after this episode, Tom appeared withdrawn from the milieu and refused to go on outings for several weeks' time. It wasn't until he went out with his mother, Jodi, one afternoon that the actual source of his struggle that day was discovered. "Don't go down Lakeview," he stated. Bewildered, Jodi turned to him. "Lakeview Drive?" she inquired. "Yeah, don't go down Lakeview," he answered. Investigating farther, Jodi discovered that being on Lakeview Drive triggered bad memories for Tom of the way he was mistreated at Lincoln Place, a community residential facility located off that street.

  (91)

CASE 13: CORRECTED VERSION

Each number in the corrected version refers to an explanation below.

- Tom is a 20 year old male diagnosed with schizophrenia, paranoid type ①. He has been living in community residential facilities for five ② years. During a recent outing with two ③ of his housemates and two ④ staff members ⑤ Tom appeared to "lose it" for no obvious reason. As the group was riding down a busy street, Tom suddenly began yelling "No, No." ⑥ He hit ⑦ himself on ⑧ the head, removed his seatbelt and laid on ⑨ the floor of the van, ⑩ crying. After pulling over and parking the van, staff members attempted to assist Tom by trying to remove him from the vehicle ⑪. Physical contact appeared to escalate Tom's behavior further ⑫. He began kicking and yelling. He was incontinent and was visibly shaking. At ⑬ a loss for how to respond, the staff called 911 for help.

- The arrival of the police and an ambulance prompted Tom ⑭ to try to run away ⑮ from his providers. He was stopped by the police and then ⑯ transported to the emergency department for an evaluation. After administering a dose of Ativan and performing a psychiatric evaluation, emergency department personnel diagnosed Tom as suffering from a psychotic episode ⑰. Six ⑱ hours after arriving at the ER, Tom was discharged ⑲ to the residential program.

cont.

EXPLANATIONS OF CORRECTIONS

1. The original sentence defined Tom in terms of his illness, which dehumanizes him. Avoid this error.
2. Spell out numbers from one through ten.
3. Spell out numbers from one through ten.
4. Spell out numbers from one through ten.
5. "Staffs" means sticks or rods. The narrator means "staff members."
6. We placed the period inside close-quotation marks.
7. We used "hit" instead of "began hitting" for parallelism with the verbs in the rest of the sentence. The alternative is to separate the two phrases into two sentences with different verb tenses.
8. Preposition error: use "on" instead of "in" because he hit the outside of his head.
9. "Laid" is correct; "lied" means he told untruths.
10. We inserted a comma between the independent clause and the one-word modifier.
11. Misplaced modifier.
12. We revised the sentence in order to use active voice; "further" is correct for concepts. Active voice clarifies who does what to whom.
13. Incorrect preposition.
14. We deleted the comma because it is not required.
15. We deleted the comma because it is not required.
16. Homophone error: than and then—"than" is for comparisons; "then" refers to time.
17. Misplaced modifier.
18. Spell out numbers from one through ten.
19. "Discharged back" is redundant.

cont.

- Following ⑳ this episode, Tom appeared withdrawn from the milieu and refused to go on outings for several weeks ㉑. Jodi, Tom's mother, discovered the source of Tom's struggle one afternoon, when they were out together ㉒. "Don't go down Lakeview," he stated. Bewildered, Jodi turned to him. "Lakeview Drive?" she inquired. "Yeah, don't go down Lakeview," he answered. Investigating farther, Jodi discovered that being on Lakeview Drive triggered bad memories for Tom, ㉓ of the way he was mistreated at Lincoln Place, a community residential facility located off that street.

EXPLANATIONS OF CORRECTIONS

20. "After" is redundant with "following."
21. "Weeks" and "time" are redundant.
22. Passive voice; "actual" and "his struggle" deleted as unnecessary verbiage.

23. We inserted a comma to indicate "the way he was mistreated" refers to "bad memories."

CASE 14: ANNUAL TREATMENT PLAN: MENTAL HEALTH DIAGNOSES

*What follows is an annual treatment plan that combines assessment
and planned interventions. There are 24 writing errors in the "Individual
Treatment Plan" section. Note how the information is written objectively.
NOS means "not otherwise specified," a standard abbreviation in
psychiatric diagnoses.*

ORIGINAL VERSION

Name: Thomas Rhodes   Effective Date: 08/01/11 – 07/31/18
Dob: 09/09/69
Client ID: 958233
AXIS I.   296.90   Mood Disorder NOS
AXIS II.   799.9   Deferred Axis II Diagnosis
AXIS III. Arthritis
AXIS IV.   Discord with Family
AXIS V.   70

Diagnosis By: Catherine Smith, LPCMH

Program Discharge Criteria: When consumer meets the discharge criteria
for Insurance Company or when consumer initiates the discharge process.

Consumer Strengths: Committed to Treatment, Organized, Intelligent

Consumer Barriers: Pessimism, Makes Excuses, Allowing/Freeing Up
Time to Do It

Consumer participation in treatment planning:

- contributed to goals and plans
- informed of plan content
- present at team meeting
- refused to participate
- unable to participate
- refused to sign
- unable to sign

INDIVIDUAL TREATMENT PLAN   (95)

Treatment Issue #1: PSYCHIATRIC – Thomas has been recently
diagnosed with Mood Disorder, NOS. He has no prior mental health
history. Consumer noted that his chief complaint is: not being
"happy", racing thoughts (about everything he has too get done),
agitation, mood swings, and etc.

Goal: Consumer wants to be "happy" and for his thoughts (daily life situations) in his mind to slow down. Therefor, consumers' symptoms' of unhappiness, agitation, and stress will decrease to allow consumer to improve his quality of life (enjoying self, employment, family/friend involvement/interaction, & etc.).

Goal Discharge Criteria: For the stated treatment period, consumers' psychiatric symptoms and mood are significantly controlled to not interfere with daily living, basic self-care, and living enviroment.

Objectives: During the Treatment Period -

1. Thomas has agreed to learn skills/techniques to reduce his stress/anxiety/agitation.
2. Thomas has agreed to learn skills/techniques in order to refrain from negative thoughts which impact on his mood.
3. Thomas has agreed to learn skills/techniques of excceptance as defined in his original service plan
4. Thomas has agreed to counciling for his effect, which is actually to flat and detached
5. Fortunately, in order to accomplish items 1–4, Thomas has agreed to attend our day treatment group three times per each week

(96)

Interventions: During the entire Treatment Period -

1. Therapist will educate Thomas on stress/anxiety/agitation reduction techniques.
2. Therapist will educate Thomas on skills/techniques to refrain from negative thoughts that impact his mood.
3. Therapist will educate Thomas on skills/techniques to of excceptance as defined in his original treatment plan

INDIVIDUAL TREATMENT PLAN

This treatment plan consists of _3_ pages and the signatures below acknowledge having read and understand the content of this Treatment Plan.

Consumer Signature *(indicates that plan has been discussed with the consumer and that the consumer has been offered a copy of his/her treatment plan):*	Date:
Therapist Signature:	Date:
Physician/Nurse Practitioner Signature:	Date:
Clinical/Program Director Signature:	Date:
Family Member Signature *(if applicable):*	Date:

Family involvement in treatment planning process. Please check one of the following:

____ family member participated   ____ consumer requests no family involvement

____ family contacted and refused   ____ no family available

____ family estranged from consumer   ____ other _____

____ family participation but not
       available for signature

CASE 14: CORRECTED VERSION

Each number in the corrected version refers to an explanation below.

INDIVIDUAL TREATMENT PLAN

Treatment Issue #1: PSYCHIATRIC – Thomas recently was ①
diagnosed with Mood Disorder, NOS. He has no prior mental health
history. Consumer noted that his chief complaints are ② ③ not being
"happy," ④ racing thoughts (about everything he has to ⑤ get done),
agitation, mood swings, ⑥ etc.

Goal: Consumer wants to be "happy" and ⑦ his thoughts (daily life
situations) ⑧ to slow down. Therefore ⑨, consumer's ⑩ symptoms ⑪
of unhappiness, agitation, and stress will decrease to allow consumer
to improve his quality of life (enjoying self, employment, family/friend
involvement/interaction, ⑫ etc.).

Goal Discharge Criteria: For the stated treatment period, consumer's ⑬
psychiatric symptoms and mood are significantly controlled to not
interfere with daily living, basic self-care, and living environment ⑭.

cont.

EXPLANATIONS OF CORRECTIONS

1. We corrected the split verb form and the incorrect verb tense.
2. We used the plural because the list has multiple items.
3. We deleted the semicolon: any punctuation would interrupt a complete thought.
4. We placed the comma inside the close-quotation mark.
5. Homophone error: to and too—"too" means excessive or also.
6. "And" and "etc." are redundant.
7. We revised and used parallel sentence construction.
8. Redundancy: "thoughts" and "in his mind" repeat the same idea.
9. We corrected a spelling error.
10. We inserted an apostrophe to indicate the singular possessive.
11. We deleted the apostrophe because no possessive is required.
12. "&" and "etc." are redundant.
13. We inserted an apostrophe to indicate the singular possessive.
14. We corrected the spelling error.

cont.

Objectives: During the Treatment Period -

1. Thomas has agreed to learn skills/techniques to reduce his stress/anxiety/agitation.
2. Thomas has agreed to learn skills/techniques in order to refrain from negative thoughts, which impact on his mood.
3. Thomas has agreed to learn skills/techniques of acceptance ⑮ as defined in his original service plan.
4. Thomas has agreed to counseling ⑯ for his affect ⑰, which is ⑱ too ⑲ flat and detached.
5. ⑳ In order to accomplish items 1–4, Thomas has agreed to attend our day treatment group three times ㉑ each week.

Interventions: During the Entire Treatment Period -

1. Therapist will educate Thomas on stress/anxiety/agitation reduction techniques.
2. Therapist will educate Thomas on skills/techniques to refrain from negative thoughts that impact his mood.
3. Therapist will educate Thomas on skills/techniques ㉒ of acceptance ㉓ as defined in his original treatment plan. ㉔

EXPLANATIONS OF CORRECTIONS

15. We corrected spelling—correct word choice.
16. Homophone error: counciling (not a word) and counseling (advising).
17. Incorrect word choice.
18. We deleted the unnecessary word.
19. Homophone error: too and to (see #5).
20. Avoid including your opinion.

21. Avoid redundancy: "each" and "per" repeat the same idea.
22. One preposition, "of" is correct, "to" is not.
23. We corrected the spelling error—correct word choice.
24. Through the entire document, we added periods at ends of sentences. The original was inconsistent.

CASE 15: DISABILITIES: CLIENT PROGRESS NOTES

These records came from an agency that serves and advocates for people with disabilities.

Note the absence of the direct article (the) in the narrative, an acceptable practice in some agencies' case notes. Also, when referring to themselves, the writers either omitted a noun or pronoun, or used "I" or "author." Learn your agency's documentation rules and protocols before attempting to write official records. There are 22 errors in this narrative. Some sentence structure (missing sentence subjects) errors are not corrected because the agency allows this omission. We corrected those that were so imprecise as to be confusing or unclear.

Participants mentioned in the document	Abbreviations used in the document
<u>Family members</u> Arnold Stevens (client) Eva Stevens (sister) Sam Stevens (father) Marsha Stevens (mother) <u>Professionals</u> Franklin DeMint, DDS (clinician) Headon Wright, MD (psychiatrist)	DDS: Department of Disabilities Services DD: developmental disabilities IEP: individual educational plan SW: social worker

ORIGINAL VERSION

Entry 1 (99)

Called, and spoke to Sam Stevens to confirm that I will attempt to get to appt.

Arnold has remained @ home with dad since mom has been in the hospital for surgery on her vains in her legs' related to circulation.

Entry 2

Called - left detailed message with service coordinator at DDS.

Entry 3

Spoke with Franklin at DDS, client has been found eligible for DD services, his IEP is coming up. Will attend this with mom.

Entry 4

Brought Arnold to Central Hospital to meet with Dr. Wright, MD, his psychiatrist.

Entry 5

Received a call from, Eva, Arnolds sister. Both have appts to see Franklin on Monday. Their is no one in the family available to assist them. I have agreed to do this. Marsha Stevens is still in the hospital. The usual staff member who works with the family is not available for this appt.

Entry 6

Brought Eva and Arnold to appt. Both, had good check-ups, and blood work. Follow-up work done as well.

Also, went to the laundry to drop off as well. Bank and grocery shopping. (100) Marsha is doing ok but surgery was not as successful as they had hoped. She will be at Fredonia Rehab Center, occupational rehabilitation.

Entry 7

Spoke to DDS Service Coordinator to update him on mothers medical status and to let him know that Arnold has not been attending his day program at Peaceful Village Counseling Center. This is to both assist dad @ home and because anxiety level @ work increases when he is not able to be home to help. The family has not been notified that there is any issue dew to Marsha's absenteeism from work.

Entry 8

Called Sam to check in on things. All is well. Marsha is still in rehab facility. She just returned after a setback that had her back in the hospital for infection in legs (pneumonia). Eva has been in the home each week to assist with groceries & errands & stuff. Sam appreciated the check-in and contact me if he needs.

Entry 9

Spoke with Franklin at DDS. Informed him that Marsha is still eligible, thank goodness. We will have the family on short term Navigation for now. [Navigation appears to be category of eligibility or service.]

Entry 10

Spoke with Franklin. Still awaiting confirmation as Adult for DDS. She needs a SW to sign Clinical Team Report. IEP is scheduled in a couple of weeks.

CASE 15: CORRECTED VERSION

Each number in the corrected version refers to an explanation below.

Case #1

Entry 1

Called ① and spoke to Sam Stevens to confirm that I will attempt to get to appt.

Arnold has remained @ home with dad since mom has been in the hospital for surgery on her veins ② in her legs ③, ④ related to circulation.

Entry 2

Called - left detailed message with service coordinator at DDS.

Entry 3

Spoke with Franklin at DDS. ⑤ Client has been found eligible for DD services. His IEP is coming up. Will attend this with mom.

Entry 4

Brought Arnold to Central Hospital to meet with Dr. Wright ⑥, his psychiatrist.

Entry 5

Received a call from Eva, Arnold's sister. Both have appts to see Franklin on Monday. There ⑦ is no one in the family available to assist them. I have agreed to do this. Marsha Stevens is still in the hospital. The usual staff member who works with the family is not available for this appt.

Entry 6

Brought Eva and Arnold to appt. Both ⑧ had good check-ups ⑨ and blood work. Follow-up work done as well.

cont.

EXPLANATIONS OF CORRECTIONS

1. We deleted the comma because it interrupts a clear thought.
2. Homophone error: vein and vain—"vein" is a blood vessel; "vain" refers to a lack of success or self indulgence (vanity).
3. We deleted the apostrophe because no possessive is required.
4. We inserted a comma between the independent clause and the following phrase.
5. We inserted a period instead of comma. We revised the run-on sentence into two sentences.
6. Avoid using a double title, choose one or the other: (Dr. and MD).
7. Homophone error: There and their—"their" indicates the possessive, as in "their hopes."
8. We deleted the comma because it is unnecessary and interrupts a clear thought.
9. We deleted the comma because it is unnecessary and interrupts a clear thought.

cont.

Also, went to the laundry to drop off ⑩. Went to bank and grocery store ⑪.
Marsha is doing ok but surgery was not as successful as they had hoped.
She will be at Fredonia Rehab Center for ⑫ occupational rehabilitation.

Entry 7

Spoke to DDS Service Coordinator to update him on mother's ⑬ medical
status and to let him know that Arnold has not been attending his day
program at Peaceful Village Counseling Center. This is to ⑭ assist dad
@ home and lower his anxiety level @ work. ⑮ His anxiety increases when he is not able
to be home to help. The family has not been notified that there is any issue
due ⑯ to [mother's] absence ⑰ from work.

Entry 8

Called Sam to check in on things. All is well. Marsha is still in rehab facility.
She just returned after a setback that had her back in the hospital for
infection in legs (pneumonia). Eva has been in the home each week to
assist with groceries, ⑱ errands & stuff. Sam appreciated the check-in and
will ⑲ contact me if he needs anything ⑳.

Entry 9

Spoke with Franklin at DDS. Informed her that Marsha is still eligible ㉑.
We will have the family on short term Navigation for now.

Entry 10

Spoke with Franklin @ DDS. Still awaiting confirmation as adult ㉒ for DDS.
She needs a SW to sign Clinical Team Report. IEP is scheduled in a
couple of weeks.

EXPLANATIONS OF CORRECTIONS

10. "Also" and "as well" are redundant.
11. We revised a sentence fragment into a complete sentence.
12. We added a word for clarity.
13. We added an apostrophe to indicate singular possessive.
14. We deleted "both" because it was confusing.
15. We revised into two sentences for clarity—previous and next.
16. Homophone error: due and dew—"due" refers to a deadline; "dew" is moisture.
17. Correct word choice: "absence" is more appropriate than "absenteeism" in this sentence.
18. We inserted a comma instead of "&" in a string of items.
19. We added "will" for clarity.
20. We added "anything" for clarity.
21. We deleted authorial opinion.
22. We deleted the capital letter because the word is not a proper noun.

CASE 16: DISABILITIES: STATUS NOTES AND PROGRESS NOTES

These "status notes" and "progress notes" are periodic summaries of clients' situations, based on information in clients' files. Each of the five notes describes a different person at some point in time. There are 25 writing errors, one of which is an optional improvement.

Client is identified as "Jim."

ORIGINAL VERSION

STATUS NOTE

(104)

Team supervisor met with Jim and his father (caregiver), at there home. Also at the meeting were client's former case manager who transferred this case to author and an RN, who stated that Jim has been in good health and nothing new to report at this time. Emergency Fact Sheet (EFS) was updated during this appointment and a new picture was taken for the EFS. Releases were given to have client's mother sign as she is his guardian. Client's father did state that Jim recently saw his cardiologist but did not have his paperwork or the information to report as he stated that client's mother takes him to these appointments.

Respectfully submitted by:

STATUS NOTE

An application was completed online at the Registry of Department of Motor Vehicles for Jim to receive a state issued identification card. The application was mailed to client's father on behalf of Jim so his dad can assist him to obtain the ID card.

Respectfully submitted by:

STATUS NOTE

(105)

Team supervisor met with Jim and his father, who is Jim's caregiver at their home. Author followed up with client's father re. the names of cardiologist, dentist, oral surgeon and eye doctor. Client's father did not have the names at this time. Client's father stated that he would not like to get the releases signed as he does not want Jim to be exploited. Will follow up further at a later date. Author also followed up regarding going to the Registry of Motor Vehicles to obtain an identification card. Jim and father have not been able to do so as of this time. Home inspection was completed at this home visit. The home does not have a working door bell at the back entrance through the kitchen and also the caregiver was instructed to place a carbon monoxide detector in the basement.

Respectfully submitted by:

STATUS NOTE (106)

Coordinator met with Jim and his father in their home. Client's father and author reviewed state Health regulations and the medical requirements for each member to have an annual physical, an eye exam every two years and dentist's exams every six months. Client's father stated he feels like Big Brother is always watching him and he also sometimes wishes he stayed with Family Support program because he doesn't want people to tell him where and what to do and what is best for Jim. Client's father stated "I know what is best for Jim ". Client's father stated that he does not want to loose control over making the decisions about what is in Jim's best interest. Author and client's father updated the caregiver log book and discarded old papers. Jim was playing with tape during the visit and twirling the sticky side in his fingers. Jim appeared very happy. Client's father stated that Jim likes to fluff his pillow a certain way at night and can be very particular about things. Client's father stated that Jim would be going to see his niece this weekend. Coordinator presented the subcontractor agreement to client's father, but client's father stated he was not comfortable with subcontractor agreement and would not sign as he had concerns with statements 7 and 9. Author agreed to get more information from supervisor before next visit. Client's father stated that Jim recently went to a Birthday Party and played skee ball. Author asked client's father if there was a particular game or puzzle that Jim likes to do and perhaps we could do one together at the next visit. Client's father stated there is nothing Jim likes to play as far as games, he mostly likes to watch his shows and do his thing. Author thanked both gentlemen for the opportunity to visit and scheduled the April visit.

Respectfully submitted by:

PROGRESS NOTE (107)

Coordinator visited Jim and his father today at their home. Jim will be going to the dentist this Thursday for a regular cleaning. Client's father stated that it is time for Jim to schedule his regular eye exam, per a reminder client's father received from FenwickVision Services. Client's father and author reviewed subcontractor agreement and client's father did sign the agreement although he did have concerns with section 9. RN was also present for the visit. Reviewed with Caregiver the policy for Jim and alternative care days allotted per year. Author stated to client's father, that client's mother is interested in becoming alternative caregiver. Client's father stated that he was also aware and had no problem with that. Client's father relayed the information that Jim has not had any medical issues this month. Client's father will get a wireless doorbell for his door and a carbon monoxide detector. Client's father maintained his furnace recently by changing his fuel filter and vacuuming in between the grids. Jim has been visiting his sisters, grandmother and mother. Has been going out to eat. Jim also went to a couple of flea markets over the weekend.

Respectfully submitted by:

CASE 16: CORRECTED VERSION

Each number in the corrected version refers to an explanation below.

STATUS NOTE

Team supervisor met with Jim and his father (caregiver), at their ① home.
Also at the meeting were client's former case manager who transferred
this case to author and an RN, who stated that Jim has been in good
health and there is ② nothing new to report ③. Emergency Fact Sheet (EFS)
was updated ④ and a new picture was taken for the EFS.
Releases were given to have client's mother sign, as she is his
guardian. Client's father did state that Jim recently saw his cardiologist but
did not have his paperwork or the information to report, ⑤ as he stated that
client's mother takes him to these appointments.

Respectfully submitted by:

STATUS NOTE

An application was completed online at the Registry of Department
of Motor Vehicles for Jim to receive a state-issued ⑥ identification card.
The application was mailed to client's father on behalf of Jim so his dad
can assist him to obtain the ID card.

Respectfully submitted by:

cont.

EXPLANATIONS OF CORRECTIONS

1. Homophone error: their and there—"their" indicates the possessive, as in "their house."
2. "There is" added for clarity and to form a complete sentence.
3. "At this time" is wordy and unnecessary.
4. "During this appointment" is wordy and unnecessary. It was also misplaced, as it applied to both items that were completed during the appointment.
5. We inserted a comma before the conjunction between two independent clauses.
6. We inserted a hyphen because "state-issued" is a compound noun.

cont.

STATUS NOTE

Team supervisor met with Jim and his father, who is Jim's caregiver at their home. Author followed up with client's father for the names of cardiologist, dentist, oral surgeon and eye doctor. Client's father did not have the names at this time. Client's father stated that he would not like to get the releases signed as he does not want Jim to be exploited. Will follow up ⑦ at a later date. Author also followed up regarding going to the Registry of Motor Vehicles to obtain an identification card. Jim and father have not been able to do so ⑧. Home inspection was completed at this home visit. The home does not have a working door bell at the back entrance behind ⑨ the kitchen. ⑩ The caregiver was instructed to place a carbon monoxide detector in the basement.

Respectfully submitted by:

cont.

EXPLANATIONS OF CORRECTIONS

7. We deleted "further" because it is inappropriate and redundant.
8. "As of this time" is wordy and unnecessary.
9. "Behind" the kitchen describes the location of the entrance; "through" describes a direction, not a location.

10. "And also" is redundant. The sentence makes two separate points, so it is more appropriate to use two sentences rather than combining the information into one sentence.

cont.

STATUS NOTE

Coordinator met with Jim and his father in their home. Client's father and author reviewed state health ⑪ regulations and the medical requirements for each member to have an annual physical, an eye exam every two years and dental ⑫ exams every six months. Client's father stated he feels like Big Brother is always watching him, ⑬ and he ⑭ sometimes wishes he stayed with Family Support program because he doesn't want people to tell him where and what to do and what is best for Jim. Client's father stated "I know what is best for Jim." ⑮ Client's father stated that he does not want to lose ⑯ control over making the decisions about what is in Jim's best interest. Author and client's father updated the caregiver log book and discarded old papers. Jim was playing with tape during the visit and twirling the sticky side in his fingers. Jim appeared very happy. Client's father stated that Jim likes to fluff his pillow a certain way at night and can be very particular about things. Client's father stated that Jim would be going to see his niece the following ⑰ weekend. Coordinator presented the subcontractor agreement to client's father, but client's father stated he was not comfortable with subcontractor agreement and would not sign, ⑱ as he had concerns with statements 7 and 9. Author agreed to get more information from supervisor before next visit. Client's father stated that Jim recently went to a Birthday Party and played skee ball. Author asked client's father if there was a particular game or puzzle that Jim likes to do and perhaps they could do one together at the next visit. Client's father stated there is nothing Jim likes to play; ⑲ he mostly likes to watch his shows and do his thing. Author thanked both gentlemen for the opportunity to visit, ⑳ and scheduled the April visit.

Respectfully submitted by:

cont.

EXPLANATIONS OF CORRECTIONS

11. "Health" is not a proper noun in this sentence. "Health Department" would make the capitalization correct.
12. "Dentist's" is a possessive pronoun; the statement requires an adjective, e.g., "dental."
13. We inserted a comma before the conjunction between two independent clauses.
14. We inserted "he" for sentence clarity.
15. We placed the period inside the close-quotation mark.
16. Word choice: lose vs. loose—"lose" means to misplace or fail; "loose" means unrestrained.
17. The phrase, "would be going to see his niece this weekend" is incorrect because the sentence is not written in the present tense. "The following weekend" is consistent with the verb form, "would be."
18. We inserted a comma before the conjunction between two independent clauses.
19. "As far as games" is an incomplete modifier as well as unnecessary and wordy. The next sentence can be combined with the previous one, using a semicolon because they are closely-related complete sentences.
20. We inserted a comma between the independent clause and phrase.

cont.

PROGRESS NOTE

Coordinator visited Jim and his father today at their home. Jim will be going to the dentist this Thursday for a regular cleaning. Client's father stated that it is time for Jim to schedule his regular eye exam, per a reminder client's father received from Fenwick Vision Services. Client's father and author reviewed subcontractor agreement, ㉑ and client's father did sign the agreement although he had ㉒ concerns with section 9. RN was also present for the visit. Reviewed with Caregiver the policy for Jim and alternative care days allotted per year. Author stated to client's father that client's mother is interested in becoming alternative caregiver. Client's father stated that he was also aware and had no problem with that. Client's father relayed the information that Jim has not had any medical issues this month. Client's father will get a wireless door bell ㉓ and a carbon monoxide detector. Client's father maintained his furnace recently by changing his fuel filter and vacuuming ㉔ between the grids. Jim has been visiting his sisters, grandmother and mother. Jim ㉕ has been going out to eat. Jim also went to a couple of flea markets over the weekend.

Respectfully submitted by:

EXPLANATIONS OF CORRECTIONS

21. We inserted a comma before the conjunction between two independent clauses.
22. (Optional) We used "had" to replace "did have" – this is a preference rather than a grammatical error.
23. "For his door" is wordy and unnecessary.
24. "In between" is a noun, an "in-between" is an agent or intermediary. "In between"

can be used to mean "between," but should be avoided in professional writing.
25. "Has been going out to eat" is an incomplete sentence, and could be confusing. Be clear. Who has been going out to eat?

4

Social Policy

In Social Work Policy class(es), students learn how institutions develop social work policies and, hopefully, how to influence them. Policy analysis is a rather involved and detailed activity, because policy-related processes are complex. In your Policy classes, students write so-called "policy briefs" and sometimes "policy analyses," based on principles taught in the class.

As social workers we have the opportunity to influence the development of policy, perhaps initiate new policy, as well as affect the implementation of existing policy. Social workers do not typically write policy analyses in practice, instead we use our understanding of where social work policy comes from so that we might write about policy in order to design, change, or modify it.

In this chapter, we have included several such texts, all written with the intention of influencing social work policies. Typically, policy-changing texts appear in newspapers, legislative committees, electronic media of all kinds, and, of course, social work websites. Regardless of where writing on policy appears, communicating clearly and effectively remains a crucial requirement for social workers; readers will dismiss error-laden and poorly reasoned writing with possible consequences for you, your agency's reputation, and social workers in general.

Each example in the following section is accompanied by a discussion of the advantages and challenges of using that type of writing to influence social work policy. Numbers on the right side of the original documents note the page locations of the corresponding content in the corrected documents.

Press Releases and News Coverage
17 – Press Release: Public Announcement of a Grant

Letters to the Editor—Newspapers
18 – A Letter to the Editor: Daily Newspaper: Giveaways to the Rich Don't Work
19 – Weekly Newspaper: State Constitutional Convention
20 – Advocacy Letter: Same-Sex Marriage

Written (and Oral) Testimony at Hearings
21 – Domestic Partner Health Benefits Bill

PRESS RELEASES AND NEWS COVERAGE

A newspaper assignment editor, guest speaking in a BSW Policy class, explained that she receives hundreds of news announcements per week, and has to make quick decisions about inclusion or rejection. She said it is usually an easy decision: "Most press releases do not tell a story; there is no action. It is usually a non-event, a reiteration of what is already going on. Those announcements do not get past my desk. The press releases that survive first review say something important. Then, it is a matter of the competition for space."

Traditional (Print and Television) Media

It can be very difficult to get media coverage for events of concern to social workers, especially if a topic lacks drama, or is of limited interest to the general public. Print and electronic media space and time, respectively, can be limited. Decisions about inclusion and exclusion of news items are not always made by local news outlets, which are increasingly owned and managed by some corporation headquartered in a far-away city. The news industry is in transition from print and over-the-air networks to Internet and cable. That is the bad news. The good news is that most changes bring new opportunities. Here are a few strategies to get your "news" published to a general audience.

First, there are many different ways to have your writing published as a social worker. But the first rule is this: whomever you send your work to, what you send must be well-written and professional. Writers have to understand their audience and to whom they write. Think about your audience—who do you hope will read what you write? Understand what you are trying to accomplish and write to that purpose. Is it to persuade? Is it to inform? Is it to respond and answer a question? Whatever your purpose, and whoever your audience, strive for a brief, accurate, well-focused, and fact-based document or news release with no writing errors. When writing to journalists, organize your writing the way they do: many use the "funnel approach," which means they organize their writing from most important to least important. Never "bury the lead." Say the most important thing first. The rest of your document should explain answers to the questions: who, what, when, and where. Who is your story about? What is at stake? What happened? When did it happen? Where did it happen? Brevity is equally important – keep your news releases to one page. Attach any documentation separately—unless the publisher specifically requests "no attachments." Find out by going to the publisher's website where you will find instructions on how to submit your material. Always make sure your facts are correct. Remember that most readers connect with the personal aspect of a story—when real people are affected by some incident, readers feel compelled to read on. If there is a compelling, personal angle in something you have witnessed, use it when writing about it. Information like this answers the question, "who is this story about?" Some of the best news stories begin and end with the personal aspect of an issue, such as a family about to lose their home because of some law or policy you and your organization are working hard to change. There is one problem with using the "personal tragedy" story as a strategy: journalists have long been accused of exploiting the suffering of people, so be careful to avoid exploiting clients or program participants. Make sure whoever you write about agrees to it, understands that they will appear in the news, and may have to answer questions by journalists or others. They should be ready to "perform" should your efforts draw media attention to the situation.

Second, know something about the publishing platform to which you are sending your work. Daily print publications have uneven news cycles. This means that some days are active days for news, while others are "slow news" days. Traditionally, Monday and Saturday events get better news coverage than the rest of the week, because they are relatively "slow news" days. That may be less of an issue in your "market" as the percentage of ink from national press services (e.g., Associated Press) increases, and local stories decrease. Look at the newspaper you hope to publish in, and get a sense of what is published and when. Larger dailies are likely to assign reporters to "beats," or topic areas. Learn who the reporters are; reach out to them; get known and respected by them. They need to report news, and if they trust and respect you, your news can help them do their jobs. In this way, your interests have some overlap with theirs. Your news announcements should go directly to your beat reporter, perhaps preceded by a courtesy call or an e-mail. Fact sheets that include documentation of sources are helpful too. A good reporter will check your facts, and when finding them accurate, respect you as a professional to be relied upon.

Third, think about your city or town's community, weekly, and special interest print media. Look at one you think reaches an important audience, and then rewrite your news release to emphasize the interests of your audience. Better, have local constituents make your announcements, if possible. For example, the announcement about an important annual meeting held by your agency, or the receipt of a large grant, offers an opportunity to stay engaged with the community. Announcements like these can be made by a board or a staff member who lives in the community served by the newspaper you hope will publish your news. Community residents almost always have more specific information about the importance of an event to their community than you will. Consider that younger people tend to be overlooked by the print media, yet they read music and entertainment publications tailored to their interests. Non-English publications abound wherever there are immigrant populations. Also, some local, weekly, and special interest publications will print your news items as you wrote them, so make sure they are well-written, well-edited, and factually accurate.

Fourth, you should know that over-the-air and some cable media play by different journalistic rules than traditional print media. Over-the-air networks—even local affiliates of national networks—need to fill at least 18 hours per day of programming. Also, they are required by law to report some amount of local news every day. You will need to develop multiple strategies for reaching out to these media outlets; to succeed you will need to tailor what you do to how they operate, but the challenge is that the rules vary from market to market. One thing is clear, though: in large cities, the national, state and city news dominates over-the-air network time—just like it does in the large daily newspaper—so an agency or community news release cannot compete.

In medium-sized cities of less than a million people, all the major news outlets compete with each other, yet they are often competing for far less news than in the major cities. The local Sunday morning talk shows and morning and afternoon drive-time news and talk radio programs need guests and are always looking for local stories. Research who the assignment editors or program directors are, and pitch your information to them. Once you know whom to talk to, you might be surprised how quickly they invite you to submit your material. Even in this circumstance, your material must be of a reliably high quality.

Cable television offers another opportunity. Cable has brought local and special interest channels, as well as public access. Federal Communications Commission (FCC) regulations require all cable markets to support non-profit community-based public access television. Community groups can arrange for training, studio, and off-site recording, and regular broadcast times, at no or little cost. Do not forget radio, which can be as powerful as TV, especially for reaching commuters. Remember: It is better to be out of the spotlight than in it and poorly prepared. Much is revealed in how we write. Professionals will judge you by how you present yourself, your agency, and for whatever cause you advocate. Be prepared.

Fifth, Internet, blogs, and social network sites like Facebook and Twitter are valuable tools for publicizing your agency's or organization's work. Again, consider your audience. Social Networking sites reach audiences who typically avoid traditional news programming. Consider a few recent examples of the power and reach of social media, especially among young people. It has become common knowledge that social media have been instrumental in world-changing events, from Barrack Obama's 2008 Presidential Campaign, to the Middle East's "Arab Spring" revolutions. Begin using your own social media activity as a way to keep informed about what is going on in the world. With social media comes hacking and identity theft, so you may consider having a skilled web master manage your agency's site. Also, anything posted on Facebook and the Internet in general is insecure, meaning likely to become public. With proper care, skill, and management, electronic media can benefit social work practice.

Sixth, you should always remember that the content of your document, news release, blog, letter to the editor, or whatever other document you create, plays a major role in any media outlet's decision to publish your news item. Community activities that garners high consensus among people, such as blood drives, charity events and holiday celebrations, are likely to be treated differently from controversial events, like a rally that accuses police of racial profiling. Depending on the perceived newsworthiness of your document, media outlets may report on controversial events, if they think their audience needs the information. For example, a rally against homelessness was covered on the 11 PM TV news, but the ground-breaking event for a new affordable housing construction project was not. The rally against homelessness consisted of students sleeping in cardboard boxes on a local college campus in the winter. The rally had visual appeal, the college campus was in the same town as the news agency, so perceived community interest was high. The event was "newsworthy." The ground-breaking ceremony, however, was relatively ordinary and was further away, so it was not covered. Still, depending on the interests of an assignment editor, the decision of which story to cover could have gone the other way.

Newspapers will treat a church spaghetti dinner to support flood or fire victims as a type of advertising for which they will not get paid. If there is space in the newspaper or website, it will probably be published, especially if it is "camera-ready," i.e., a document requiring no rewriting or reformatting. Your own photos are more likely to be printed by weeklies and special interest newspapers than a daily newspaper, and web-sites and social networking sites give you even more options. Always remember: photos should be clear, uncluttered images that convey a message, a lot like your writing.

Whenever you submit your work to a news publisher, always include your name as the contact person, with your phone and e-mail contact information. An editor may need to reach you in order to verify authenticity and facts. Finally, be sure to be prepared and always to do your best. Decisions may be made based upon the writing you prepare and submit. It is better to be out of the spotlight than in it, and unprepared.

CASE 17: PRESS RELEASE: PUBLIC ANNOUNCEMENT OF A GRANT

The Fredonia Housing Coalition (FHC) sent the following press release to all the media outlets in Fenwick, capital of Fredonia. The FHC is a housing education and advocacy organization of 30 community groups, churches, and labor unions. FHC received a small grant ($10,000) from the largest independent bank in the state. For the FHC, the grant symbolizes their legitimacy, because when banks give money, it is a clear sign of recognition and respect for the agency. It is a sign that the community endorses the agency's work. A grant is a form of encouragement to go on doing the work you are doing. The FHC wrote the following press release with the dual goals of attracting more attention and publicly thanking the bank.

The are 27 writing errors in the following press release.

ORIGINAL VERSION

First Bank of Fredonia awards Housing Coalition (115)

First Bank of Fredonia has awarded a $10,000 grant to Fredonia Housing Coalition; recognizing the important roll played by the development of long-term affordable homes in Fredonia's economic future. The funds are helping to insure that Fredonia has accurate, useful and timely information on the affordability of homes in our state.

"Fredonia Housing Coalition is a proven source of reliable data and analysis that helps to educate stakeholders across Fredonia about the connection between housing and economic development", said Charity Banks, Market President, First Bank of Fredonia. "These funds will be critically important to insuring that Fredonia Housing Coalition will be able to continue to provide credible and timely information regarding the housing climate, not only to financial institutions, but to the public at large".

First Bank of Fredonia is the latest of several charitable organizations in funding FHC's efforts to identify best practices, conduct research, and analyzing data to support: policy recommendations, public education strategies, and communication initiatives. Thru they're philanthropic efforts, First Bank of Fredonia is commited to creating meaningful change in the (116) communities they serve including community development activities.

"We appreciate First Bank of Fredonia's recognition of the important roll long-term affordable housing plays in our economy", said May King-Holmes, Executive Director of FHC. "This $10,000 grant will help FHC to offer up-to-date research and analysis on long-term affordable homes in Fredonia and the positive impact the development of these homes has on our economy".

Contact person: B. Anna D'Akry (bad@fhcfa.org).

CASE 17: CORRECTED VERSION

Each number in the corrected version refers to an explanation below.

First Bank of Fredonia Awards Grant to Housing Coalition (*)

First Bank of Fredonia has awarded a $10,000 grant to Fredonia Housing Coalition (FHC)①, ② in recognition of ③ the important role ④ ⑤ of long-term affordable homes in Fredonia's economic future. The funds will help ensure ⑥ ⑦ that Fredonia has accurate, useful and timely information on the affordability of homes in our state.

"Fredonia Housing Coalition is a proven source of reliable data and analyses ⑧ that help ⑨ educate stakeholders across Fredonia about the connection between housing and economic development," ⑩ said Charity Banks, Market President, First Bank of Fredonia. "These funds will be critically important to ensuring ⑪ that Fredonia Housing Coalition will be able to continue to provide credible and timely information regarding the housing climate to both ⑫ financial institutions and the public at large." ⑬

First Bank of Fredonia joins ⑭ several charitable organizations in funding FHC's efforts to identify best practices, conduct research, and analyze ⑮ data to support ⑯ policy recommendations, public education strategies,

cont.

EXPLANATIONS OF CORRECTIONS

* The title of the News Release should be in all capital letters. The title is the "headline" and should be brief, clear, and informative.

1. The agency's initials should be given in parentheses immediately after the writer names the agency for the first time. From then on use only the initials when naming the agency.

2. We replaced the semicolon with a comma because a semicolon requires two independent clauses before and after it.

3. We rephrased this because "recognizing" does not agree with the past tense of the sentence. In "recognition" makes the sentence clear and consistent.

4. We tightened things up here and deleted unnecessary words.

5. Homophone error: role and roll: "role" refers to activity, importance, or purpose.

6. We used future tense in this correction because the grant was just awarded and the outcomes were still in the future.

7. Word choice and near homophone error: "ensure" and "insure."

8. We used the plural "analyses."

9. "To educate" is grammatically correct but "to" is unnecessary. We changed "helps" to "help" because the subject is plural (data and analyses).

10. The comma belongs before the close-quotation mark.

11. Word choice: ensure and insure: "insure" refers to insurance.

12. The tone was too informal and wordy.

13. The period belongs inside the close-quotation mark.

14. We corrected the passive voice so now it is clear who does what to whom.

15. Strive for parallelism and pattern in your writing. Be sure the verbs are all in the same tense: identify, conduct, analyze.

16. There is no colon needed, even though there is a list of sorts in the sentence. The sentence flows smoothly without it.

cont.

and communication initiatives. Through ⑰ its ⑱ philanthropic efforts, First Bank of Fredonia demonstrates its commitment ⑲ to creating meaningful change in the communities it serves, ⑳ ㉑ including community development activities.

"We appreciate First Bank of Fredonia's recognition of the important role ㉒ long-term affordable housing plays in our economy," ㉓ said May King-Holmes, Executive Director of FHC. "This $10,000 grant will help FHC ㉔ offer up-to-date research and analysis on long-term affordable homes in Fredonia, positively impacting ㉕ our state economy." ㉖

Contact person: B. Anna D'Akry (bad@fhcfa.org).

EXPLANATIONS OF CORRECTIONS

17. "Thru" is not a word—choose between "threw" or "through."

18. "Its" because the bank is singular; they're is not possessive.

19. Spelling.

20. "It serves" because bank is singular. We also rephrased part of this sentence using more active, specific language.

21. We inserted a comma because it is needed to separate an independent clause from a phrase, or "dependent clause," which is a phrase that cannot stand alone as a complete sentence.

22. Homophone error: role and roll (see #5).

23. We inserted the comma before the close-quotation mark.

24. "To" before the verb is unnecessary though grammatically acceptable.

25. The original sentence had a parallelism problem: the part of the sentence that reads ". . . and the positive impact the development of these homes has on our economy" did not connect to "help," the verb from which the phrase should take action.

26. The period belongs inside the close-quotation mark.

LETTERS TO (NEWSPAPER) EDITORS

A relatively low-cost way to influence public policy is through a letter to the editor of a daily or weekly newspaper. Daily newspapers tend to be read by more people across a broader area than papers published weekly, and consequently enjoy more influence. But local and special interest papers with weekly and monthly publication tend to be read more completely and by a higher percentage of targeted populations, including publications that target the county, or town, or even smaller local groups within the town, for example, faith-based organizations. They also tend to accept more letters and other submissions, often just as they have been written. Even so, remember that when writing to editors, be mindful about how you approach them and that your writing is appropriate for their community. As always, your professional reputation along with your agency's is on the line, so get the facts right, use respectful language, and make your message clear and well-reasoned.

Each newspaper has its own rules, guidelines, and policies for letters. You can find this information on the publication's website or often in the editorial section of the print version. In daily newspapers, editors prefer shorter letters because space is limited. We try to stick to between three and five paragraphs when writing a letter to the editor.

Introduction: Briefly introduce the topic and why you care about it. In your introduction you define the topic and its importance. If it is a high-profile issue, as might be the case when writing about state budget issue, there may not be much need to argue for the importance of your topic. However, if your topic is less familiar to most readers—for example, a call to increase funding for parent literacy programs—the letter writer should discuss the incidence rate and prevalence of the problem and highlight consequences of inaction. Incidence is the number of people newly affected each year; prevalence is the total number of people typically affected at any given time; consequence is the harm (or benefit) attributable to the topic. If what you are arguing for is an unpopular position (such as creating pre-release programs for prison inmates), be sure to emphasize why you think your position represents a win-win situation for all involved. When arguing against the other side, gently debunk arguments the opposition might use against you. Try to work against stereotypes many people carry. Use a specific sympathetic example in order to humanize the topic.

In the body of the letter, strive to make your points follow a logical progression; use clear language and be sure to cite compelling examples. Examples serve as evidence for your cause. Depending on the topic, the body of the letter can take several tacts. When deciding how best to approach your topic, consider the degree of support or opposition your topic has among the public. What is the availability of concrete examples and how much are you relying on a theoretical argument? Though the ultimate purpose of the letter may vary, every letter needs an ultimate purpose. What's yours? Is it to instigate? To educate? To criticize? To persuade? Or to offer support? Avoid personal attacks against the opposition. Stick to the topic. Remember to consider whom you are writing to and use appropriate language: avoid jargon and smugness.

When concluding, briefly summarize the reasons for your position and consider making a recommendation for action.

CASE 18: A LETTER TO THE EDITOR—DAILY NEWSPAPER GIVEAWAYS TO THE RICH DO NOT WORK

This is a letter to the Fenwick Journal, a daily newspaper, similar in circulation and influence to a mid-size city's daily newspaper. At the time of the writing of this letter, the state legislature was considering the state budget, with proposals coming from all sides of the political spectrum. As a social worker, the writer of this letter to the editor was interested in challenging the popular idea that lower taxes for the wealthy, coupled with cuts in programs for those in need, would improve the state's business climate, consequently creating more jobs and increased state revenues. There are 34 errors in the letter.

Afterwards, we discuss some additional pointers for writing letters to editors.

ORIGINAL VERSION

Giveaways to the rich don't work

Tuesday, May 29, 2007   (120)

As our legislatures go into the final process of determining the Fredonia state Budget, they should revisit last years' decisions again, which embraced cuts in state services rather then rising additional revenue, and which disproportionately benefitted those who need help the least at the expense of those, who are most vulnerable. The governor's current proposed budget would carry that sorry legacy into 2008 and beyond into the future.

Here is one example of how the cut-only strategy effects Fredonians. I teach at Fredonia State College. My students are hard-working, tax paying state residents who play by the rules but keep loosing ground. Most are the first in their family's to attend college. What happens is that every year, because of decisions made at the state house, a smaller percentage of public higher education costs are subsidized by the state, driving college students' farther into debt or out from college altogether to boot. My students have to work more and more each year (often coming to class   (121) bleary-eyed from their third-shift jobs, and hurrying off after class to their afternoon job), just to pay ever-higher tuition, fees and bookstore bills. It is no wonder they don't have time for assigned readings and important out-of-class educational activities, like field trips or there own research.

When my students graduate this place, they will find that other policy decisions, like privatization of state jobs and reduced reimbursements' to state vendors, have resulted in lower incomes with which to pay off their college debts. (Financial aid has devolved from scholarships to loans in the last two decades). Meanwhile, the state's capitol-gains tax is set to expire this year, resulting in yet another tax cut in the tens of millions of dollars for the state's wealthiest residents. And last year's income-tax cut, which also benefitts only the wealthiest and many out-of-staters, will cost Fredonia $70 million a year when fully implemented.

I have a bold proposal; Base state fiscal policy on evidence rather than intuition and unproven theory. Enact revenue and spending practices that work rather then feel good. Their has yet to be conclusive evidence that subsidizing the rich results in better economic climates, more jobs, enhanced public revenues or improvements in the quality of life for the majority of citizens. In fact, the opposite is more evident: Pandering to those that need assistance the least are more likely the engine that drives the race to the bottom for everyone else.

Mai-King Goode

Social Worker

CASE 18: CORRECTED VERSION:

Each number in the corrected version refers to an explanation below.

Giveaways to the Rich Don't Work (*)

Tuesday, May 29, 2007

As our legislators ① go into the final process of determining the Fredonia state budget ②, they should revisit last year's ③ decisions ④, which embraced cuts in state services rather than ⑤ raising ⑥ additional revenue, and which disproportionately benefited ⑦ those who need help the least at the expense of those ⑧ who are most vulnerable. The governor's current ["current" was included to differentiate this year from previous years, but it is not necessary] proposed budget would carry that sorry legacy into 2008 and beyond ⑨.

Here is one example of how the cut-only strategy affects ⑩ Fredonians. I teach at Fredonia State College. My students are hard-working, tax-paying ⑪ state residents who play by the rules but keep losing ⑫ ground. Most are the first in their families ⑬ to attend college. Every year, because of decisions made at the State House ⑭, the state subsidizes a smaller percentage of public higher education costs ⑮, driving college students ⑯

cont.

EXPLANATIONS OF CORRECTIONS

* Every word in a title should be capitalized.

1. Word choice is off here probably because of homophone error: "Legislatures" is plural of "legislature," the entire legislative body. The appropriate words are "legislators"— multiple members of the legislature— or "legislature"—the singular body made up of legislators.

2. We removed the capital letter because "budget" is not a proper noun.

3. We added an apostrophe indicating the singular possessive.

4. We deleted "again" because it is redundant with "revisit."

5. Homophone error: "than" and "then." Use "than" to compare, "then" to indicate time.

6. Word choice is off here. Use "raising" revenues; "rising" in this context is incurred because it means getting up or "rising" higher, as in bread rising.

7. Misspelling. "benefited" has one "t."

8. We deleted the comma because it interrupts a clear thought and is unnecessary.

9. We deleted "into the future" because it is redundant with "beyond."

10. Word choice is off here: affect and effect— "affect" is the verb, meaning to influence. "Effect" refers to things, as in the specific outcomes, or "effects."

11. "Tax-paying" is a hyphenated compound adjective.

12. Word choice: losing and loosing—"to lose" means to no longer possess.

13. "Families" is the correct way to indicate non-possessive plural.

14. "State House" is a proper noun and should be capitalized.

15. We corrected the passive construction, "is subsidized" and made it active: "the state subsidizes." Also, the subject is percentage, not costs. "Costs" is the object of the sentence, so the verb must be singular, as in, "the percentage is . . ."

16. We deleted the apostrophe because no possessive is required.

cont.

further ⑰ into debt or out of ⑱ college altogether ⑲. My students have to work more and more each year (often coming to class bleary-eyed from their third-shift jobs, and hurrying off after class to their afternoon jobs ⑳), just to pay ever-higher tuition, fees and bookstore bills. It is no wonder they don't have time for assigned readings and important out-of-class educational activities, like field trips or their ㉑ own research.

When my students graduate ㉒, they will find that other policy decisions, like privatization of state jobs and reduced reimbursements ㉓ to state vendors, have resulted in lower incomes with which to pay ㉔ their college debts. (Financial aid has devolved from scholarships to loans in the last two decades). Meanwhile, the state's capital-gains ㉕ tax is set to expire this year, resulting in yet another tax cut in the tens of millions of dollars for the state's wealthiest residents. And last year's income-tax cut, which also benefits ㉖ only the wealthiest and many out-of-staters, will cost Fredonia $70 million a year when fully implemented.

I have a bold proposal: ㉗ Base state fiscal policy on evidence rather than intuition and unproven theory. Enact revenue and spending practices that work rather than ㉘ feel good. There ㉙ has yet to be conclusive evidence that subsidizing the rich results in better economic climates, more jobs, enhanced public revenues or improvements in the quality of life of ㉚ the majority of citizens. In fact, the opposite is more evident: Pandering to those who ㉛ need assistance the least are more likely the engine that drives the race to the bottom for everyone else.

EXPLANATIONS OF CORRECTIONS

17. "Further" is correct when there is no measurable unit specified in the sentence. Debt is a concept.
18. We corrected a preposition error: "out of college" is correct; "out <u>from</u> college" is incorrect.
19. "To boot" is informal language and unnecessary.
20. The subject is "students" who have different "jobs"—make sure you are consistent and parallel with the use of singular or plural.
21. Homophone error: their and there—"their" is the possessive. The phrase, "this place" is too informal, and the preposition "from" should proceed it. We left the sentence without naming the school.
22. We deleted the apostrophe because no possessive is required.
23. We deleted the comma because it interrupts a clear thought and is unnecessary.

24. We deleted "off" because it is redundant with "pay."
25. Word choice is off here: "capital" applies to money while "capitol" refers to the State House. The hyphenation is correct.
26. Spelling error.
27. We used a colon rather than a semicolon because the next sentence specifies the "bold proposal."
28. Word choice is off here: "than" is for comparisons.
29. Homophone error: there and their—"their" is possessive.
30. We corrected a preposition error.
31. "Who" is the correct pronoun when a sentence refers to people; "what" applies to things. The subject is singular and so the noun should be singular, e.g., "pandering is . . ."

CASE 19: A LETTER TO THE EDITOR OF A WEEKLY NEWSPAPER STATE CONSTITUTIONAL CONVENTION

Fredonia's state capital is the small city of Fenwick, located in central Fredonia. The Fenwick Gazette is a weekly newspaper that serves the city. As we mentioned earlier, weeklies tend to be more generous than dailies in accepting and printing verbatim letters written by individuals who are members of the community and who represent one or more interest groups within the community. Elected officials and community residents tend to read local papers more completely than larger, more distant daily newspapers serving larger areas and larger populations. Here is a letter written by a Fenwick resident who happened to be a social work student on the Fenwick campus of the University of Fredonia.

In this letter the writer presents a proposal for a state-wide "constitutional convention," which, if held, would recommend changes to the Fredonia constitution. In the past, such conventions have presented more challenges than opportunities for social workers. In recent years such changes have resulted in proposed amendments that ban abortions and restrict the voting rights of first-generation citizens. At the time the following letter to the editor appeared, the constitutional convention, or "con-con," had received considerable attention, with arguments on both sides filling the media. The Fredonia chapter of the National Association of Social Workers (NASW) asked social workers to write letters to their local newspapers, most of which were weekly newspapers. NASW asked social workers to present the social work perspective on issues related to the "con-con." What follows is a letter to the editor responding to the NASW request. There are 17 errors.

ORIGINAL VERSION

Dear Editor: (124)

I must say that I read with interest your coverage of the campaign for a constitutional convention. Constitutional conventions are more affective methods for problem solving then the regular legislative process, claim proponents. I strongly disagree.

Around the country "Con-Con's" have become vehicles for well organized groups to push agendas that are harmful to the civil rights' of others, such as anti-choice, anti-gay, and anti-immigrant amendments. Delegates tend to be choosen in low-turnout off-year elections, and have no accountability to anyone, the reason being because they do not run for re-election. They can address any issue, usually in a short time period with minimal open discussion, and in so doing, tamper with our most precious document; the state Constitution.

The situation is rife for well-funded special interests to bypass our routine policy-making processes and push there often-divisive agendas on the public.

The annual General Assembly session being an affective legislative process. The fact of the matter is that when a constitutional amendment has sufficient support, the regular legislative process has a mechanism for submitting amendments to the public, as is happening this year with the Separation of Powers Amendment. Legislation can be messy and frustrating, the reason being because many policy decisions require the balancing of competing interests and values in the context of available resources. It is called Democracy, and no one has figured out an exceptable alternative.

(125)

On the surface, a statewide convention to improve our constitution sounds reasonable: bring together all Constituencies and hammer out needed changes to the Fredonia Constitution. It doesn't quiet happen that way.

Steamboat Willy

Fenwick

CASE 19: CORRECTED VERSION

Each number in the corrected version refers to an explanation below.

Dear Editor:

① I read with interest your coverage of the campaign for a constitutional convention. ② Proponents claim that constitutional conventions are more effective ③ methods for problem solving than ④ the regular legislative process. I strongly disagree.

Around the country "Con-Con's" have become vehicles for well organized groups to push agendas that are harmful to the civil rights ⑤ of others, such as anti-choice, anti-gay, and anti-immigrant amendments. Delegates tend to be chosen ⑥ in low-turnout off-year elections, and have no accountability to anyone, ⑦ because they do not run for re-election. They can address any issue, usually in a short time period with minimal open discussion, and in so doing, tamper with our most precious document: ⑧ the state Constitution.

The situation is ripe ⑨ for well-funded special interests to bypass our routine policy-making processes and push their ⑩ often-divisive agendas on the public.

The annual General Assembly session is ⑪ an effective ⑫ legislative process. ⑬ When a constitutional amendment has sufficient support, the regular legislative process has a mechanism for submitting amendments to the public, as is happening this year with the Separation of Powers

cont.

EXPLANATIONS OF CORRECTIONS:

1. We deleted unnecessary language that made the original sentence wordy and a touch too informal.
2. We moved the controlling verb "claim" into the first phrase of the sentence. This tends to add clarity.
3. Word choice is off here: use "effect" when referring to nouns; use "affect" when you mean "to influence" as a verb.
4. Homophone error: than and then—"than" is for comparisons.
5. We deleted the apostrophe. No possessive required.
6. Spelling error. "Choosen" is not a word.
7. We cut unnecessary language that made the original sentence wordy and a touch too informal.
8. We inserted a colon because the next statement is an elaboration of the previous one.
9. Word choice is off here: ripe and rife— "ripe" means ready, well-suited, well-timed while "rife" means widespread.
10. Homophone error: Their and there—"their" is the possessive.
11. "Being" is the wrong form of the "to be" verb. We replaced it with "is."
12. Word choice is off here: use "effective" when referring to nouns; use "affective" when you mean "to influence" as a verb.
13. We cut unnecessary language that made the original sentence wordy and a touch too informal.

cont.

Amendment. Legislation can be messy and frustrating ⑭ because many policy decisions require the balancing of competing interests and values in the context of available resources. It is called Democracy, and no one has figured out an acceptable ⑮ alternative.

On the surface, a statewide convention to improve our constitution sounds reasonable: bring together all constituencies ⑯ and hammer out needed changes to the Fredonia Constitution. It doesn't quite ⑰ happen that way.

Sincerely,

Steamboat Willy

Fenwick River Dock

EXPLANATIONS OF CORRECTIONS

14. We cut unnecessary language that made the original sentence wordy and a touch too informal.

15. Spelling error.

16. The word "constituency" is a common noun and should not be capitalized.

17. Word choice is off here, or a spelling error, or a homophone error: quite and quiet—"quiet" means silent, quite means completely, or absolutely.

CASE 20: ADVOCACY LETTER: SAME-SEX MARRIAGE

In several states around the country, legislators are debating the relative merits of civil unions, same-sex marriage, and the question of defining marriage as a union of two "opposite-sex-only" individuals. The next example is a letter to members of a state legislature's Judiciary Committee from the executive director of that state's chapter of the National Association of Social Workers (NASW). In Fredonia, the NASW endorsed same-sex marriage, and opposed civil unions. If you disagree with the position taken by Fredonia's NASW, that's a good discussion to have in class. There are 34 writing errors in the letter.

ORIGINAL VERSION

DATE: May 11, 2011   (127)
TO: House Judicial Committee
RE: Testimony in Opposition to H – 6103 (Civil Unions)

The National Association of Social Workers – Fredonia Chapter as it has in the past is in opposition to civil unions. We do not beleive a civil union is equal to a civil marriage. This position is primarily based on the premise that "separate but equal is inherently unequal". Although, we appreciate the sentiment of the sponsors to provide legal protection for same gender couples. We feel as though the passage of this legislation would actually impede the progress towards true, actual **marriage equality**.

As long as we do not recognize the writes and priveleges of any specific group within our community fully, we are supporting institutional discrimination. Civil unions is not an inclusive concept; and can only result in segregation in the hearts and minds of Fredonians'. It is our belief that by utilizing such procedures as civil unions to try to insure equality results   (128) in confusion by the public (especially our young citizens) and negatively impacts the understanding of fairness and civil rights in Fredonia. No community can be truly healthy until it rids itself of such practices, cleans up it's attitudes, educates it's citizens, ect.

We urge that the members of this committee, the sponsors of this legislation, and all the members of the Fredonia State Legislator to focus their efforts to pass a true marriage equality bill, which has not only been our committment for the last ten years, but is good public policy.

Respectively submitted by:
Dr. Moe Larry, Ph.D, LICSW
Executive Director

CASE 20: CORRECTED VERSION

Each number in the corrected version refers to an explanation below.

DATE: May 11, 2011
TO: House Judicial Committee
RE: Testimony in Opposition to H – 6103 (Civil Unions)

The Fredonia Chapter of the National Association of Social Workers opposes civil unions just as it has in the past. ① ② ③ We do not believe ④ a civil union is equal to a civil marriage. This position is based primarily ⑤ on the premise that "separate but equal is inherently unequal." ⑥ Although ⑦ we appreciate the sentiment of the sponsors to provide legal protection for same gender couples, ⑧ we believe ⑨ ⑩ passage of this legislation would ⑪ impede ⑫ progress towards true ⑬ **marriage equality**.

As long as we do not fully ⑭ recognize the rights ⑮ and privileges ⑯ of any specific group within our community, we are supporting institutional discrimination. Civil union is not an inclusive concept ⑰ and can only result in segregation in the hearts and minds of Fredonians. ⑱ We

cont.

EXPLANATIONS OF CORRECTIONS

1. We corrected the "syntax" or word order of the sentence. It is always best to avoid convoluted word order. Avoid the need for too many clauses offset by commas. This makes a sentence harder to follow. You do not want to tax the patience of your reader.
2. See above.
3. The active voice: NASW opposes rather than NASW is in opposition to.
4. Spelling error.
5. "Is primarily based" contains a split verb form; we moved "primarily" outside the verb phrase. Some grammarians allow for "split infinitives" as in "to boldly go," while others do not.
6. The period belongs inside the quotation mark.
7. The original was an incomplete sentence because it lacked a verb. When some conjunctions—in this case, the word "although"— begins a sentence, there should be no comma following them.
8. We changed the period at the end of the incomplete sentence to a comma and combined the subordinate and independent clauses to create a complete sentence.
9. "Feel as though" is informal and passive writing. Use the word "believe" when dealing with facts and information. To believe something about a situation is different from feeling something about a situation. Do not confuse the two.
10. We deleted "the" because it is not necessary.
11. We deleted "actually" because it is unnecessary.
12. We deleted "the" because it is not necessary.
13. We deleted the words "true, actual" because they are redundant, and neither is necessary.
14. "Fully" is a misplaced modifier, placed at the end of the sentence instead of close to "recognize."
15. Homophone error. Write and right—"right" means correct or refers to direction.
16. Spelling error.
17. We deleted the semicolon because the second phrase is not an independent clause and so a semicolon is incorrect. Use a comma with or without a conjunction.
18. We deleted the apostrophe because the sentence does not require the possessive. "Fredonians" is plural without possessive.

cont.

believe ⑲ that by utilizing such procedures as civil unions to try to ensure ⑳ equality, we promote ㉑ confusion in ㉒ the public (especially our young citizens) and negatively impact ㉓ people's ㉔ understanding of fairness and civil rights in Fredonia. No community can be truly healthy until it rids itself of such practices, cleans up its ㉕ attitudes, educates its ㉖ citizens, etc. ㉗

We urge ㉘ the members of this committee, the sponsors of this legislation, and all the members of the Fredonia State Legislature ㉙ ㉚ to pass a true marriage equality bill, which has been our commitment ㉛ for the last ten years ㉜.

Respectfully ㉝ submitted by:
Moe Larry, Ph.D, LICSW ㉞
Executive Director

EXPLANATIONS OF CORRECTIONS

19. We made the sentence more active and changed "our belief" to "we believe," which makes it more clear. Who believes? We do.

20. Word choice is off here: ensure and insure— "ensure" means to guarantee; "insure" means to provide an insurance policy.

21. This is a convoluted sentence. The writer did not complete the thought, "we believe that by. . ." We completed it in the corrected version.

22. Preposition error: confusion should be <u>in</u> the public, not <u>by</u> the public.

23. "Impact" is a verb; its noun is we. So "impact<u>s</u>" (we impacts) is incorrect.

24. "The" was confusing; we changed it to "people's," which makes more sense.

25. Homophone error: its and it's —"its" is the possessive; "it's" is a contraction of "it is."

26. Homophone: error: See # 25

27. Etc. is the correct abbreviation for "et cetera." Ect. is incorrect.

28. "That" creates an unnecessary passive voice. Active writing is "We urge the members. . ."

29. A legislator refers to an individual; a legislature is a deliberative body made up of legislators.

30. "Focus their attention" is an unnecessary phrase; it adds nothing to the sentence and may even be offensive to the legislators, because it could imply the writer thinks that they are not focused.

31. Spelling error.

32. "Not only . . . but" is unprofessional writing, and it diminishes the first point by labeling it as "not only." We eliminated the second point referring to "good public policy" because it was redundant, but if we wanted to keep both points we could have written: "We urge the members of this committee, the sponsors of this legislation, and all the members of the Fredonia State Legislature to pass a true marriage equality bill, which has been our commitment for the last ten years, and is good public policy."

33. Word choice is off here: respectfully and respectively—"respectfully" conveys respect; "respectively" refers to the order of things in a list.

34. Avoid redundant titles: select one but not both—Dr. or PhD.

WRITTEN (AND ORAL) TESTIMONY AT HEARINGS

In Fredonia, same-sex marriage is not legal, but domestic partnerships have some protections. For several years, state employees who enter into domestic partnerships have received the same health benefits that married couples enjoy, thanks to the sensitivities of the state's elected officials, who were lobbied by state employee unions in the 1990s. Suddenly, in 2005, the Internal Revenue Service (IRS) discovered a regulation in the Tax Code that required the federal government to consider health and other benefits provided to unmarried employees' partners as taxable income. This meant that when employers provide workers who are married with benefits, such as health insurance, those benefits cannot be taxed as income. But those same benefits can be taxed as income if the employee is not married. In January of 2006, Fredonia's state employees began receiving letters from the IRS with bills for unpaid federal taxes on 2004 health benefits they had received for their partners. In Fredonia, like many states, state income taxes are calculated as a percentage of federal income taxes, meaning the new IRS ruling would result in an additional state income tax for domestic partners. Consequently, the state employees' union asked the state legislature to exclude the domestic partner benefit from its calculation of state income taxes, and take all possible steps to minimize the impact of the IRS ruling. Two bills were introduced in the State House: H 7679 (sponsored by Rep. Halfright), and H 7804 (Rep. Alright). Case 21 is testimony given in writing and presented orally, during hearings held on H 7679.

This is a true and somewhat typical story about policy-making process. States invent their own tax policies, but only up to a point. The U.S. Tax Code addresses taxes owed to the federal government, and some states "piggyback" their income taxes on federal income taxes, sometimes with consequences as described here. Often multiple bills will be submitted during a legislative session addressing the same problem, because legislators have different interpretations, views, and constituents. Sometimes multiple bills will be combined in committee hearings for the convenience of legislators and/or the public. Other times, for a variety of reasons, bills addressing the same topic are not considered together, as was the case in this scenario.

Providing testimony is not uncommon for social workers. If and when you are asked to present, consider the following rules for giving testimony: state who you are, where you live, and whom you represent. Brevity is a virtue. Legislators hear a lot of testimony; they appreciate direct, clear, and brief statements. Be accurate and factually correct. Sometimes comments are limited to three minutes or less, because of the need to hear a long line-up of speakers. Prepare a three-minute version of your testimony, but be ready to go into more detail if asked to.

Lies and exaggerations will be discovered. Cite relevant facts and experiences of other jurisdictions, if possible. The human side of policy is very compelling, so demonstrate consequences for real people. If you are directly affected and you are there advocating for yourself as well as others, you may want to say so and explain how and why that is. If your testimony includes a proposal that has costs, say what they are and defend them. Always connect argument to relevant human values.

There is no right way to order your testimony logically, other than to follow a reasonable and well-organized progression of relevant points that lead to a conclusion. If you know of individuals affected by the policy in question, you can begin and end with the human side, but do not disclose identities without permission. If you have data, use them in ways that clearly support your argument but do not overwhelm the audience. You can always attach data or refer legislators to relevant sources. Personal attacks are ineffective and usually counterproductive. Serve the task, not your ego.

CASE 21: DOMESTIC PARTNER HEALTH BENEFITS BILL

Here is written testimony given by an eminent member of the social work faculty at Fredonia State College. The first version has 19 writing errors.

Facts:

- Fredonia provides health benefits to domestic partners of state employees
- The IRS has a rule that only heterosexual married partners can receive untaxed benefits
- The IRS treats health benefits for domestic partners and same-sex married partners as taxable income
- The IRS sent tax bills to Fredonia state employees for federal taxes on their domestic partners' health benefits
- Fredonia's state income tax is calculated as a percentage of the federal income tax

State-level proposed remedies:

H. 7804 – Rep. Alright's Bill – would amend state statutes on health insurance coverage, family leave, and income tax to include domestic partners and exempt health benefits from all state tax liability.

H. 7679 – Rep Halfright's Bill – Would implement a loan program for those state employees affected by the income tax liability due to the extension of health insurance coverage to a non-domestic partner.

The state employees' union endorsed H. 7804 and opposes H. 7679.

ORIGINAL VERSION

Testimony at Fredonia House Finance Committee
In opposition to H. 7679
March 10, 2006

Honorable Committee Members: (132)

My name is Clem N. Say. I am a professor of social work at Fredonia State College. I am here representing the Fredonia State College faculty union, to propose changes to H. 7679 (Rep. Halfright) that would bring it closer to H. 7804 (Rep. Alright). 4 of my colleagues in the School of Social Work at FSC are directly effected by this issue.

222 state employees are caught in a financial bind created by the state's provision of domestic partner benefits without taxing those benefits, as required by a discriminatory federal law. For some of those state workers, the sudden unexpected bills for back taxes come to thousands of dollars.

These co-workers of mine are no different from me in there work or loyalty to our jobs, but the US Tax Code singles' them out as less valued then the rest of us. Now the state is trying to help.

The FSC faculty union commends Rep. Halfright for the provisions proposed in H. 7679, recognizing the difficulties the state's inadvertent error caused, and for creating a loan program to help my fellow state employees' pay these surprise bills.

But, it seems to us that H. 7679 doesn't go far enough. There are 3 serious omissions:
1. There's no language in the bill indicating that the loans would be interest free.
2. H. 7679 proposes that state employees will be paying back <u>state income tax</u> (Page 2, line 9) in addition to federal taxes, because our state's income tax largely piggybacks on the federal income tax. The state can not do anything about the federal income tax, but it can — and should — forgive any state income tax owed as a result of the federal law.

Precisely, because state law (unlike federal law) recognizes the   (133)
legitimacy of domestic partnership for health insurance purposes, it should not be penalizing these employees in ways that married employees are not, for having this insurance coverage. In the same vain, we also farther urge that the bill be amended to contain a provision similar to that contained in H. 7804, Rep. Alright's bill, that would also make clear that the health insurance coverage will not be taxed by the state for future years either.

3. Regrettably, to add insult to injury, the Department of Administration also recently issued a memo stating that domestic partners of state employees will no longer be covered by either COBRA or the Family Medical Leave Act. Rep. Alright's legislation provides that domestic partners of state employees are entitled to the protections of COBRA and too the states version of the FMLA. H. 7679 is silent on this issue.

Last week, the Fredonia Daily Gazette reported that it had assessed the fiscal impact of these three amendments, and estimated that the loss to the state would be fewer than $60,000 a year. In the arena of discrimination remedies, and as a symbol of this state's historic inclusion of minority groups, this is a bargain.

CASE 21: CORRECTED VERSION:

Each number in the corrected version refers to an explanation below.

Honorable Committee Members:

My name is Clem N. Say. I am a professor of social work at Fredonia State College. I am here representing the Fredonia State College faculty union, to propose changes to H. 7679 (Rep. Halfright) that would bring it closer to H. 7804 (Rep. Alright). Four ① of my colleagues in the School of Social Work at FSC are directly affected ② by this issue.

Two hundred twenty two ③ state employees are caught in a financial bind created by the state's provision of domestic partner benefits without taxing those benefits, as required by a discriminatory federal law. For some of those state workers, the sudden unexpected bills for back taxes come to thousands of dollars.

These co-workers of mine are no different from me in their ④ work or loyalty to our jobs, but the US Tax Code singles ⑤ them out as less valued than ⑥ the rest of us. Now the state is trying to help.

The FSC faculty union commends Rep. Halfright for the provisions proposed in H. 7679, recognizing the difficulties the state's inadvertent error caused, and for creating a loan program to help my fellow state employees ⑦ pay these surprise bills.

But ⑧ H. 7679 doesn't go far enough. There are three ⑨ serious omissions:
1. There is ⑩ no language in the bill indicating that the loans would be interest-free ⑪.
2. H. 7679 proposes that state employees will be paying back <u>state income tax</u> (Page 2, line 9) in addition to federal taxes, because our state's income tax largely piggybacks on the federal income tax. The state cannot ⑫ do anything about the federal income tax, but it can — and should — forgive any state income tax owed as a result of the federal law.

cont.

EXPLANATIONS OF CORRECTIONS:

1. Spell out numbers from one through ten.
2. Word choice is off here: affected and effected—use affected as a verb.
3. Spell out numbers that begin sentences; three-digit numbers are not hyphenated.
4. Homophone error: their and there—"their" is the possessive.
5. No apostrophe because the sentence did not require the possessive.
6. Homophone error: than and then—"than" is for comparison.
7. No apostrophe because the sentence did not require the possessive.
8. We re-phrased and cut out unnecessary language.
9. Spell out numbers between one through ten.
10. Avoid using contractions.
11. Hyphenate interest-free because it is a two-word modifier.
12. "Cannot" is one word.

cont.

Precisely ⑬ because state law (unlike federal law) recognizes the legitimacy of domestic partnership for health insurance purposes, it should not be penalizing these employees in ways that married employees are not, for having this insurance coverage. In the same vein ⑭, we further ⑮ urge that the bill be amended to contain a provision similar to that contained in H. 7804, Rep. Alright's bill, that would also make clear that the health insurance coverage will not be taxed by the state for future years ⑯.

3. Regrettably, to add insult to injury, the Department of Administration also recently issued a memo stating that domestic partners of state employees will no longer be covered by either COBRA or the Family Medical Leave Act. Rep. Alright's legislation provides that domestic partners of state employees are entitled to the protections of COBRA and to ⑰ the state's ⑱ version of the FMLA. H. 7679 is silent on this issue.

Last week, the Fredonia Daily Gazette reported that it had assessed the fiscal impact of these three amendments, and estimated that the loss to the state would be less ⑲ than $60,000 a year. In the arena of discrimination remedies, and as a symbol of this state's historic inclusion of minority groups, this is a bargain.

EXPLANATIONS OF CORRECTIONS

13. We deleted the comma because it interrupts a clear thought and is not necessary.
14. Homophone error: vein and vain—"vein" is a blood vessel; "vain" means unsuccessful, or extremely proud.
15. Word choice is off here: further and farther—use "further" for concepts that do not have measurable units of one – "urge" is such a concept. "Also" and "further" are redundant.
16. "Either" and "also" are redundant.
17. Homophone error: too and to—"too" means excessive or also.
18. We inserted an apostrophe to indicate the possessive in "the state's."
19. Word choice is off here: less and fewer—use "less" when referring to units of one that can be measured, as in dollars.

III

Agency-Based Writing
Writing Research Reports, Grants, and Letters

Social service agencies have many needs for written products. Chapters 5, 6, and 7 contain some examples of agency-based writing: reports of research and program data, applications for small and medium-sized grants, and letters to various constituencies. Each chapter begins with an introduction explaining the specific writing issues involved.

Chapter 5, Writing Research Reports, includes a PowerPoint presentation of service utilization, two survey reports, a report of a focus group meeting, and an op-ed article that uses data to influence social policy.

Agency-based research need not be formal studies with large samples and statistical data analysis. As explained in Chapter Five, simple frequency distributions often form the basis for reports of agencies' work. Also, qualitative data (people's words rather than numbers) can form the basis of some reports.

Chapter 6 contains several examples of applications for small grants. In these situations, small, sometimes local, family, religious, special interest, and/or other kind of charitable foundations make funds available for issues that concern them. Often no rules or protocols are specified, and we have to research these foundations to learn their procedures. Sometimes personal contacts can be helpful. The chapter contains several letters to small foundations that resulted in grants. In each case, the applicant did her homework to ascertain the foundation's contact person, service interest, level of funding, application cycle, and expectations.

Chapter 7 includes several kinds of letters social workers write: to clients, other agencies, governmental entities, funders, and constituents. Social work education programs should teach students how to write these kinds of letters. One of my social work jobs required almost monthly condolence letters to constituents who lost family members, and another half that amount of letters to funding agencies, in support of grant applications written by colleague agencies. Looking back, I believe I've written more letters as a social worker than any other kind of writing.

All three categories of agency-based writing require competent writing. While brevity may be less important than in case documentation, awkward or convoluted sentences detract from the clarity of our communication. Other writing rules typically apply, as discussed in Part 2. At stake is our standing in our community of colleague agencies, funders, and governmental entities. At risk is successful attraction of resources, our influence, and our credibility.

5

Writing Research Reports

In this chapter we learn about social work research reports and how to write them. The opportunity for social workers to use their research skills occurs frequently in human service situations. Types of research reports include: needs assessments, client satisfaction surveys, evaluation of interventions, assessment of program results, and measurement of outcomes for accreditation reviews. Social workers deal with all of these types of reports routinely. The need for social workers to be able to handle research reports is especially important when you work for an agency that receives grants and contracts from foundations and state and federal departments. All of these entities expect full reporting about how the agency is spending its resources. In addition to regular program and practice assessments, the opportunity occasionally arises for social workers to research a particular social topic and write about it with the intent to impact policies that affect clients and service-delivery agencies.

For the most part, **frequency distributions** provide sufficient basis for research reports. Frequency distributions are groupings of data into various categories: how many participants fall into each category. If appropriate, we can report **averages** and/or **medians**, and sometimes **standard deviations,** as ways to describe groupings of participants. Let us do a quick review, in case you have not covered how to handle these statistics yet, or have forgotten how.

The instructor begins by asking the students to count the coins they have with them that day. Each takes out her or his change from wherever they keep it. Some have to reach to the bottom of back packs, through pencils and paper and any number of things that got buried there three semesters earlier.

At some point, most students clatter their coins to the desk and the class finally gets results. Here is an example for a class with ten students:

Student	Number of coins	Total value
1	3	.45
2	1	.25
3	0	0
4	7	1.20
5	2	.50
6	7	1.35
7	3	.40
8	3	.75
9	5	1.10
10	0	0
Totals: 10 students	35	6.00

Frequency tables would look like these:

A. Coins

	Frequency	Percent	Cumulative Percent
0	2	20	20
1	1	10	30
2	1	10	40
3	3	30	70
5	1	10	80
7	2	20	100
Totals	10	100	

B. Value

	Frequency	Percent	Cumulative Percent
0	2	20	20
.25	1	10	30
.40	1	10	40
.45	1	10	50
.50	1	10	60
.75	1	10	70
1.10	1	10	80
1.20	1	10	90
1.35	1	10	100
Totals	10	100	

Frequency tables reorganize the information recorded from each individual, one at a time, and allow us to report in percentages: for example, 30% of the students in class (the largest grouping), had three coins. The fourth column, cumulative percent, adds the percentages from each reply up to that point, so 70% of the students in class that day had three or fewer coins; 50% had 40 cents or less.

We can also calculate averages by dividing the totals by the number of participants: 35 coins divided by ten students comes to an average of 3.5 coins per student; $6.00 divided by ten students comes to an average of 60 cents per student. So, using the coins example, now the report might say that of the ten students who attended class, eight carried coins with them. The group averaged 3.5 coins and 60 cents. Medians (midpoints) were slightly lower, 2.3 coins and 45 cents. Means and medians are useful in describing midpoints or averages. Research reports also include information about "dispersion," how far people are from the average. A group with an average of 45 cents can consist of everyone having 45 cents (no dispersion) or any combination that averages 45 cents, in which case there will be dispersion because some people will have less or more than 45 cents. Researchers usually need to report dispersion so readers can understand the sample's characteristics. The statistic "standard deviation" is used to report dispersion. The higher the standard deviation, the average amount each person is away from the mean, the more dispersion there is in the sample. Organizing information in tables enormously facilitates report writing. Sometimes you can collect the information you need from a computer, but sometimes you will be doing your own calculations with data you have collected.

Let us look at a satisfaction survey as another example. Suppose you ask your clients a set of questions about their levels of satisfaction with various aspects of your programs, and conclude with a final summary question: Overall, how satisfied are you with the services of XYZ Agency?

Administering this survey is a way to collect data. Using reporting tables and statistics allows the data you collect to be taken up and understood quickly by service agencies.

If your satisfaction survey frequency table reads like the following example, you would be pretty happy with the results:

	Frequency	Percent	Cumulative Percent
Very satisfied	31	62.0	62.0
Somewhat satisfied	15	30.0	92.0
Somewhat dissatisfied	3	6.0	98.0
Very dissatisfied	1	2.0	100
Totals	50	100	

From this table you can see that, by a large majority, clients are very satisfied (62%) and almost everyone reports that they are very or somewhat satisfied—the cumulative percent of very and somewhat satisfied, 92%, indicates this. Now if we represent the answers with a number, for instance: very dissatisfied = 1; somewhat dissatisfied = 2;

somewhat satisfied = 3; very dissatisfied = 4, the data tell us that the average response and the median response are both above 3.5, which is true for nearly all the ratings. We might very well be content simply to say 62% were very satisfied, and 92% were very or somewhat satisfied. The same computer program that gives us these frequency distributions can generate pie charts, bar graphs, and other visual representations of how people answered our survey questions. You can do this in spread sheet software also.

It is important to collect this kind of assessment data because it represents one way we find out if we are successfully fulfilling our duties. For example, a social work professor asked her students what they like best and least about the Research class, and got the following results:

Students liked best:
- The way the professor explains things (3)
- The professor's teaching style (2)
- The professor's sense of humor (2)
- Miscellaneous comments (no duplicates; 7)

Students liked least:
- The readings (4)
- The assignments/papers (2)
- The class meeting time (2)
- The professor's teaching style (2)
- Miscellaneous comments (no duplicates; 5)

Note that the total comments for both questions exceed the ten participants. When asked for comments, sometimes people will say two or more things. Also, the professor's teaching style is liked and disliked (two students each). How would we average these comments or find a median comment? Averaging is not possible because there are no numbers to add up and divide. A median may be possible if we can figure out a way to rank-order the comments, but this almost impossible. The comments and their interpretations often are too subjective. So we are left with a data set experts call "qualitative data" because it cannot be numerically scaled into a table. The examples of students' coins and clients' satisfaction involve "quantitative data." "Quantitative data" represents numbers or information that can be translated to numbers, scaled, and used in calculations. Qualitative data refers to how people feel about a particular topic expressed in words, ideas, and images.

The research reports in this section include both quantitative and qualitative data. The quantitative data reports rely mostly on frequency distributions. Occasionally, there is a correlation and/or probability statistic. I explain what these concepts mean where necessary.

We gather qualitative data often by face-to-face discussions that take place in a focus group. Focus group facilitators record participants' responses and then later organize the data in clusters and by categories. In Chapter 4, the organizational needs assessment of Tender Mercies Homeless Shelter is based on qualitative data.

Whether you use qualitative or quantitative data, always report the results dispassionately. Advocacy and enthusiasm for a particular interpretation of the data does not belong in research reports. That is not to say we should not have a position or seek to advance it with our research. Be enthusiastic when you present your report and advocate for a course of action based on the data in the report. But be sure the data in the report are objective and credible. Such writing is depersonalized. This is why you may notice that the following reports lack a strong voice or personality. This is a deliberate writing choice. The style of the research report allows for the reader to figure out what the results mean, with only a modicum of assistance by the author in the discussion section or summary of the report. Numbers on the right side of the original documents note the page locations of the corresponding content in the corrected documents.

Case 22 – Client Report Using Frequency Distributions: Project Restore
Case 23 – Survey Report to the State Legislature: Gun Ownership and Domestic Violence
Case 24 – Satisfaction Survey of BSW Students at a Social Work Program: Report and Executive Summary
Case 25 – Focus Group Report: Parents and Teachers Program
Case 26 – Reporting Research Results to Influence Public Policy: The Fredonia Estate Tax

CASE 22: CLIENT REPORT USING FREQUENCY DISTRIBUTIONS: PROJECT RESTORE

A social worker presented the following client report to the steering committee of a demonstration program called "Project Restore." "Project Restore" is a demonstration program of the Fredonia Office of Child Support Services (OCSS) and is responsible for "helping" non-custodial parents make their child support payments. As you might imagine, non-custodial parents sometimes do not welcome "help" from OCSS. Some non-custodial parents—usually fathers—have abandoned their families and have no interest in supporting them. In cases like these, "help" becomes "enforcement" of court orders, and often involves law enforcement. "Project Restore" reaches out to dads who, at one point in the past, supported their children, but recently they stopped because of a job loss or other financial crisis. "Help" from "Project Restore" takes the form of case management with the explicit aim of helping the non-custodial parent remove barriers interfering with employment, work toward enhancing job skills, and generally help the client find a better job and keep it. All "Project Restore" clients are voluntary and represent people who are looking to improve their employment situations and consequently resume making child support payments.

There are 48 writing errors in the report.

Abbreviations
AA: Associate of Arts (two year) degree
CP: Custodial parent
NCP: Non-custodial parent
DCYF: Fredonia's child welfare department, also called DCPS (Department of Child Protective Services)
OCSS: (Fredonia) Office of Child Support Services

ORIGINAL VERSION

PARTICIPANT'S CHARACTERISTICS

Project
Restore

Helping families. Restoring support.

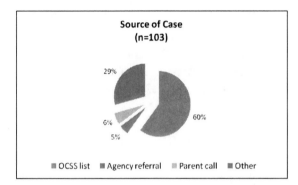

Thru 7 months of operations, most cases (60%) have come form lists. We have provided services to 103 cases. This includes 98 NCPs and 5 CPs. In 3 cases, we have served both the NCP and CP. (151)

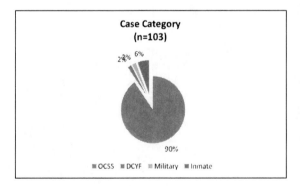

There are 4 case categories: (1) veterans, (2) child welfare cases, (3) incarcerated parents, and (4) regular OCSS enforcement cases. 90 percent of the parents interviewed to date have been from the regular OCSS enforcement caseload.

cont.

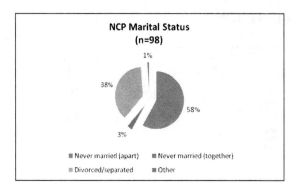

More than half of the parents (152) we have interviewed (58%) were never married to the other (e.g., custodial) parent. Another 38 percent are divorced or seperated from the other parent and their are a few other NCPs with different marital statuses.

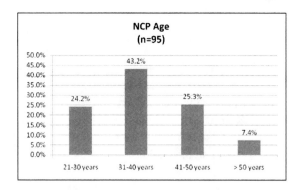

The plurality of NCPs are between the ages of 31–40 and the average age of all NCPs is 37.8 years.

cont.

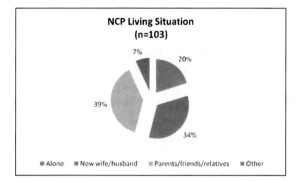

About two-fifths of the NCPs (153)
(39%) are living with parents,
friends or relatives a third (34%)
are living with a new partner and a
fifth (20%) are living alone.

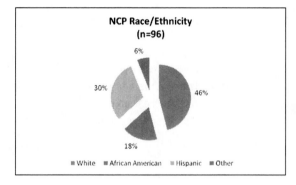

Almost a majority of the NCPs
are white while another third
are Hispanic. (Case manager's
Spanish language skills has been
useful in a few cases). The "other"
category includes Asians, Pacific
Islanders, and others.

cont.

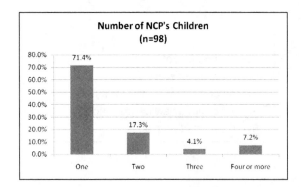

Most of the NCPs have only a single child they are supporting with the other parent, although, a few NCPs had four or more children. (The highest number of reported children was 6). (154)

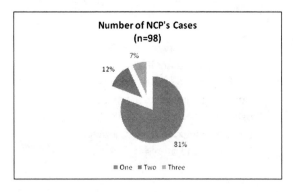

While, most NCPs (81%) only have a single case, the remainder 19 percent have more than one case. [Case: child support order]

cont.

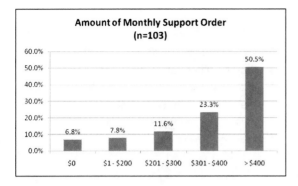

The average monthly support order for the cases we have interviewed is $445. This average has increased in each set of data tables as the proportion of NCPs with higher order levels has increased.

(155)

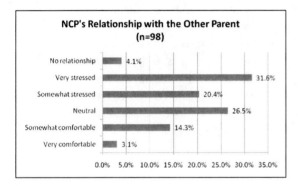

In addition to restoring child support as a reliable source of income to the family; Project Restore hopes to improve parental relationships, parent-child relationships, and family stability. More than half of the NCPs interviewed (52.0%) described their relationship with the other parent as very or somewhat stressed. Only 17.4% described the relationship as very or somewhat comfortable.

cont.

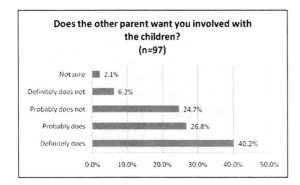

Two-third of NCPs (67.0%) believe   (156)
that the other parent definitely or
probably wants them involved with
their children. 30.9 percent do not
believe the other parent wants
them involved.

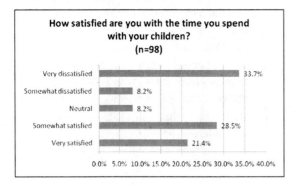

NCPs are divided in their
satisfaction with the amount of
time they spend with their children.
Almost a majority (49.9%) are
very or somewhat <u>satisfied</u> with
the amount of time they spend
with their children now, while 41.9
percent are very or somewhat
<u>dissatisfied</u> with their access.

cont.

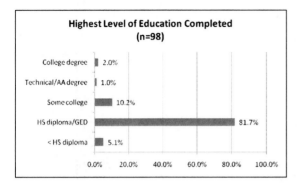

Educational levels of the parents (157) we have interviewed are fairly low, with more than 86.8 percent, saying they're highest level of education is a high school diploma or less. Only 3 percent have a technical/AA or college degree. When we compare employment status and educational level, we do not find a relationship between education and the NCP's employment status.

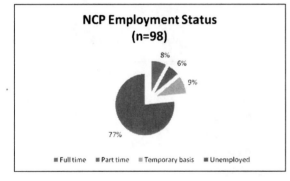

A key project objective is to help parents' find employment. As indicated in this chart, 77% of the parents we have interviewed are unemployed and another 9% are in part-time or temporary jobs.

cont.

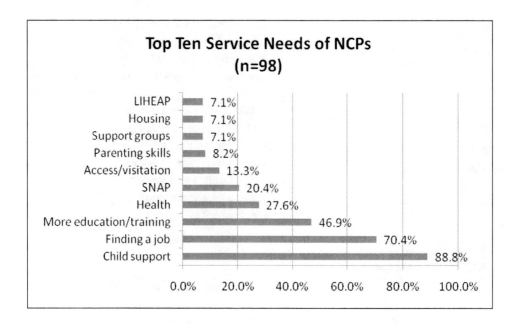

The chart above displays the proportion of all NCPs interviewed who mentioned a specific service need. Child support was mentioned by almost all NCPs (88.8%) as an issue they needed assistance addressing. NCPs have a wide range of needs; and although, this chart only displays the top 10 needs. Other needs also were mentioned (e.g., improved relationship with the other parent, transportation, legal assistance, etc.).

(158)

CASE 22: CORRECTED VERSION

PARTICIPANTS' ① CHARACTERISTICS

Project **R**estore

Helping families. Restoring support.

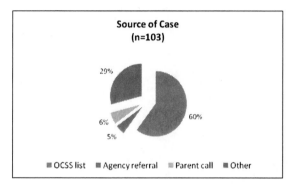

Source of Case (n=103)

29%

60%

6%

5%

▨ OCSS list   ▨ Agency referral   ▨ Parent call   ▨ Other

Through ② seven ③ months of operations, most cases (60%) have come from ④ lists. We have provided services to 103 individuals ⑤. This includes 98 NCPs and five ⑥ CPs. In three ⑦ cases, we have served both the NCP and CP.

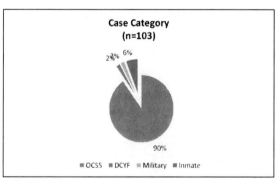

Case Category (n=103)

2% 2% 6%

90%

▨ OCSS   ▨ DCYF   ▨ Military   ▨ Inmate

There are four ⑧ case categories: (1) veterans, (2) child welfare cases, (3) incarcerated parents, and (4) regular OCSS enforcement cases. Ninety ⑨ percent of the parents are ⑩ ⑪ from the regular OCSS enforcement caseload.

cont.

EXPLANATIONS OF CORRECTIONS

1. Plural possessive.
2. "Thru" is not a word. Use "through."
3. Spell out numbers from one through ten.
4. Word error: use from, not form.
5. The report appears to confuse individuals with cases; there are 103 different individuals and 100 families (mother-father partnerships). The author should have clarified the distinction between cases and individuals.
6. Spell out numbers from one through ten.
7. Spell out numbers from one through ten.
8. Spell out numbers from one through ten.
9. Always spell out numbers that begin sentences.
10. We deleted unnecessary language.
11. The author used incorrect verb tense. Because the cases are ongoing; all are open, use the present tense.

cont.

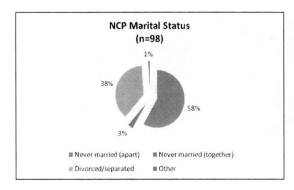

More than half of the parents ⑫ (58%) were never married to the other (e.g., custodial) parent. Another 38 percent are divorced or separated ⑬ from the other parent and there ⑭ are a few other NCPs with different marital statuses.

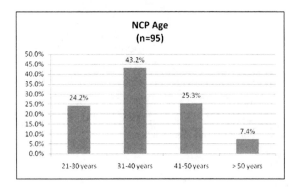

The plurality of NCPs is ⑮ between the ages of 31–40; ⑯ the average age of all NCPs is 37.8 years.

cont.

EXPLANATIONS OF CORRECTIONS

12. We deleted unnecessary language.
13. Spelling error correction.
14. Homophone error: there and their—"their" is the possessive.
15. The word "plurality" refers to a singular idea, so the verb should be "is" and not "are."

16. The two sentences connected by "and" are not of equal significance. In cases like these a semicolon may be more appropriate than "and."

cont.

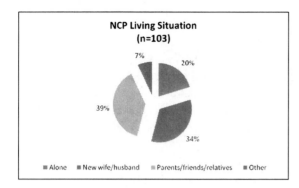

About two-fifths of the NCPs
(39%) are living with parents,
friends or relatives; ⑰ a third (34%)
are living with a new partner; ⑱ a
fifth (20%) are living alone.

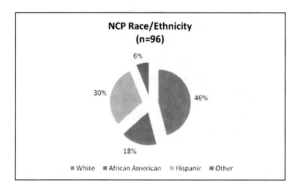

Almost half ⑲ of the NCPs
are white while another third
are Hispanic. (Case manager's
Spanish language skills have ⑳
been useful in a few cases). The
"other" category includes Asians
and Pacific Islanders ㉑.

cont.

EXPLANATIONS OF CORRECTIONS

17. The original was a run-on sentence,
consisting of three complete sentences
linked by commas. To correct we used
semicolons to separate the three complete
sentences.

18. See #17, semicolon corrects a run-on sentence.

19. "Almost a majority" is misleading and
implies authorial bias given that the actual
statistic was 46%.

20. The word "skills" is plural.

21. Corrected phrase: "The other category
includes" . . . "Asians and Pacific Islanders."

cont.

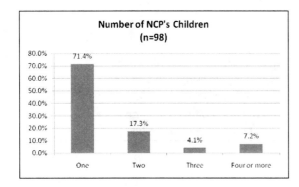

Most of the NCPs are supporting a single child ㉒, although a few have four or more children. (The highest number of reported children was six. ㉓ ㉔)

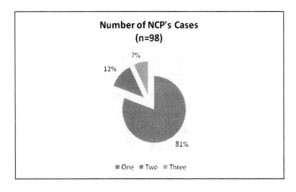

While ㉕ most NCPs (81%) ㉖ have a single case, the remaining ㉗ 19 percent have more than one case [㉘ case: child support order]. ㉙

cont.

EXPLANATIONS OF CORRECTIONS

22. Excess verbiage eliminated by combining two sentences. Say more with less.
23. Spell out numbers from one through ten.
24. The period belongs inside the close-parenthesis.
25. The comma is not necessary after a one-word introductory phrase.
26. "Only" is unnecessary and judgmental.
27. Word choice is off here: remaining and remainder mean different things.
28. Capital letter is not required because there is no new sentence.
29. The period belongs at the end of the full sentence.

cont.

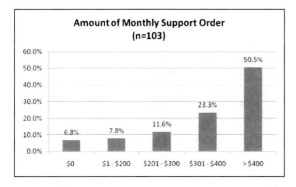

The average monthly support order for the caseload ㉚ is $445. This average has increased in each set of data tables, as the proportion of NCPs with higher order levels has increased.

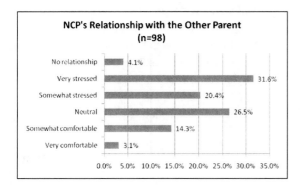

In addition to restoring child support as a reliable source of income to the family, ㉛ Project Restore hopes to improve parental relationships, parent-child relationships, and family stability. More than half of the NCPs ㉜ (52.0%) described their relationship with the other parent as very or somewhat stressed. Less than one-fifth ㉝ 17.4% described the relationship as very or somewhat comfortable.

cont.

EXPLANATIONS OF CORRECTIONS

30. We edited excess verbiage.

31. Use a comma instead of the semicolon when linking an independent clause to a subordinate clause or phrase.

32. "Interviewed" is unnecessary.

33. "Only" is opinion; "Less than one-fifth" is statistically accurate.

cont.

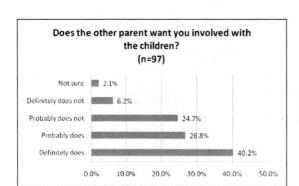

Two-thirds ③④ of NCPs (67.0%) believe that the other parent definitely or probably wants them involved with their children. Almost one-third (30.9 %) ③⑤ do not believe the other parent wants them involved.

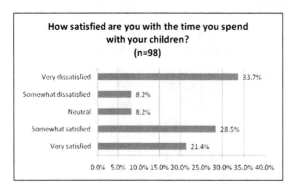

NCPs are divided in their satisfaction with the amount of time they spend with their children. Almost a majority (49.9%) are very or somewhat satisfied, while 41.9 percent are very or somewhat dissatisfied ③⑥.

cont.

EXPLANATIONS OF CORRECTIONS

34. "Two-thirds" should end with "s."

35. We re-wrote the sentence to avoid beginning it with a percentage.

36. We deleted excess verbiage.

cont.

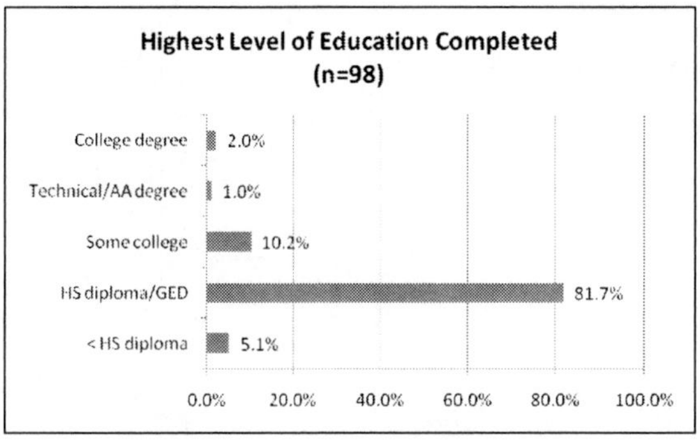

A large majority (86.8 %) of the parents have a high school diploma or less schooling ㊲. Three ㊳ percent have a technical/AA or college degree. When we compare employment status and educational level, we do not find a correlation ㊴.

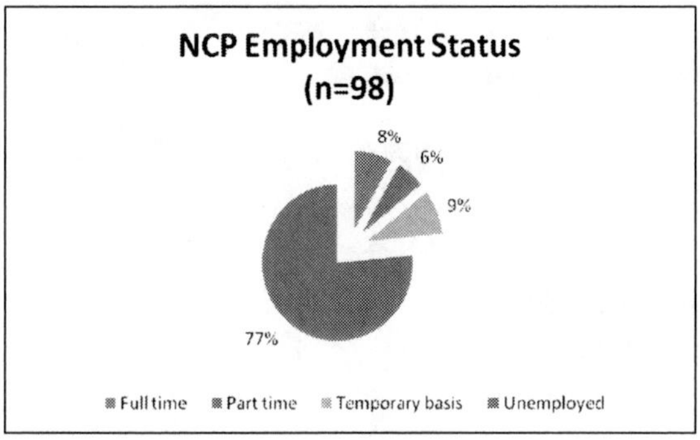

A key project objective is to help parents ㊵ find employment. As indicated in this chart, 77% of the parents ㊶ are unemployed, ㊷ and another 9% are in part-time or temporary jobs.

cont.

EXPLANATIONS OF CORRECTIONS

37. We deleted authorial opinion.
38. The word "only" represents authorial opinion; sentence begins with "three," which should be spelled out.
39. Excess verbiage deleted.
40. No apostrophe because no possessive is required.
41. We deleted unnecessary verbiage.
42. Comma before a connecting conjunction ("but" not "however") between two independent clauses.

cont.

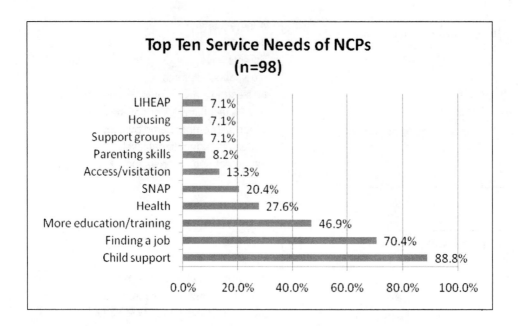

The chart above displays the proportion of all NCPs interviewed who mentioned a specific service need. Child support was mentioned by almost all NCPs (88.8%) ④③. NCPs have a wide range of needs ④④ and although ④⑤ this chart only displays the top 10 needs, ④⑥ other needs ④⑦ were mentioned (e.g., improved relationship with the other parent, transportation, legal assistance ④⑧).

EXPLANATIONS OF CORRECTIONS

43. We deleted unnecessary verbiage.

44. No comma required.

45. No comma required.

46. This was an incomplete sentence; We inserted a comma between subordinate and independent clauses to form one sentence.

47. "Also" is redundant with "other needs."

48. We deleted "etc." after e.g.

CASE 23: SURVEY REPORT TO THE STATE LEGISLATURE: GUN OWNERSHIP AND DOMESTIC VIOLENCE

The following case represents an example of how survey results can influence state legislation. A student-run telephone survey gathered data about voters' attitudes toward firearms and domestic violence. The students submitted their survey report to the state legislature, in support of legislation that would prohibit people convicted of domestic violence from buying or possessing firearms if a restraining order has been issued against them and is in place. With the assistance of the survey report, a coalition of community groups was able to get the legislation passed. There are 40 writing errors in the report. Because this is a submission to the state legislature, we added a brief executive summary with no errors, which you will find after the explanation of corrections.

ORIGINAL VERSION

FREDONIA STATE COLLEGE SCHOOL OF SOCIAL WORK FREDONIANS' ATTITUDES ABOUT DOMESTIC VIOLENCE AND FIREARMS REPORT OF A STATEWIDE SURVEY

Background of the Study   (162)

The Fredonia Coalition Against Domestic Violence (F-CADV) wanted to determine the attitudes of fellow Fredonians about gun possession amoung perpetrators of domestic violence against whom there is a permanent restraining order, in preparation for legislation that had been re-introduced in the Fredonia legislature during the current session, after failing for the passed few years.

Methods

The Coalition had obtained a random-digit dialing list of Fredonian households from Survey Masters Inc. The list contained a total of 2700 randomly selected telephone numbers. Dr. Stan R. De Viashon, an eminent professor at the Fredonia State College (FSC) School of Social Work, conducted an impressive statistical power analysis to determine the number of households who would need to be contacted to insure validity of the results at margin of error of $\pm$ 5 percentage points (the .05 confidence level.) A total of 400 completed calls was required. Dr. De Viashon also applied for and received permission to conduct the study from the FSC research ethics board (IRB). Students' placed the phone calls; asking just 5 questions: 3 demographic questions – age, gender, and gun ownership – and 2 substantive questions – weather or not judges should have authority to remove firearms when a permanent restraining order exists, and if perpetrators who require a gun for work should be allowed to continue to use there weapons at work.

Data resulting from the survey was analyzed using the Statistical Program   (163)
for the Social Sciences (SPSS). Frequencies, cross-tabulations, and
regression analysis were done to determine the overall results.

Results

434 phone calls were completed. Every jurisdiction in Fredonia was
represented, and all responses were used in the analysis. The largest
group of respondents was 35–49 years of age (N=143, 33%). 31%
(N=133) were 50–65 years old. 36 percent of respondents were male
(N=155) and 64 percent were female (N=276). 19 percent of respondents
(N=81) owned a firearm and 79 percent did not (N=343).

90 percent of respondents (N=389) believe that judges should be able
to remove firearms from perpetrators' that have a permanent restraining
order against them.

55 percent of respondents (N=236) believe that perpetrators that require
firearms in they're work should be allowed to continue to use them at work
and 38 percent (N=166) believe they should not be permitted to continue
using there weapons at work.

Among every age group more than 80 percent of respondents believe that
guns should be removed. Within the largest age group of respondents,
those 35–49 years old, 95 percent of respondents (N=135) expressed
that preference. Ninety percent of those aged 51–65 (N=120) stated that
opinion.

More than half of respondents in every age group believe perpetrators   (164)
who use their guns for work should be allowed to continue using them.
Fifty-seven percent of those in the largest age group of respondents
(N=81) thought that perpetrators needing weapons for work should be
allowed to keep them and Fifty-three percent (N=71) of those aged 50–65
believed this as well. Eighty-nine percent of men (N=138) and 90 percent
of women (N=249) supported the removal of firearms for perpetrators with
a permanent restraining order. Fifty-five percent of men (N=85) and 54
percent of women (N=150) believed that those perpetrators who needed a
weapon for work should continue to use them for work.

Among gun owners, 77 percent (N=62) expressed support for judges
removing weapons of those who had a permanent restraining order
against them, while 19 percent (N=15) did not support removal. Sixty-one
percent of gun owners (N=49) believe that those who require guns for
work should be allowed to keep them and 39 percent (N=32) believe they
should not.

Discussion

Clearly, Fredonians support the passage of the bill regarding the removal of firearms from those whom have a permanent restraining order filed against them. This finding held across all age groups, was strong for both men and women, and was very strong among those who own guns.

Not so clear are the results for the question regarding retention of weapons among those who need them for work. Slightly more than half of respondents supported retention of weapons for work.

Respectively submitted,

Dr. Stan R. DeViashon
Proffessor of Social Work
Fredonia State College

CASE 23: CORRECTED VERSION

Each number in the corrected version refers to an explanation below.

Background of the Study

The Fredonia Coalition Against Domestic Violence (F-CADV) surveyed ① the attitudes of fellow Fredonians about gun possession among ② perpetrators of domestic violence against whom there is a permanent restraining order, in preparation for legislation that had been re-introduced in the Fredonia legislature during the current session, after failing for the past ③ few years.

Methods

The Coalition had obtained a random-digit dialing list of Fredonian households from Survey Masters Inc. The list contained ④ 2700 randomly selected telephone numbers. Dr. Stan R. De Viashon, a ⑤ professor at the Fredonia State College (FSC) School of Social Work, determined that a random sample of 400 would generate results with a margin of error of ± five percent ⑥ (.05 confidence level). ⑦ Dr. De Viashon also applied for and received permission to conduct the study from the FSC research ethics board (IRB). Students ⑧ placed the phone calls, ⑨ asking ⑩ five ⑪ questions: three ⑫ demographic questions – age, gender, and gun ownership – and two ⑬ substantive questions – whether ⑭ ⑮ judges should have authority to remove firearms when a permanent restraining order exists, and whether ⑯ perpetrators who require a gun for work should be allowed to continue to use their ⑰ weapons at work.

cont.

EXPLANATIONS OF CORRECTIONS

1. We used simpler and clearer language.
2. Spelling error.
3. Homophone error: past and passed—
   "passed" means went by; "past" refers to ago.
4. We deleted unnecessary verbiage.
5. We deleted authorial opinion about the professor's status.
6. We used a more direct, active voice, combining two sentences while eliminating unnecessary verbiage.
7. The period belongs outside the close-bracket.
8. There is no possessive required.
9. Use a comma (not a semicolon) between an independent clause and a long subordinate clause.
10. "Just" is opinion and so we deleted it.
11. Spell out numbers from one through ten.
12. Spell out numbers from one through ten.
13. Spell out numbers from one through ten.
14. Homophone error: whether and weather—"whether" means if.
15. "Whether" and "or not" are redundant.
16. In professional writing it is common to use whether instead of "if" when possible.
17. Homophone error: their and there—to indicate the possessive use "their".

cont.

The Coalition analyzed the data resulting from the survey ⑱ ⑲ using the Statistical Program for the Social Sciences (SPSS). Frequencies, cross-tabulations, and regression analysis were done to determine the overall results.

Results

Students completed 434 phone calls ⑳. Every jurisdiction in Fredonia was represented, and all responses were used in the analyses ㉑. The largest group of respondents was 35–49 years of age (N=143, 33%). Thirty-one percent ㉒ (N=133) were 50–65 years old. Thirty-six ㉓ percent of respondents were male (N=155) and 64 percent were female (N=276). Nineteen ㉔ percent of respondents (N=81) owned a firearm and 79 percent did not (N=343).

A large majority (90%) ㉕ of respondents (N=389) believe that judges should be able to remove firearms from perpetrators ㉖ who ㉗ have a permanent restraining order against them.

Fifty-five ㉘ percent of respondents (N=236) believe that perpetrators who ㉙ require firearms in their ㉚ work should be allowed to continue to use them at work, ㉛ and 38 percent (N=166) believe they should not be permitted to continue using their ㉜ weapons at work.

Among every age group more than 80 percent of respondents believe that guns should be removed. In ㉝ the largest age group of respondents, those 35–49 years old, 95 percent of respondents (N=135) expressed that preference. Ninety percent of those aged 51–65 (N=120) stated that opinion.

cont.

EXPLANATIONS OF CORRECTIONS

18. Corrected the passive voice and made it active.
19. The word "data" is plural—an error in the original.
20. We corrected the passive voice and made it clear who was doing what. We also moved 434 to later in the sentence, thereby avoiding having to spell out any number that begins a sentence.
21. The sentence requires verb and noun agreement—all should be plural.
22. Spell out numbers when they begin sentences.
23. Spell out numbers when they begin sentences.
24. Spell out numbers when they begin sentences.
25. Spell out numbers when they begin sentences, or substitute other language – in this case, "A large majority" is true and important.
26. No possessive required.
27. Use "who" as the pronoun when referring to people.
28. Spell out numbers when they begin sentences.
29. "Who" is the pronoun when referring to people.
30. Homophone error: their and they're— "they're" is a contraction of they are.
31. Use a comma before a connecting conjunction that links two independent clauses.
32. Homophone error: their and there (see #30).
33. Word choice is off here: use "in" because it refers to an age group "in total," not as just a part to a larger whole.

cont.

More than half of respondents in every age group believe perpetrators who use their guns for work should be allowed to continue using them. Fifty-seven percent of those in the largest age group of respondents (N=81) thought that perpetrators needing weapons for work should be allowed to keep them; ㉞ fifty-three ㉟ percent (N=71) of those aged 50–65 believed this as well. Eighty-nine percent of men (N=138) and 90 percent of women (N=249) supported the removal of firearms for perpetrators with a permanent restraining order. Fifty-five percent of men (N=85) and 54 percent of women (N=150) believed ㊱ those perpetrators who needed a weapon for work should continue to use them for work.

Among gun owners, 77 percent (N=62) expressed support for judges removing weapons of those who had a permanent restraining order against them, while 19 percent (N=15) did not support removal. Sixty-one percent of gun owners (N=49) believe that those who require guns for work should be allowed to keep them, ㊲ and 39 percent (N=32) believe they should not.

Discussion

Clearly, Fredonians support the passage of the bill regarding the removal of firearms from those who ㊳ have a permanent restraining order filed against them. This finding held across all age groups, was strong for both men and women, and was very strong among those who own guns.

Not so clear are the results for the question regarding retention of weapons among those who need them for work. Slightly more than half of respondents supported retention of weapons for work.

Respectfully ㊴ submitted,

Dr. Stan R. DeViashon
Professor ㊵ of Social Work
Fredonia State College

EXPLANATIONS OF CORRECTIONS

34. We used a semicolon instead of "and," which allows "as well" to stay.
35. No capital letter is required.
36. We deleted "that" because it is not needed.
37. Use a comma before a connecting conjunction that links two independent clauses.
38. "Who" takes a verb, in this case "have" — "whom" does not take a verb.
39. Word choice is off here: "respectfully" conveys respect; "respectively" refers to the order of things in a list.
40. Spelling error.

Executive Summary

In order to determine the level of support for legislation barring people from owning firearms if they have convictions for domestic violence along with restraining orders, students surveyed a randomly selected sample of Fredonian households on May 29 and 30. The results, with a margin of error of ± five percentage points, indicate that 90% of respondents support such restrictions on gun ownership, except when the individual needs a gun for his or her job (45% support the restriction). The consensus view that except when work requires a firearm, those convicted of domestic violence and having restraining orders should not be allowed to own guns, held in all tested demographic groups, including households with gun owners.

CASE 24: SATISFACTION SURVEY OF BSW STUDENTS AT A SOCIAL WORK PROGRAM: REPORT AND EXECUTIVE SUMMARY

Client satisfaction surveys are important tools for monitoring clients' reactions to services, and for identifying unmet needs. In some ways, satisfaction research is similar to needs assessments. While satisfaction surveys can tell us a lot about how clients perceive our work with them, and help us identify unmet needs, this kind of research cannot assess conclusively the quality or impact of our work. To achieve the latter requires outcomes-based research, which measures the positive consequences of interventions like changes in the client's cognition, skills-based action, and other relevant behaviors. With an understanding of the strengths and limits of client satisfaction research, practitioners can develop useful feedback about our work with clients, and make appropriate adjustments.

As a way to learn how to conduct and analyze client satisfaction research, students in the Research class (SW 302) in the BSW program at Fredonia State College conducted a satisfaction survey among BSW and MSW students who attend the School of Social Work (SSW). The students analyzed the survey results in class. The professor subsequently reported the results for the consideration of the SSW and the College. The following is the professor's report of the results.

In the professor's report of 100 BSW students' responses to a written survey, he follows a logical outline for presenting research results: first, he introduces the topic; then he states his research question and explains his methodology for administering the survey; next he presents his results and the limitations of the study; he ends with a summary. See if you can note the use of authorial opinion in the original version and compare what you see with the corrected version. Research reports should present the methods and results objectively while reporting the facts in a logical order. In the corrected summary section, the author included some interpretive comments, but they were all backed up by the data. In some reports, there might be a Discussion section for interpretation of the results where the author may speculate more broadly about what the survey results mean. Note that the report includes information about student satisfaction (Fieldwork) and possible unmet needs (course scheduling, food service, and elective course offerings). The open-ended question about other topics gave respondents the chance to indicate additional unmet needs and/or their satisfaction with other aspects of the SSW.

There are 59 writing errors in the report. At the end of the correction section, we added an "executive summary," a brief report of the study and findings, with 23 writing errors.

ORIGINAL VERSION

Report on Student Satisfaction Survey – 2011

Report to the Dean, SSW

Abbreviations: SSW: School of Social Work (Fredonia State College)

BSW: Bachelor of Social Work

MSW: Masters of Social Work

Introduction and Methodology

(170)

In the 2011 spring semester students' in SW 302, Research and Evaluation, conducted a Survey of student satisfaction with various aspects of the SSW Experience. The survey was composed by students enrolled in SW 302, who polled students in their other classes for topics to include. The one-page/two-sided survey forms (consisting mostly of Likert-formatted questions about course scheduling, fieldwork, food, electronic resources and elective course topics) was distributed to student mailboxes, and to non-social-work-majoring students via their professors, the week-before spring break. A box was placed in the student lounge for students to deposit there responses. Approximately 400 blank forms were distributed; 178 were returned: for an approximate response rate of 44.5%. We estimate that 180 forms were distributed to BSW students; Students returned 100 forms (response rate = 55.6%). This is a report of BSW student satisfaction, the full survey form is attached to this report. This was an exploratory study about Student Satisfaction and needs in the SSW.

Results

1. Course scheduling

   The survey asked for respondents interest in attending classes during each of the four 3 hour time slots (8–11, 11–2, 2–5, 5–8). There was considerable interest (more than 50% of the full sample) across all the times, enough to assure sufficient enrollment in each time period. (171) Mid-mornings was most popular (acceptable to more than 70%); early afternoons and evenings were approved by more than 60%; early mornings were least popular (okay for 55%).

   Students' expressed fewer interest in weekend classes: about 1/3 checked Saturday's; less than 20% checked Sunday's. A large majority (75%) would like to see more summer social work offerings and sections of all required courses available every semester. There is considerable interest in alternative course formatting: about 60% would like us to schedule more online or hybrid courses. As you know, some of us on the faculty have been arguing this point for years. Now we have evidence to support our views.

2. Fieldwork

    When we were planning the survey, students expressed strong feeling about field, both positive and negatively. The survey results, howsoever, were considerably positive about field. Of 9 aspects of field listed on the survey, a majority of students were dissatisfied by only one item: lack of reimbursement for expenses incurred in field (22 of 43 responding, 13 of whom were very dissatisfied). Large majorities' of respondents were satisfied with the other 8 items. Factor analysis identified two clusters: 1) high satisfaction with the agency, the amount and relevance of work students due in field, student's input into selection of they're placements, and the on-site field supervisor; 2) location of the agency and lack of reimbursement. Students were very satisfied with their field liaisons (97% satisfied or very satisfied); and communications with the SSW Field Office (more than 85%).

3. Food and beverages on campus   (172)

    The main cafeteria is on the other side of the campus, a 10- 15-minute walk each way. The auxiliary café near the SSW is convenient but offers a reduced menu. 4 questions addressed the importance of food and beverage service. Ratings of importance ranged from about 70% (hot snacks) to 85% (healthy snacks), with more then 90% saying "overall improvements to food and/or beverage service" is important. 72% said they knew the nearby café exists; 2/3 said they would patronize the café at least once per week if it's hours were extended beyond the current 3 PM closing time.

4. Access to electronic resources

    The main congregation area of the SSW has WiFi. There are 3 networked desk-top computers and one-printer in the student lounge. 3 questions where about satisfaction with these resources. About 60% of respondents were dissatisfied with the availability of printers in the SSW. About 55% were satisfied with availability of computers; 75% were satisfied with power plug availability. On a separate question, almost 90% said they'd like to see wireless printing available in the School. Good luck in this economic environment!

5. Elective course offerings

    Over the years, students have asked for more elective courses. The survey listed 11 possible topics for social work electives. 4 topics attracted the most interest: domestic violence (57%), children and youth (50%), substance abuse (49%), and mental health (42%). No other topics received more than 30 votes. When asked about credit allocation for electives. The plurality of students (43%) said they'd be interested in taking an elective course for 3 credits.

6. Written comments (173)

28 BSW students wrote comments in response to an open-ended question about dissatisfaction related to the nine field topics. A few comments covered two topics:

- Unreimbursed expenses and distance to field placement=11
- Not the population or topic of interest=7
- The work is not interesting, not enough to do=6
- The agency is disorganized or not supportive of students=5
- Communication with the SSW field office=2
- One student wrote, "love my placement"; another: "I hate, hate my field."

Their were space for students to write in any additional topics of interest they'd like to add. Ten did: two were about electronic resources; the rest were miscellaneous compliments and concerns.

Summary

I would say that the response rate of 55% among BSW students (and about 30% among MSW students) was typical and acceptable. This report is based on BSW responses only, MSWs are not included.

Surprisingly, the data indicates considerable satisfaction with the BSW Program and the SSW. Lord knows, there's plenty to complain about. Areas of greatest satisfaction are most aspects of fieldwork, and availability of power plugs for laptops and other devices. What students said was areas of concern are unreimbursed expenses related to fieldwork, and availability of printers' (including wireless capability) and computers. [Crybabies!!] Written comments reflect some dissatisfaction with the level of work and support offered at some field placements.

There is considerable student interest in more coarse offerings (including (174)
electives), at more times (in the day and across semesters), and with more options for distance-instruction. Also, students are interested in more food and beverage service, with more choice of products and times of operation for the East Campus Café.

Limitations include unknown validity, low response rate (and missing values), researcher error (and bias, e.g., qualitative data analyses, etc.), the reactive effect (e.g., students in SW 302 took and administered the survey with the instructors involvement) and history (e.g., spring break). Alphas were acceptable on all three scales (fieldwork, food and beverages, and electronic resources). All results were consistent with previous years findings (suggesting concurrent validity). The design and sampling methods, as well as response rate and limitations, were appropriate for an exploratory study.

Respectively submitted,

Dr. Stan R. De Viashon

CASE 24: CORRECTED VERSION

Each number in the corrected version refers to an explanation below.

Introduction and Methodology

In the 2011 spring semester, ① students ② in SW 302, Research and Evaluation, conducted a survey ③ of student satisfaction with various aspects of the SSW Experience. Students who were enrolled in SW 302 composed this survey, and, who polled students in their other classes,④ for topics to include. Researchers distributed the one-page/two-sided survey forms (consisting mostly of Likert-formatted questions about course scheduling, fieldwork, food, electronic resources and elective course topics) to student mailboxes and to non-social-work-majoring students via their professors, the week-before spring break. Researchers placed a box in the student lounge for students to deposit their ⑤ responses. Approximately 400 blank forms went out to students; 178 were returned, ⑥ for an approximate response rate of 44.5%. We estimate that researchers distributed 180 forms to BSW students; students returned 100 (response rate = 55.6%). This is a report of BSW student satisfaction; ⑦ we have attached the full survey form to this report. This was an exploratory study about student satisfaction ⑧ and needs in the SSW.

Results

1. Course scheduling
   The survey asked for respondents' ⑨ interest in attending classes during each of the four three-hour ⑩ time slots (8–11, 11–2, 2–5, 5–8). There was considerable interest (more than 50% of the full sample) across all

   cont.

EXPLANATIONS OF CORRECTIONS

1. We inserted a comma after the introductory phrase.
2. No apostrophe because there is no possessive.
3. No capital "s" required because "survey" is a common noun.
4. (optional) we included a comma for brief pause, but the general rule is to use commas sparingly and only when grammatically necessary or to make the idea more clear. Passive voice corrected to active voice.
5. Homophone error: their and there—"their" is used to indicate the possessive. Passive voice corrected to active voice.
6. Comma instead of a semicolon to link an independent and a subordinate clause. Passive voice corrected to active voice.
7. Semicolon instead of a comma because it links two complete sentences. With a comma, it becomes a run-on sentence. Passive voice corrected to active voice.
8. No capital "s" required because "student satisfaction" is not a proper noun.
9. An apostrophe is required to indicate the possessive.
10. "Three-hour" because we spell out numbers one through ten; also, the compound adjective (three-hour) should be hyphenated.

cont.

the times, enough to assure sufficient enrollment in each time period.
Mid-mornings were ⑪ most popular (acceptable to more than 70%); early
afternoons and evenings were approved by more than 60%; early
mornings were least popular (okay for 55%).

Students ⑫ expressed less ⑬ interest in weekend classes: about one-third ⑭
checked Saturdays ⑮; less than 20% checked Sundays ⑯. A large
majority (75%) would like to see more summer social work offerings,
and sections of all required courses available every semester. There is
considerable interest in alternative course formatting: about 60% would
like us to schedule more online or hybrid courses. ⑰

2. Fieldwork
   When we were planning the survey, students expressed strong feelings ⑱
   about field, both positive and negative ⑲. The survey results, however ⑳,
   were considerably positive about field. Of nine ㉑ aspects of field listed
   on the survey, a majority of students was ㉒ dissatisfied by only one
   item: lack of reimbursement for expenses incurred in field (22 of 43
   responding, 13 of whom were very dissatisfied). Large majorities ㉓ of
   respondents were satisfied with the other eight ㉔ items. Factor analysis
   identified two clusters: 1) high satisfaction with the agency, the amount
   and relevance of work students do ㉕ in field, students' ㉖ input into
   selection of their ㉗ placements, and the on-site field supervisor;
   2) location of the agency and lack of reimbursement. Students were
   very satisfied with their field liaisons (97% satisfied or very satisfied) ㉘
   and communications with the SSW Field Office (more than 85%).

cont.

EXPLANATIONS OF CORRECTIONS

11. Verb and noun agreement: the plural subject (mornings) must link to a verb, which is also in the plural.
12. No apostrophe because there is no possessive.
13. Word choice here: "less" is correct for concepts (interest); "fewer" is used when the noun has a measurable unit of one – there is no way to measure "cognitive interest" with measurable units. Use "less."
14. Always spell out and hyphenate fractions.
15. Do not use an apostrophe except to indicate the possessive.
16. Do not use an apostrophe except to indicate the possessive.
17. The first sentence is unnecessary information in a research report. The second sentence is opinion.

18. Use the plural case consistently, or the singular, but avoid mixing them in one sentence.
19. Use parallelism: if you write positive, then use negative, or if you write positively, then use negatively.
20. "Howsoever" is a word, but not the clearest professional writing.
21. Spell out numbers from one through ten.
22. Singular case: "majority" is singular.
23. No apostrophe because there is no possessive.
24. Spell out numbers from one through ten.
25. Homophone error: do and due—"do" is a verb; "due" refers to a deadline.
26. Apostrophe to indicate the plural possessive.
27. Homophone error: their and they're—see #5.
28. No semicolon because the following phrase is not a complete sentence.

cont.

3. Food and beverages on campus

   The main cafeteria is on the other side of the campus, a 10–15-minute walk each way. The auxiliary café near the SSW is convenient but offers a reduced menu. Four ㉙ questions addressed the importance of food and beverage service. Ratings of importance ranged from about 70% (hot snacks) to 85% (healthy snacks), with more than ㉚ 90% saying "overall improvements to food and/or beverage service" is important. Seventy-two percent ㉛ said they knew the nearby café exists; two-thirds said they would patronize the café at least once per week if its ㉜ hours were extended beyond the current 3 PM closing time.

4. Access to electronic resources

   The main congregation area of the SSW has WiFi. There are three networked desk-top computers and one ㉝ printer in the student lounge. Three ㉞ questions were ㉟ about satisfaction with these resources. About 60% of respondents were dissatisfied with the availability of printers in the SSW. About 55% were satisfied with the ㊱ availability of computers; 75% were satisfied with power plug availability. On a separate question, almost 90% said they would ㊲ like to see wireless printing available in the School. ㊳

5. Elective course offerings

   Over the years, students have asked for more elective courses. The survey listed 11 possible topics for social work electives. Four ㊴ topics attracted the most interest: domestic violence (57%), children and youth (50%), substance abuse (49%), and mental health (42%). No other topics received more than 30 votes. When asked about credit allocation for electives, the plurality of students (43%) said they would ㊵ be interested in taking an elective course for three credits ㊶.

   cont.

EXPLANATIONS OF CORRECTIONS

29. Spell out numbers from one through ten.
30. Homophone error: than and then—"than" is for comparisons.
31. Always spell out numbers and percentages when they begin sentences.
32. Homophone error: its and it's—"its" is possessive; "it's" is the contracted form of it is.
33. No hyphen because the two words do not combine to form a single item.
34. Spell out numbers from one through ten.
35. Word choice is off here: were and where—"where" refers to a place.
36. We included "the" before availability.
37. Avoid using contractions in professional writing.
38. We deleted authorial opinion.
39. Spell out numbers from one through ten.
40. Avoid using contractions in professional writing.
41. The first phrase was an incomplete sentence; a comma (or conjunction) combines the two statements into one complete sentence. Spell out numbers from one through ten.

cont.

6. Written comments
   Twenty-eight ㊷ BSW students wrote comments in response to an open-ended question about dissatisfaction related to the nine field topics. A few comments covered two topics:

   - Unreimbursed expenses and distance to field placement=11
   - Not the population or topic of interest=7
   - The work is not interesting, not enough to do=6
   - The agency is disorganized or not supportive of students=5
   - Communication with the SSW field office=2
   - One student wrote, "love my placement"; another: "I hate, hate my field"

   There ㊸ was ㊹ space for students to write in any additional topics of interest ㊺. Ten did: two were about electronic resources; the rest were miscellaneous compliments and concerns.

Summary

㊻ The response rate of 55% among BSW students (and about 30% among MSW students) was typical and acceptable. This report is based on BSW responses only; ㊼ MSWs are not included.

㊽ The data indicate ㊾ considerable satisfaction with the BSW Program and the SSW. ㊿ The data also indicates students have the greatest satisfaction in most aspects of fieldwork (51) and the availability of power plugs for laptops and other devices. (52) Students' concerns are unreimbursed expenses related to fieldwork, and availability of printers (53) (including wireless capability) and computers. (54) Written comments reflect some dissatisfaction with the level of work and support offered at some field placements.

cont.

EXPLANATIONS OF CORRECTIONS

42. Always spell out numbers when they begin sentences.
43. Homophone error: their and there (see #5)
44. Verb and noun agreement: "space" is singular, so the verb "to be" should be singular, e.g., "was."
45. "They'd like to add" is redundant with "additional topics" and it is a contraction of "they would."
46. Delete "I would say" because it is unnecessary.
47. Semicolon instead of comma because it links two independent clauses, and if you use a comma you create a comma-splice, or run-on sentence.
48. We deleted authorial opinion.
49. "Data" is plural, as in "the data are useful."
50. "Lord knows, there's plenty to complain about" is opinion.
51. We deleted the comma because it is unnecessary.
52. We deleted unnecessary language and revised passive construction.
53. No possessive.
54. Avoid authorial opinion and self-righteous judgment.

cont.

There is considerable student interest in more course ⑤⑤ offerings (including electives), at more times (in the day and across semesters), and with more options for distance-instruction. Also, students are interested in more food and beverage service, with more choice of products and times of operation for the East Campus Café.

Limitations include unknown validity, low response rate (and missing values), researcher error (and bias, e.g., qualitative data analyses ⑤⑥), the reactive effect (e.g., students in SW 302 took and administered the survey with the instructor's ⑤⑦ involvement) and history (e.g., spring break). All results were consistent with previous years' ⑤⑧ findings (suggesting concurrent validity). The design and sampling methods, as well as response rate and limitations, were appropriate for an exploratory study.

Respectfully ⑤⑨ submitted,

Dr. Stan R. De Viashon

EXPLANATIONS OF CORRECTIONS

55. Homophone error: course and coarse—"coarse" means rough, uneven, or vulgar. Also, this may border on opinion, but it appears defensible in that it interprets the data. Ultimately, the writer would have to be able to defend the statement.

56. Avoid using "etc." with e.g.

57. We inserted an apostrophe to indicate the possessive.

58. We inserted an apostrophe to indicate the possessive.

59. Word choice is off here: respectfully and respectively—"respectfully" conveys respect; "respectively" refers to the order of things in a list.

Executive Summary   (176)

The 2011 student survey addressed students satisfaction with fieldwork-related issues and assessed students possible unmet needs' in areas of course scheduling, food services and electronic resources in the SSW. The survey topics were identified by students. One hundred BSW students' returned completed surveys, a response rate of about 55%.

Findings

What students said was they want more flexability in the scheduling of classes. Majorities' of students expressed interest in attending classes in each available time slot (8 AM–8 PM) and during the summer. Majorities were also interested in taking hybrid or online classes, and having all required courses offered during all semesters as well. Smaller numbers of students said they will take courses on weekends, especially Saturdays (about one third). The data says their was considerable satisfaction with the field education program, with the exception of reimbursement of expenses incurred in field (the majority were dissatisfied). Students expressed interest in expanded food and beverage service on the East Campus (variety and availability). Computer and printer availability continued to be a student concern: 45% and 75%, respectfully, expressed the need for more computing and printing capabilities, 90% said they'd like to see wire-less printing (from their laptops) available. 4 topics for   (177) elective courses were indicated. What the students wrote in comments sections tended to reinforce these findings too.

The surveys credability is limited mostly by the response rate (slightly above 50% of BSW students). Other validity threats are discussed, but appear to not seriously challenge these results.

Respectfully submitted,

Dr. Stan R. De Viashon

CORRECTIONS TO THE EXECUTIVE SUMMARY:

Each number in the corrected version refers to an explanation below.

Executive Summary

The 2011 student survey addressed students' ① satisfaction with fieldwork-related issues and assessed students' ② possible unmet needs ③ in areas of course scheduling, food services and electronic resources in the SSW. Students identified the survey topics. One hundred BSW students ④ returned completed surveys, a response rate of approximately 55%.

Findings

⑤ Students want more flexibility ⑥ in the scheduling of classes. Majorities ⑦ of students expressed interest in attending classes in each available time slot (8 AM – 8 PM) and during the summer. Majorities indicated interest in taking hybrid or online classes, and having all required courses offered during all semesters ⑧. Smaller numbers of students said they would ⑨ take courses on weekends, especially Saturdays—about one-third ⑩. ⑪ There is ⑫ considerable satisfaction with the field education program, with the exception of reimbursement of expenses incurred in field—the majority expressed dissatisfaction ⑬. Students expressed interest in expanded food and beverage service on the East Campus (variety and availability). Computer and printer availability continue ⑭ to be a student concern: 45% and 75%, respectively ⑮, expressed the need for more computing and printing capabilities, 90% said they would ⑯

cont.

EXPLANATIONS OF CORRECTIONS TO THE EXECUTIVE SUMMARY

1. Apostrophe to indicate the plural possessive.
2. Apostrophe to indicate the plural possessive.
3. No apostrophe because there is no possessive.
4. No apostrophe because there is no possessive.
5. Unnecessary verbiage.
6. Spelling error.
7. No apostrophe because no possessive is required.
8. Redundant: "and" and "as well."
9. Use the conditional tense, not future tense.
10. Hyphenate fractions when you spell them out.
11. "The data says their" is incorrect: "data" is plural so "says" should be "say"; "their" is possessive; the entire lead-in is unnecessary because the report is based on the data.
12. There are word order and verb tense issues here: because students filled out the survey in the past, "respondents said" is okay; sentiments, beliefs, and perceptions are likely to continue a few months after the survey was completed, so those items are still occurring in the present.
13. Same issue as above: students expressed satisfaction in the past, but they are likely to be dissatisfied about the same items today.
14. Use the present tense: those concerns continue into the present; use the singular because the subject of the sentence is "availability," not "computers and printers."
15. Word usage: respectively and respectfully— "respectfully" conveys respect; "respectively" refers to the order of things in a list.
16. Avoid contractions. Spell out "they would."

cont.

like to see wireless ⑰ printing (from their laptops) available. Four ⑱ topics for elective courses were indicated. Students' comments ⑲ tended to reinforce these findings ⑳. The survey's ㉑ credibility ㉒ is limited mostly by the response rate (slightly above 50% of BSW students). The report presents other validity threats, but they do not ㉓ challenge these results.

Respectfully submitted,

Dr. Stan R. De Viashon

EXPLANATIONS OF CORRECTIONS TO THE EXECUTIVE SUMMARY

17. "Wireless" is not hyphenated

18. Spell out numbers from one through ten.

19. We deleted unnecessary verbiage.

20. We edited to avoid redundancy: "reinforce" and "too" are redundant.

21. Apostrophe for the singular possessive.

22. Spelling error.

23. We corrected the passive voice construction so it is clear who is doing what to whom.

FOCUS GROUP REPORTS

Focus groups are used to collect data that are more difficult to obtain than data produced by surveys. When people are sensitive about, or they are not completely aware of, their views, perspectives, or feelings, peer-group process may be the most effective way to help people articulate what they believe, know, or feel about a certain topic. Focus groups rely on an interactive process of group conversation, with members expressing themselves at greater depth and with more detail than they would in a one-on-one interview or in a pencil-and-paper survey. By contrast, group interviews follow a more orderly procedure, with participants taking turns answering pre-determined questions, or indicating agreement or disagreement to items in an interview protocol. Focus group process involves a semi-structured discussion, in which the facilitator manages a probing conversation, encouraging participants to react to each other. Data may be recorded by audio and sometimes video tape. There is often a separate note taker.

Focus group data are qualitative in nature because the data gathered takes the form of words rather than numbers or statistics. There are no averages, medians, or dispersions to calculate. Instead, focus group reports indicate a range of expressed views, including topics of consensus and disagreement. Focus group reports can be less conclusive than quantitative data reports while at the same time summarization can be more difficult because the views expressed by the group may be diffuse and difficult to summarize.

CASE 25: FOCUS GROUP REPORT: PARENTS AND TEACHERS PROGRAM

The following is a report about a focus group session with 12 mothers who participated in a program called Parents and Teachers (PAT). PAT involved home visits, drop-in chats, play groups, screenings, and information and referral. A PAT independent evaluator convened and managed the focus group in order to add insight to a parent survey that had been conducted the previous month. Regarding report format: always report consensus responses in regular font; you should present illustrative direct quotes in italics. We added an executive summary (with errors) at the end of the report. There are 66 writing errors in the report and executive summary; sentence structure errors are not corrected in direct quotes from clients (the quotes in italics).

ORIGINAL VERSION

Focus Group Report (184)

A focus group was held on June 2, at a public Elementary School in the District. Recruitment was conducted two ways; the survey to all PAT parents included an information and sign-up form, and PAT administrators made announcements during PAT activities in May. A consent procedure was administered at the beginning of the session. A small honorarium was given to parents and child care was provided in another location in the school by PAT staff while the evaluator and an assistant conducted the focus group meeting.

12 parents arrived very punctually, dinner was served to the children and the parents, and the children were taken to another part of the building for the 90 minute duration of the focus group. All 12 parents were women, and one husband arrived about an hour into the session, stayed until the end, but did not speak. The question stream was developed by the evaluator, in consultation with the PAT staff and based on the national PAT focus group protocol.

The guiding evaluation question for the focus group, based on the quantitative survey data, was; what elements of the PAT program are most and least affective in promoting positive outcomes for parents' and/

or children alike? Following, is summaries of responses with illustrative,   (185)
quotes in italics:

Q: How would you describe the program to us as outsiders? What is this
   program?
   • Networking among themselves
   • Parenting expertise knowledge
   • Child life-stage development
   • *They respect parents; some programs' look down on us*

Q: How do you know they respect you?
   • *Every time they see you, they tell you what a great job your doing.*
     Their supportive, ect. Even when your feeling discouraged, they find
     a way to say some-thing positive. They don't use your words against
     you (only answer given.)

Q: Do you know anyone that has left the program? Have you ever thought
   about leaving the program? Why do people leave PAT?
   • You must want it, be ready for it, invest yourself in it
   • *(My friend) felt there was no value added to it and didn't want to*
     spend the time that way. I really don't know why (she) left. She's the
     one who told me about PAT.

Q: Do other neighbors or relatives seeing you use the program label you?
   Is their that risk?
   [General consensus that this is not an issue because PAT's staff
   vehicles are not labeled and many peoples use the program.]

Q: Do you use the home visits/parent educator? When they make a home   (186)
   visit, what happens? What do they do best? What makes a home visit
   what it is?
   • Developmental, entertaining, age-appropriate activities with the
     children
   • *There's lots of affirmation. It makes me think about how I can help*
     (my son) later on.
   • *They're not afraid to use math or science in simple down-to-earth*
     ways. For example, they used measuring tape to measure things, the
     bed, the rug, how tall he was, other stuff, it was basic math.

Q: Do they prepare you for this? It sounds like you really have to trust
   them. . .If someone came into my house with a measuring tape. . .

   • General Affirmation of trust
   • *It's all age appropriate activities .....I'm the tester. They try things out*
     on my kids and they know we'll like it.

Q: Do they take into account you're unique values? If your a minority or have certain belief's, do they take that into account? How?
- General affirmation – they get to know you
- *They ask you about you're live and stress.*
- *I get a cents of calmness. Afterwards my interactions are much more loving with my daughter. Its because I'm not in a vaccuum. This is the hardest work I've ever done. I feel sorry for anyone that doesn't have this.*

Q: Can you think of any ways you haven't said yet that the program has helped you?
- Connect with resources
- Provide information
- Provide support and understanding
- *I'm a young mother. I feel depressed that my friends' are all out doing things and I can't go out. None of my friends have kids; so she (parent educator) gave me her home number. I call her and she supports me and tells me I'm a good mother.* (187)
- *You can ask the questions you can't ask anyone else.*

Q: Let's talk about drop-in-and-chat group meetings. What works well, what doesn't?
- Informative
- Convenient
- *It helps built confidence in me as a parent.*
- *I can bring the knowledge I gain home to my spouse. Including when my husband and I disagree.*
- *Its a refresher for you're second or third child. Or sometimes your son and daughter are so different you deal with different issues.*

Q: Let's talk about playgroups. What works well, what doesn't?
- Positive pear interaction
- *Social developement, especially for the shy kids.*
- *There's no cost. If your kid isn't having a good day or you're not having a good day, you can leave.*

Q: Let's talk about screenings, Ages & Stages, hearing & vision, ect. Are you involved in it, what works well, what doesn't?
- Skills' and tools' to evaluate, understand and help your child.
- *It helped me to look at behaviors I didn't like and reinterpret them in a way so I could enjoy that part of my son.*

[No suggestions for improvement.]

Q: Let's talk about community resources, linking you up with community resources. Are you aware of or use resources?

There were 2 categories of thought: some use their own networks and/or other involvements for linking with resources; others rely on PAT staff and always find the information useful, accurate, appropriate and honest.

Q: What barriers are there to resources even when you know whom to call? (Recorder's note: *Those with barriers are not at the focus group. Clear self-selection.)* (188)

Q: Are there any other changes in you or the way your functioning as a parent as a result of the PAT program? [Note: This is an outcomes question]
- More knowledgable, skilled, affective
- More self-confidence, calmer, connected with other mom's
- *I'm more honest with my kids. I admit when I don't know what I'm doing.*
- *If you don't apologize to them, they won't neither. How can you expect them too grow up with good values?*
- *When I had my daughter it was really stressful and it was like dropping into an abyss. I've gained empowerment and confidence. This program helps us and our kids' to be the best versions of ourselves. It gives me confidence to be myself as a parent. Thats been a gift.*
- *I have less money, I'm by myself all the time, than I got pregnant again. I was depressed and I came to this group and people have the same problems I do. The educator said this was normal and I started looking forward to it. The other mothers' and I try to get together on our own, even in the summer.*
- *We call each other.*

Q: Last question. Are there changes in your children that you've scene as a result of this program? [Outcomes item] (189)
- *Sharing and interacting with the other children. My child is much less clingy.* [Others affirm]
- *My child has gained confidence and a sense of importance.* [Others affirm]
- *My child was shy but now goes up too everybody. The older kids are role models for the younger kids.*
- *I have tools to apply to kids – hundreds of them.*

Executive Summary

12 PAT participant's attended a focus-group in May. They expressed very high satisfaction with the program, for several different reasons, usually with a high degree of consensus.

Reasons for high satisfaction were:
- Skills, flexibility and sensitivity of PAT staff;
- Conveniance;
- Many needs' met;
- Networking;
- Resource linkages;
- Empowerment of mothers;
- Informative and skill-building.

Outcomes' identified by participants:
- Knowledge, skills and improved behavior's regarding parenting;
- Improved child behavior and developement;
- Improved self-confidence, self-esteem;
- Networking.

In view of the self-selected (voluntary) sample, representativeness of the full PAT client population are questionable.

CASE 25: CORRECTED VERSION

Each number in the corrected version refers to an explanation below.

Focus Group Report

The PAT evaluator and assistant conducted a focus group at a public elementary school ① in the district ②. PAT conducted recruitment two ways: ③ the survey to all PAT parents included an information and sign-up form, and PAT administrators made announcements during PAT activities in May. Staff administered a consent procedure at the beginning of the session. PAT staff gave a small honorarium to parents, ④ while other PAT staff provided child care in another location in the school. ⑤ The evaluator and an assistant conducted the focus group meeting.

Twelve ⑥ parents arrived punctually; staff served dinner to the children and the parents; later the staff members took the children to another part of the building for the 90-minute ⑦ duration of the focus group. All 12 parents were women, and one husband arrived about an hour into the session, stayed until the end, but did not speak. The evaluator developed the question stream, in consultation with the PAT staff and based on the national PAT focus group protocol.

The guiding evaluation question for the focus group grew out of the quantitative survey data: ⑧ what elements of the PAT program are most and least effective ⑨ in promoting positive outcomes for parents ⑩ and/

cont.

EXPLANATIONS OF CORRECTIONS

1. Corrected passive voice. Also, no capital letter required because, no specific school is named.
2. School district is not named, so no capital letter required.
3. We used a colon because an elaboration follows. We also corrected the passive voice construction.
4. Comma before a connecting conjunction between two independent clauses. We also corrected passive voice.
5. Comma between two subordinate clauses. We corrected the passive voice.
6. Spell out and capitalize numbers that begin sentences.
7. This was a run-on sentence with multiple problems. We rewrote the sentence to eliminate "very" (unnecessary with punctually), and correct sentence structure by using semicolons to separate independent clauses. We hyphenated 90-minute.
8. This was a convoluted sentence. We used a colon to create two independent clauses. The second is an elaboration of the first.
9. Word choice is off here: effective and affective—effective refers to the influence or consequence of an intervention; affective refers to emotion or compelling power.
10. No apostrophe because there is no possessive.

cont.

or children alike? Following ⑪ are ⑫ summaries of responses with illustrative ⑬ quotes in italics. ⑭

Q: How would you describe the program to us, ⑮ as outsiders? What is this program?
- Networking among themselves
- Parenting expertise knowledge
- Child life-stage development
- *They respect parents; some programs* ⑯ *look down on us*

Q: How do you know they respect you?
- *Every time they see you, they tell you what a great job you're* ⑰ *doing. They're* ⑱ *supportive, etc.* ⑲ *Even when you're* ⑳ *feeling discouraged, they find a way to say something* ㉑ *positive. They don't use your words against you* (only answer given). ㉒

Q: Do you know anyone who ㉓ has left the program? Have you ever thought about leaving the program? Why do people leave PAT?
- You must want it, be ready for it, invest yourself in it.
- *(My friend) felt there was no value added to it and didn't want to spend the time that way. I really don't know why (she) left. She's the one who told me about PAT.*

Q: Do other neighbors or relatives seeing you use the program label you? Is there ㉔ that risk?
[General consensus that this is not an issue because PAT's staff vehicles are not labeled and many people ㉕ use the program.]

cont.

EXPLANATIONS OF CORRECTIONS

11. We deleted the comma because it is unnecessary.
12. "Summaries" is plural.
13. The comma is unnecessary.
14. We inserted a period rather than a colon, which indicated that all that follows is one sentence.
15. The comma indicates that we, not the participants, are the outsiders.
16. No apostrophe because the sentence does not require the possessive.
17. Homophone error: you're and your— "you're" is the contraction of you are.

18. Homophone error: they're and there— "they're" is the contraction of they are.
19. "Etc."—not ect.
20. Homophone error: you're and your (see #17).
21. Use "something"—"some-thing" is not a word.
22. The period belongs after close-parenthesis mark.
23. "Who" is the pronoun for people when it takes a verb—"whom" when it does not.
24. Homophone error: there and their—"their" is the possessive.
25. "People" is plural.

cont.

Q: Do you use the home visits/parent educator? When they make a home visit, what happens? What do they do best? What makes a home visit what it is?

- Developmental, entertaining, age-appropriate activities with the children
- *There's lots of affirmation. It makes me think about how I can help (my son) later on.*
- *They're [correct: they are] not afraid to use math or science in simple down-to-earth ways. For example, they used measuring tape to measure things:* ㉖ *the bed, the rug, how tall he was, other stuff.* ㉗ *It was basic math.*

Q: Do they prepare you for this? It sounds like you really have to trust them. . .If someone came into my house with a measuring tape. . .

- General Affirmation of trust
- *It's all age-appropriate* ㉘ *activities .....I'm the tester. They try things out on my kids and they know we'll like it.*

Q: Do they take into account your ㉙ unique values? If you're ㉚ a minority or have certain beliefs ㉛, do they take that into account? How?

- General affirmation – they get to know you.
- *They ask you about your* ㉜ *life* ㉝ *and stress.*
- *I get a sense* ㉞ *of calmness. Afterwards my interactions are much more loving with my daughter. It's* ㉟ *because I'm not in a vacuum* ㊱. *This is the hardest work I've ever done. I feel sorry for anyone that [incorrect (who) but a quote] doesn't have this.*

Q: Can you think of any ways you haven't said yet that the program has helped you?

- Connect with resources
- Provide information
- Provide support and understanding

cont.

EXPLANATIONS OF CORRECTIONS

26. Use a colon when a list follows.
27. Run on sentence; use a comma with a conjunction, a semicolon to make one sentence out of it, or a period if you want to make two separate sentences.
28. Hyphenate two-word adjectives.
29. Homophone error: your and you're (see #17).
30. Homophone error: you're and your (see #17).
31. "Beliefs" is plural, no apostrophe required.
32. Homophone error: your and you're (see #17).
33. Word choice is off here: life is a noun and live is a verb.
34. Homophone error: sense and cents— "sense" is perception or wisdom; "cents" refers to money.
35. Homophone error: it's and its—"its" is the possessive; "it's" is the contraction of it is.
36. Spelling error.

cont.

- *I'm a young mother. I feel depressed that my friends* ㊲ *are all out doing things and I can't go out. None of my friends have kids; so she (parent educator) gave me her home number. I call her and she supports me and tells me I'm a good mother.*
- *You can ask the questions you can't ask anyone else.*

Q: Let's talk about drop-in-and-chat-group ㊳ meetings. What works well, what doesn't?
- Informative
- Convenient
- *It helps built confidence in me as a parent.*
- *I can bring the knowledge I gain home to my spouse. Including when my husband and I disagree.*
- *It's* ㊴ *a refresher for your* ㊵ *second or third child. Or sometimes your son and daughter are so different you deal with different issues.*

Q: Let's talk about playgroups. What works well, what doesn't?
- Positive peer ㊶ interaction
- *Social development* ㊷*, especially for the shy kids.*
- *There's no cost. If your kid isn't having a good day or you're not having a good day, you can leave.*

Q: Let's talk about screenings, Ages & Stages, hearing & vision, etc. ㊸ Are you involved in it, what works well, what doesn't?
- Skills ㊹ and tools ㊺ to evaluate, to understand and to help your child.
- *It helped me to look at behaviors I didn't like and reinterpret them in a way so I could enjoy that part of my son.*
[No suggestions for improvement.]

Q: Let's talk about community resources, linking you up with community resources. Are you aware of or use resources?
   There were 2 categories of thought: some use their own networks and/or other involvements for linking with resources; others rely on PAT staff and always find the information useful, accurate, appropriate and honest.

cont.

EXPLANATIONS OF CORRECTIONS

37. No apostrophe because the sentence did not require the possessive.

38. This is a hyphenated four-word adjective.

39. Homophone error: it's and its (see #35).

40. Homophone error: your and you're (see #17).

41. Homophone error: peer and pear—"peer" refers to one's equal; "pear" is a fruit.

42. Spelling error.

43. "Etc.," not ect.

44. No apostrophe because the sentence requires no possessive.

45. No possessive. See #44.

cont.

Q: What barriers are there to resources even when you know whom [correct] to call? (Recorder's note: *Those with barriers are not at the focus group. Clear self-selection.*)

Q: Are there any other changes in you or the way you're ⁴⁶ functioning as a parent as a result of the PAT program? [Note: This is an outcomes question]

- More knowledgeable ⁴⁷, skilled, effective ⁴⁸
- More self-confidence, calmer, connected with other moms ⁴⁹
- *I'm more honest with my kids. I admit when I don't know what I'm doing.*
- *If you don't apologize to them, they won't either ⁵⁰. How can you expect them to ⁵¹ grow up with good values?*
- *When I had my daughter it was really stressful and it was like dropping into an abyss. I've gained empowerment and confidence. This program helps us and our kids ⁵² to be the best versions of ourselves. It gives me confidence to be myself as a parent. That has ⁵³ been a gift.*
- *I have less money, I'm by myself all the time, then ⁵⁴ I got pregnant again. I was depressed and I came to this group and people have the same problems I do. [Syntax error (switch tenses) but a quote] The educator said this was normal, ⁵⁵ and I started looking forward to it. The other mothers ⁵⁶ and I try to get together on our own, even in the summer.*
- *We call each other.*

cont.

EXPLANATIONS OF CORRECTIONS

46. Homophone error: you're and your (see #17).
47. Spelling error.
48. Word choice is off here: effective and affective (see #9).
49. No possessive. See #44.
50. Avoid the double negative—"won't" and "neither" cancel each other out.
51. Homophone error: to and too—"too" means also or excessive.
52. No possessive. See #44.
53. Avoid using contractions: "that has"
54. Word choice is off here: then and than— "then" refers to time; "than" is for comparisons.
55. Use a comma before a connective conjunction linking two independent clauses.
56. No possessive. See #44.

cont.

Q: Last question. Are there changes in your children that you've seen ⑤⑦ as
a result of this program? [Outcomes item]

- *Sharing and interacting with the other children. My child is much less clingy.* [Others affirm]
- *My child has gained confidence and a sense of importance.* [Others affirm]
- *My child was shy but now goes up to ⑤⑧ everybody. The older kids are role models for the younger kids.*
- *I have tools to apply to kids – hundreds of them.*

Executive Summary

Twelve ⑤⑨ PAT participants ⑥⓪ attended a focus group in May. They expressed very
high satisfaction with the program, for several different reasons, usually
with a high degree of consensus.

Reasons for high satisfaction were:
- Skills, flexibility and sensitivity of PAT staff;
- Convenience ⑥①;
- Many needs ⑥② met;
- Networking;
- Resource linkages;
- Empowerment of mothers;
- Informative and skill-building.

Outcomes ⑥③ identified by participants:
- Knowledge, skills and improved behaviors ⑥④ regarding parenting;
- Improved child behavior and development ⑥⑤;
- Improved self-confidence, self-esteem;
- Networking.

In view of the self-selected (voluntary) sample, representativeness of the
full PAT client population is ⑥⑥ questionable.

EXPLANATIONS OF CORRECTIONS

57. Homophone error: seen and scene—"seen" is past tense for see; "scene" is a vista or part of a play or film.
58. Homophone error: to and too (see #51).
59. Always spell out numbers that begin sentences.
60. No possessive. See #44.

61. Spelling error.
62. No possessive. See #44.
63. No possessive. See #44.
64. No possessive. See #44.
65. Spelling error.
66. Verb and noun agreement: "population" is singular, so the verb "is" should be singular.

CASE 26: REPORTING RESEARCH RESULTS TO INFLUENCE PUBLIC POLICY: THE FREDONIA ESTATE TAX

Fredonia, like most states, taxes money when passed from one generation to the next in the form of an inheritance. When someone dies and bequeaths an estate to someone else, the inheritor pays an estate tax to the state. A business organization in Fredonia has been arguing that Fredonia's estate tax drives wealthy people to other states, where estate taxes are lower or non-existent. Fredonia exempts the first $850,000 from taxation, which is less generous than most other states. This opinion article, published in a weekly state business newspaper, argues that the data do not support the anti-tax argument. We inserted 59 errors.

"Op-ed" is short for "opposite the editorial," meaning the space in the newspaper or magazine across from the editorial section where senior staff of the newspaper publish their opinions. Op-eds are opinion pieces that can be written by staff columnists, guest columnists, or readers. Op-eds differ from letters to the editor in length and substance. In the Policy section of this book, we suggest that letters to editors should be three to four paragraphs. Op-eds are longer, generally eight or more paragraphs. Letters can be reactive, provocative, questioning, complaining, accusatory, and one-sided. Op-eds, on the other hand, should contribute to a public dialogue (as do some letters), by integrating evidence—theoretical, empirical or both—in order to argue a point in greater detail than most letters do. Op-eds generally take longer than letters to make their points because they are more deliberate and sophisticated. Op-eds are more difficult than letters to get published, because they take so much more space and editors demand higher quality in the writing.

Even so, a good process for writing an op-ed begins about the same way as one for writing a letter to the editor: 1) introduce the topic and state why it is important. 2) Develop an argument by supporting a position while nullifying opposing views. 3) Finish your argument with a conclusion that re-states your main claim and summarizes the data and the argument you have made for it. Tie it all together in your conclusion. Effective writers organize their argument around particular themes or ideas that they introduce early and return to often, and especially in the concluding paragraph.

The following op-ed combines research results and logic. In the following example, the original article—the one about the estate tax possibly costing the state revenue—relied on financial data to makes its argument. The social work professor's response to the original article also relied upon data to make a counter-argument. He researched websites for information about interstate migration. When he found that interstate migration was a more complex phenomenon than portrayed in the original article, he decided there was enough information to support an op-ed because the material was more complex than a letter to the editor would typically allow. The op-ed, with 60 errors, represents a research report in that it uses data and existing research to help the author make his point.

ORIGINAL VERSION

Is the Estate Tax a Factor in Migration Patterns Affecting Fredonia?

(194)

By Stan R. DeViashon, Professor of Social Work, Fredonia State College

A friend of mine, recently retired; took his pension and moved from Fredonia to a small town in a Red State where marijuana laws are not enforced very rigorously. Recreational pot is very important to him. Does this mean Fredonia should legalize drugs for personal use? Become a Red State? How do we know that my friend isn't more representative then rich people whom supposedly left because of our relatively high tax burden? Which scenario should inform state policy? The answer: neither.

The Fredonia Business Association commissioned a study that claimed to "prove" that our estate tax causes out-migration, and loss of jobs' and tax revenue. Although, the assertion appears plausable, the data is not there.

In 2008, the most recent year for which official statistics about migration between the states are available, 4 states accounted for a net loss of almost 2000 former Fredonians: Massachusetts, Florida, New York and Connecticut. Besides, being the leading destinations for people leaving our state, all 4 states were also highest as sources of migration into Fredonia too. Migration occurs in all directions, the business group study only counted people that left.

Even if we limit our sites to those that left tax burden is almost irrelevant because of the fact that differences across the states' are not that great. Looking closely at Fredonia's data, our 2008 tax burden (10.2%) was less then 1 percent higher than the U.S. median of 9.4%. The 33 most tax-costly states all fall within a 2% range of tax burdens: 11.8% - 9.8%. Fredonia (# 10 in the U.S.) is on the low side of midrange of these 33 states. Given the array of factors that contribute to the decision to leave one state and move to another, a 1% or 2% decrease in tax burden is likely to pail in comparison to consideration's like quality of life, nearness of family, jobs', schools', climate, access to health care and other necessities', total cost of living, and so on, etc. Based on all state and local taxes, 2 of the 4 states to which Fredonians relocated the most in 2008 (MA and FL) had less tax burdens then Fredonia, and two (CT and NY) had higher taxes.

(195)

According to a study of human migration between New England and other parts of the country in 2003–2004, conducted by the New England Policy Center, all New England states lost population, particularly to Florida and the southeast, do to a variety of National and regional issues which did not include state tax burdens. [http://www.bos.frb.org/economic/neppc/dp/2006/neppcdp0601.pdf]

New Hampshire, (fifth lowest tax burden in the country and lowest in New England), is an instructive example. 8 New Hampshire counties share borders with eleven Vermont, Massachusetts and Maine counties, all with higher tax burdens. When contiguous counties across state lines are compared; no clear migration patterns are evident. Slightly more N.H. counties gained population, but they included both counties that do not border other states. If people simply chased lower taxes, there would have been more consistent migration into N.H. from neighboring counties in Massachusetts, Vermont and Maine. (196)

What I think is that with unemployment rates at persistently high levels, jobs probably explain more then tax burdens. All 4 of Fredonia's highest migration partners had lower unemployment statistics than our's, as did the entire country, with the occassional acception of Michigan. Sure enough, Massachusetts, with the lowest unemployment rate among the 4 states (more than 3% less than Fredonia's 10.1%), was the relocation target for the majority of leavers (4,732), but also the source of the majority of migration to Fredonia (3,927). Our 3 other leading migration trading partners had very similar unemployment rates (7% - 8%), and were abandoned for Fredonia by almost equal numbers of peoples (about 1,100 each).

But Florida is different. With a very low tax burden (47th), almost 3% less then Fredonia's, and a similar unemployment rate in comparison to N.Y. and CT, Florida experienced almost 50% more in-migration from Fredonia then those states. Why? Another friend of mine retired to Florida. He hates taxes, but brags that he's playing golf while we shovel, not that his tax burden has decreased. Maybe his golf partners' are members of the Fredonia Business Association.

Parenthetically, for these 4 states there is no correlation between tax burden and employment rates; challenging yet another anti-tax myth. (197)

In sum many factors contribute to the decision where to live. We all know individuals that make decisions that appear to support or refute a favorite theory, but policy decisions which effect all of us should not be made on the basis of episodic data or hunches. As much as the evidence is varied, it also clearly refutes tax burden as a major determinant of where people decide to live.

2008 Migration Patterns Involving R.I. and its Four Largest Migration Partners

	Moved into FA (from)	Moved out of FA (to)	Net change in FA	Tax Burden of each state	State unemployment rate in 2008
MA	3927	4732	−805	9.5% (23rd)	6.9%
FL	1133	1912	−779	7.4% (47th)	8.1%
NY	1123	1284	−161	11.7% (2nd)	7.0%
CT	1149	1269	−120	11.1% (3rd)	7.1%
FA Totals	7332	9197	−1865	10.2% (10th)	10.1%

Sources:
http://www.golocalprov.com/news/moving-out-of-ri-top-5-destination-states/
http://www.golocalprov.com/news/where-do-ri-immigrants-come-from-top-5-places/
http://www.taxfoundation.org/taxdata/show/478.html
http://www.bls.gov/news.release/archives/laus_01272009.pdf

CASE 26: CORRECTED VERSION:

Each number in the corrected version refers to an explanation below.

Is the Estate Tax a Factor in Migration Patterns Affecting Fredonia?
By Stan R. DeViashon, Professor of Social Work, Fredonia State College

A friend of mine ① recently retired, ② took his pension, and moved from Fredonia to a small town in a red state ③ where the police do not enforce marijuana laws very rigorously. Recreational pot is very important to him. Does this mean Fredonia should legalize drugs for personal use? Become a red state ④? How do we know that my friend is not more representative than ⑤ rich people who ⑥ supposedly left Fredonia because of our relatively high tax burden? Which scenario should inform state policy? The answer: neither.

The Fredonia Business Association commissioned a study that claimed to "prove" that the Fredonia estate tax causes out-migration, and loss of jobs ⑦ and tax revenue. Although ⑧ the assertion appears plausible ⑨, the data are ⑩ not there.

In 2008, the most recent year for which official statistics about migration among ⑪ the states are available, four ⑫ states accounted for a net loss of almost 2,000 former Fredonians: Massachusetts, Florida, New York and Connecticut. Besides ⑬ being the leading destinations for people leaving our state, all four ⑭ states were also highest as sources of migration into Fredonia ⑮. Migration occurs in all directions; ⑯ the business group study only counted people who ⑰ left, and not people who arrived.

cont.

EXPLANATIONS OF CORRECTIONS

1. We deleted the comma because it interrupted a clear thought.
2. Use a comma instead of semicolon between an independent clause and a phrase.
3. "Red state" is not a proper noun – no capital letters required.
4. See #3.
5. Homophone error: than and then—"than" is for comparisons; "then" refers to time. The contraction "isn't" has been corrected to "is not."
6. Use "who" because "who" takes a verb: "who supposedly left. . ."
7. No apostrophe because the sentence requires no possessive.
8. No comma required after "although" as an introductory phrase.
9. Spelling error.
10. "Data" is plural as in "the data are accurate."
11. Use "among" when comparing three or more items.
12. Always spell out numbers between one and ten.
13. No comma after a one-word sentence introduction.
14. Always spell out numbers between one and ten.
15. "Also" and "too" are redundant.
16. Use a semicolon when linking two independent clauses.
17. "Who" is the pronoun when you are referring to people; "that" is a pronoun for things.

cont.

Even if we limit our sights ⑱ to those who ⑲ left, ⑳ tax burden is almost irrelevant because ㉑ differences across the states ㉒ are not that great. ㉓ Fredonia's 2008 tax burden (10.2%) was less than ㉔ one ㉕ percent higher than the U.S. median of 9.4%. The 33 most tax-costly states all fall within a 2% range of tax burdens: 11.8% - 9.8%. Fredonia (number ten ㉖ in the U.S.) is on the low side of midrange of these 33 states. Given the array of factors that contribute to the decision to leave one state and move to another, a 1% or 2% decrease in tax burden is likely to pale ㉗ in comparison to considerations ㉘ like quality of life, nearness of family, jobs ㉙, schools ㉚, climate, access to health care and other necessities ㉛, total cost of living, and so on ㉜. Based on all state and local taxes, two ㉝ of the four ㉞ states to which Fredonians relocated the most in 2008 (MA and FL) had lower ㉟ tax burdens than ㊱ Fredonia, and two (CT and NY) had higher taxes.

According to a study of human migration between New England and other parts of the country in 2003–2004, conducted by the New England Policy Center, all New England states lost population, particularly to Florida and the Southeast ㊲, due ㊳ to a variety of national ㊴ and regional issues, ㊵ which did not include state tax burdens. [http://www.bos.frb.org/economic/neppc/dp/2006/neppcdp0601.pdf]

cont.

EXPLANATIONS OF CORRECTIONS

18. Homophone error: sight and site—"sight" refers to vision; "site" refers to a place.
19. Who is the correct pronoun when referring to people.
20. Use a comma between subordinate and independent clauses.
21. We deleted "of the fact that" because it is unnecessary verbiage.
22. No apostrophe because the sentence requires no possessive.
23. "Looking closely at Fredonia's data" is wordy and unnecessary verbiage.
24. Homophone error: than and then (see #5).
25. Always spell out numbers from one through ten.
26. Spell out both the word "number" and the numbers from one through ten. Also, "1%" or "one percent" is correct.
27. Homophone error: pail and pale—"pail" is a bucket; "pale" is colorless. Also, the colon is correct because an elaboration follows.
28. No apostrophe because the sentence requires no possessive.
29. No apostrophe because the sentence requires no possessive.
30. No apostrophe because the sentence requires no possessive.
31. No apostrophe because the sentence requires no possessive.
32. "Etc." and "and so on" are redundant.
33. Always spell out numbers from one through ten.
34. Always spell out numbers from one through ten.
35. Word choice is off here: "less" is appropriate for items with countable units of one; "tax burden" does not fit that category.
36. Homophone error: than and then (see #5).
37. "Southeast" is a region, not a direction, so it should be capitalized as a proper noun.
38. Homophone error: due and do—"due" refers to a deadline; "do" is a verb.
39. "National" is not a title or part of a proper noun.
40. Use a comma between independent clause and a phrase.

cont.

New Hampshire has the fifth lowest tax burden in the country and lowest in New England, which makes it an instructive example. Eight ④¹ New Hampshire counties share borders with eleven Vermont, Massachusetts and Maine counties, all with higher tax burdens than NH counties. When contiguous counties across state lines are compared, ④² no clear migration patterns are evident. Slightly more NH counties gained population, but they included both counties that do not border other states. If people simply chased lower taxes, there would have been more consistent migration into NH from neighboring counties in Massachusetts, Vermont and Maine.

④³ With unemployment rates at persistently high levels, jobs probably explain more than ④⁴ tax burdens. All four ④⁵ of Fredonia's highest migration partners had lower unemployment statistics than ours ④⁶, as did the entire country, with the occasional ④⁷ exception ④⁸ of Michigan. Sure enough, Massachusetts, with the lowest unemployment rate among the four ④⁹ states (more than 3% less than Fredonia's 10.1%), was the relocation target for the majority of leavers (4,732), but also the source of the majority of migration to Fredonia (3,927). Our three ⑤⁰ other leading migration trading partners had very similar unemployment rates (7% - 8%), and were abandoned for Fredonia by almost equal numbers of people ⑤¹ (about 1,100 each).

But Florida is different. With a very low tax burden (47th), almost 3% less then Fredonia's, and a similar unemployment rate in comparison to NY and CT, Florida experienced almost 50% more in-migration from Fredonia than ⑤² those states. Why? Another friend of mine retired to FL. He hates taxes, but brags that he's playing golf while we shovel, not that his tax burden has decreased. Maybe his golf partners ⑤³ are members of the Fredonia Business Association.

cont.

EXPLANATIONS OF CORRECTIONS

41. Always spell out numbers from one through ten.
42. Use a comma, not a semicolon, between subordinate and independent clauses.
43. We deleted unnecessary verbiage.
44. Homophone error: than and then (see #5).
45. Always spell out numbers from one through ten.
46. No apostrophe because the sentence requires no possessive.
47. Spelling error.
48. Spelling error.
49. Always spell out numbers from one through ten.
50. Always spell out numbers from one through ten.
51. "People" is the proper word – "peoples" means collections (multiple groups) of people.
52. Homophone error: than and then (see #5).
53. No apostrophe because the sentence requires no possessive.

cont.

Parenthetically, for these four ⑤④ states, ⑤⑤ there is no correlation between tax burden and employment rates, ⑤⑥ challenging ⑤⑦ another anti-tax myth.

In sum, ⑤⑧ many factors contribute to the decision where to live. We all know individuals who ⑤⑨ make decisions that appear to support or refute a favorite theory, but policy decisions that affect ⑥⓪ all of us should not be made on the basis of episodic data or hunches. As much as the evidence is varied, it also clearly refutes tax burden as a major determinant of where people decide to live.

EXPLANATIONS OF CORRECTIONS

54. Always spell out numbers from one through ten.

55. Use a comma after an introductory phrase.

56. Use a comma, not a semicolon, between independent clause and phrase.

57. "Yet" is unnecessary verbiage.

58. Use a comma after an introductory phrase.

59. "Who" is the pronoun for people, "that" for things.

60. Word choice is off here: affect and effect. Use "affect" as the verb form meaning to influence.

6

Grant Writing

In the best of times, social service agencies and organizations struggle to obtain sufficient resources to support their work. Just about every agency frequently, if not continually, experiences greater demand for its services than it can afford to deliver. Given these circumstances, social workers often must help find additional sources of funding to support an agency's work, which is why grant writing represents such an important professional activity.

Governmental agencies and large foundations often publish "Requests For Proposals" (RFPs), that announce the availability of grants or contracts. RFPs typically delineate the criteria for eligibility. For example, an RFP will solicit grant proposals from non-profit corporations, educational institutions, or religious organizations. An RFP will explain the dimensions of the grant, including the time period, the amount of funds available, and the application deadline. Finally, RFPs outline what the funding organization's expectations are regarding how your agency will spend the grant money, how to document results, the types of evaluation requirements the funding institution requires that serve to demonstrate whether your agency has produced the results you proposed, and other details. Sometimes a granting agency announces a "bidders' conference." A "bidder's conference" is a meeting—sometimes open, and sometimes by invitation or advance registration—at which the funding institution explains the grant's requirements and procedures. Sometimes bidder's conferences are conducted online or by conference call. Organizations that offer funds usually post appropriate forms on their websites. RFP grants tend to be competitive and substantial in size.

Funding organizations offer smaller grants as well—typically up to $50,000 per year—and criteria and procedures for applications may be as formal as described above, or informal to the point of no published procedures at all. Smaller grants come from government agencies, large or small foundations, religious organizations, family or special-interest foundations, or charities.

In this chapter, we will focus on smaller grants, which may be the type you most frequently encounter in social work practice. The larger grants usually come with their own instructions and forms. Because smaller grants usually require less formal applications, sometimes a simple but well-written descriptive narrative is sufficient. Effective grant writing represents a powerful skill for serving your agency, your clients, and your own professional development.

Grants of more than $10,000 usually require a "logic model," which is a document that explains the rationale for the proposed intervention your agency hopes to undertake, and how progress toward "outcomes"—positive results—will be measured. "Logic models" have six basic components:

- Inputs: Inputs represent your agency's funds and other financial resources, including cash and non-cash resources, other grant funds your agency may have already obtained, and other sources of an agency's overall financial status; some granting agencies like to see that their funding "leverages" other funds from other sources. In this way, an agency's proposed service agenda might be sustainable, and granting institutions would prefer to invest in an effective project that can be sustained until its mission is complete.
- Activities or interventions: "Activities or interventions" refers to the work your service agency will do with the grant money. This section should include a description of your "intervention plans." What is the problem you are seeking to address? How will you intervene? Ideally, what will your clients (or participants) experience as recipients of your agency's intervention?
- Outputs: "Outputs" refers to the total amount of agency time and agency resources necessary to effectively execute the work listed in the "activities or interventions" section. Be sure to indicate the cost of agency personnel in terms of hours spent on the project. For example, an after-school socialization and tutorial program will provide 150 hours of peer mentoring. Be sure to outline how those hours will be structured, who will be involved, and the cost of the personnel per hour of service. How much does one social worker cost per hour? How many weeks or months should you extend the 150 hours? Is this program ten hours a week, or forty? These are some of the questions you need to consider as you write your grant. A logic model outputs statement calculates the total people-hours of each kind of service involved in the intervention.
- Outcomes: "Outcomes" refers to what you believe will be the positive consequences of your agency's intervention should you receive the grant money and implement it successfully. What will your clients or participants learn? How will it change their lives for the better? Think of clients' cognition, skills, and behaviors that will change as a consequence of the intervention. Be clear and realistic, but also appropriately ambitious. Outline your vision:
  - Immediate results: What will your clients take-away from the intervention or activity within the first six months of participation?
  - Intermediate results: What do you believe will be the situation after six to eighteen months?
  - Long-range results: If you successfully implement your intervention and your participants actively engage with your services, what do you believe will be the results eighteen months to three or more years after your agency's intervention?
- Can you prove it? Can you prove with evidence that you will have succeeded? How will you prove it? Be sure to discuss how your agency will measure intervention "outcomes." Provide a short plan of how you will evaluate your efforts.

- To be persuasive you will need to organize your argument around a "theory of change," which means a concept that supports your claim about why the intervention of your agency will actually lead to the changes you claim.

This is a good outline to incorporate into a proposal for more than $10,000, even if this information is not requested explicitly. It is also the beginning of a good proposal for larger grants. Other information you should include in a short grant proposal is documentation of the community need, a description of your agency's expertise and legitimacy in terms of the interventions you seek to provide, and the identification and professional credentials of the "principal investigator" (PI), the person responsible for managing the grant. This indicates clearly whether your agency is fully behind your grant proposal. Your PI should have agency authority. Be sure to indicate the sustainability of the grant program after the funds expire, and include the legal tax status of your agency. Grant proposals should be complete, professionally written, and sufficiently detailed.

To identify organizations and institutions that offer grants of any size, begin by researching and locating the grant-funding foundations in your community. As tax-exempt organizations, foundations must be registered with their home state's tax-exempt-granting department—e.g., the state Department of Business Regulation. You may research by size, or by purpose, among other ways. Begin by using your agency contacts to access the people involved in the foundation. For example, you may find that someone on your agency's board of directors, or a community supporter of your agency, can help you contact the foundation's leadership. You may also want to partner with other agencies and write collaborative grant proposals, pooling resources and expertise. Collaborating is an excellent way to learn from more experienced or successful grant writers. If there is a social work educational program in your area (BSW and/or MSW), its field placement office may know of potential partners. Also, consider local social work faculty. Many of them may be available to help identify grant sources, and to participate in the grant writing process.

Here are some national web sites that may prove useful as sources of information about available grants.

- As of 2012: Catalog of Federal Domestic Assistance [https://www.cfda.gov/], which "contains detailed program descriptions for **2,167** Federal assistance programs."
- A Guide to Funding Resources: http://www.nal.usda.gov/ric/ricpubs/fundguide.html This site includes "links to searchable databases offering funding opportunities from government and/or private sources that are available to local governments, community organizations, and individuals. It provides web links to more than sixty full-text online guides, manuals, and tips to assist grant writers prepare successful proposals. The section of *"Additional Resources"* is a bibliographic listing of published grant writing resources and funding directories."
- http://www.grants.gov. is a "source to FIND and APPLY for federal grants. The U.S. Department of Health and Human Services is proud to be the managing partner for Grants.gov, an initiative that is having an unparalleled impact on the grant community."

- HHS Grants Forecast—http://www.acf.hhs.gov/hhsgrantsforecast/ is "a database of planned grant opportunities proposed by its <u>agencies</u>. Each Forecast record contains actual or estimated dates and funding levels for grants that the agency intends to award during the fiscal year. Forecast opportunities are subject to change based on enactment of congressional appropriations."
- Michigan State University Libraries http://staff.lib.msu.edu/harris23/grants/2socser.html is "a compilation of web pages and books of potential interest to nonprofit organizations seeking funding opportunities related to social services" in Michigan and nationwide.
- Rural Assistance Center http://www.raconline.org/info_guides/funding/grantwriting.php provides advice and listings of organizations who support activities and interventions aimed at people who live in rural areas.

FOUR GRANT APPLICATIONS

What follows are four grant applications of various sizes. They do not always represent the logic model as described above, possibly because the granters have that information, or do not need it. Regardless of how well you think you know a granting institution, it is always a good idea to compose a "logic model" and include it in the grant proposal. Numbers on the right side of the original documents note the page locations of the corresponding content in the corrected documents.

27 – Grant Application: Small Religious or Family Foundations
28 – Letter to a Private Foundation
29 – Letter Soliciting a Grant from a For-Profit Corporation
30 – Application for a New Grant from a State Department ($120,000)

CASE 27: GRANT APPLICATION: SMALL RELIGIOUS OR FAMILY FOUNDATIONS

This is an application for a $1,000 grant, written by a non-profit mental health advocacy organization—Mental Health Advocacy, Inc. of Fredonia (MHAFA). The mental health agency's target is a family foundation that has a history of supporting local, community-based mental health services. As you read it note how the writer has formatted the application as a letter, only a page-and a-half in length. The foundation is so small and local that it has no required forms. The foundation invites applicants to submit letters that explain how the grant money will be used. The following grant application represents an example of a successful proposal. An informal approach is appropriate for small foundations with informal application procedures. But always be sure! Never assume! In this case, the foundation awards grants that range from $500 to $10,000, and may be renewable. Research your local foundations: find out about their community interests, the methods they use to choose who to fund, their funding cycle and deadlines, and whom they have recently funded. As you prepare to write your grant proposal, try to make contact with the person who processes applications for the foundation.

Finally, experienced grant writers learn one important truth about this process: It may take a few years of unfunded proposals before a foundation or funding institution takes you on as their priority. It may take time to be recognized by them. Do not give up.

As your read the proposal, notice the outline it follows:

1) A brief introduction to the agency with an emphasis on the topic of the proposal—
2) The amount requested and what the money is for—
3) The legitimacy and expertise of the agency—
4) The agency's purpose or mission—
5) Current and recent agency activities that compliment the proposal's mission—
6) The agency's recent accomplishments—
7) How the money will be used—
8) What is the agency's tax-exempt status?

- Note how the proposal's format fulfills in its own way the requirements of the "logic model." The more you understand the "logic model" of your proposal, the easier it will be to write a less formal proposal letter like the one that follows.

For larger grant requests and for most RFPs, you will need to add a separate page that specifically outlines the proposal's budget along with a sentence or two identifying the "principal investigator" (PI), and measurable outcomes with due dates as discussed above.

There are 49 writing errors in this letter.

ORIGINAL VERSION

Mental Health Association of Fredonia (MHAFA)
1732 Route 2
Fenwick, FA 00055
June 3, 2009

Dee Pockets, Trustee
Good Intentions Trust
300 World Peace Street
Fenwick, FA 00055

Dear Mrs. Pockets, (206)

Mental Health Advocacy Inc. of Fredonia (MHAFA), supports an adequate and organized system of behavioral health care for children and they're families, which include early detection and treatment, and advocates for recovery-based systems of evidence-based health care, and accessibility to treatments and medications based on affectiveness rather then cost.

Please consider a grant allocation of $1000 for community outreach, support our mental health screening, stigma reduction, and improving our referral activities in Fenwick, FA.

MHAFA was foundated in 1916, as the Fredonia Assoc'n of Mental Hygiene, too help brake the chains of mental illness, and promote awareness of how fundamental mental health is to overall health and (207) well-being, thru the promotion of mental health, the prevention mental illness and working to improve the system of care for mental health thru advocacy, education, services and the dissemination of research.

To achieve this, we promote the intergration of behavioral health and general health, mental wellness and cultural and linguistic competency. MHAFA is commited to parity between mental health care and substance abuse treatment with general medical care in insurance coverage to insure affordability of treatment.

I am please to inform you that MHAFA is a founding member of the National Mental Health Advocacy League (now known as Mental Health League) and also the Fredonia statewide outreach partner of the National Center for Mental Health.

All funds raised will be used to promote our mission and help absorb the cost of all of our education events throughout the year; including informational and screening materials for distribution thru our speakers' bureau and thru our participation in health and community fairs as well. Each year we provide and send to community organization and colleges annual screening kits to help us provide Depression screenings in October, Eating Disorder screenings in February, Anxiety screenings in March, and Alcohol screenings in April.

(208)

As early identification and treatment provides the best opportunities for improved mental health and recovery we wish too increase this collaborative outreach in more settings, including primary healthcare.

Attached please find a copy of our IRS 501C3 charitable status statement, our most recent financial statement, a list of our Board of Directors, and a brochure describing all of our programs and services. Please contract me if you need any farther information or wish to discuss this request.

Thank you for you're kind and generous consideration.

Sincerely yours,

Shirley Hope

CASE 27: CORRECTED VERSION

Each number in the corrected version refers to an explanation below.

Dear Ms. ① Pockets,

Mental Health Advocacy Inc. of Fredonia (MHAFA) ② supports an adequate and organized system of behavioral health care for children and their ③ families, which includes ④ early detection and treatment. ⑤ MHAFA advocates for recovery-based systems of evidence-based health care, including ⑥ accessibility to treatment ⑦ and medication, ⑧ ⑨ based on effectiveness ⑩ rather than ⑪ cost.

Please consider a grant allocation of $1000 for community outreach, mental health screening, stigma reduction, and improvement of our referral activities in Fenwick, FA. ⑫

MHAFA was founded ⑬ in 1916, as the Fredonia Association ⑭ of Mental Hygiene, to ⑮ help break ⑯ the chains of mental illness, and to promote awareness

cont.

EXPLANATIONS OF CORRECTIONS

1. Ms. is the preferred title when addressing women.
2. We deleted the comma because the sentence did not require it.
3. Homophone error: their and they're—"their" is possessive; "they're" is the contraction of they are.
4. "Includes" refers to "system" and should be in the singular, e.g., *the system of behavioral care which includes . . .*
5. Run-on sentence corrected by creating two sentences.
6. Word choice for clarity: "Including" is more appropriate than "and" because the information that follows is a component of advocacy.
7. The word "treatment" should be singular because it refers to a broad category of care, rather than to specific treatments for multiple people.
8. "Medication" should be singular because it refers to a broad category of care, rather than to specific treatments for multiple people.
9. Always insert a comma between an independent clause and a dependent phrase.
10. "Affectiveness" is not a word. "Effectiveness" is a word.
11. Homophone error: than and then—use "than" to compare; "then" refers to time.
12. Use parallelism for style and clarity: note how all items in the list are now nouns.
13. "Foundated" is not a word.
14. "Association" rather than "assoc'n". In professional writing it is best to avoid abbreviations.
15. Homophone error: to and too—"too" means also or excessive.
16. Homophone error: break and brake—"break" means destroy or allowance, as in "give me a break"; to "brake" refers to stopping.

cont.

of mental health as fundamental for overall health and well-being ⑰.
⑱ MHAFA's activities include promoting mental health, preventing ⑲
mental illness and working to improve the system of care for mental health,
⑳ through ㉑ advocacy, education, services and ㉒ dissemination of research.

To achieve this, we promote the integration ㉓ of behavioral health and
general health, mental wellness and cultural and linguistic competency.
MHAFA is committed ㉔ to parity between mental health care and substance
abuse treatment, ㉕ with general medical care in insurance coverage to ensure ㉖
affordability of treatment.

㉗ MHAFA is a founding member of the National Mental Health
Advocacy League (now known as Mental Health League) and ㉘
statewide outreach partner of the National Center for Mental Health,
representing Fredonia ㉙.

The grant will support our education events throughout
the year ㉚, ㉛ including informational and screening
materials for distribution through ㉜ our speakers' bureau and
㉝ our participation in health and community fairs ㉞.
Each year we provide annual screening kits ㉟ ㊱ to
community organizations ㊲ and colleges, ㊳ for depression

cont.

EXPLANATIONS OF CORRECTIONS

17. We simplified the prose style.
18. Run-on sentence corrected by creating two sentences.
19. Use parallelism for style and clarity: not how all items on the list are now led by gerunds—"ing" verbs that become nouns.
20. Always use a comma to link an independent clause and dependent phrase.
21. "Thru" is not a word.
22. We deleted "the" because the sentence does not require it.
23. Spelling error.
24. Spelling error.
25. Always use a comma to link an independent clause and a dependent phrase.
26. Word usage: "ensure" means guarantee; "insure" refers to insurance.
27. Unnecessary verbiage.
28. "And" and "also" are redundant.
29. Use parallelism for style and clarity: "Founding partner" and "statewide out-

reach partner" now clearly represent the two roles played by MHSFA, with "representing Fredonia" at the end of the sentence, for clarity.
30. Unnecessary verbiage.
31. Use a comma, not a semicolon, because the next statement is not a complete sentence.
32. "Thru" is not a word.
33. "Thru" is not a word; "through" is unnecessary because this phrase refers back to the previous "through."
34. "As well" is redundant with "and."
35. Misplaced modifiers make a sentence harder to understand: "the kits" should be placed as close as possible to "provide" for clarity.
36. "And send" is redundant with "provide."
37. Syntax: we made all items in the sentence consistently plural.
38. "To help us" is unnecessary; the kits are <u>for</u> the screenings.

cont.

③⑨ screenings in October, eating disorder ④⓪ screenings in February,
anxiety ④① screenings in March, and alcohol ④② screenings in April.

As early identification and treatment provides the best opportunity
④③ for improved mental health and recovery, ④④ we wish to ④⑤ increase
this collaborative outreach in more settings, including primary healthcare.

Attached please find a copy of our IRS 501C3 charitable status statement,
our most recent financial statement, a list of our Board of Directors, and a
brochure describing all of our programs and services. Please contact ④⑥ me
if you need any further ④⑦ information or wish to discuss this request.

Thank you for your ④⑧ ④⑨ consideration.

Sincerely yours,

Shirley Hope

EXPLANATIONS OF CORRECTIONS

39. No capital letter required: items 39–42 are not proper nouns.

40. No capital letter required because it is not a proper noun.

41. No capital letter required because it is not a proper noun.

42. No capital letter required because it is not a proper noun.

43. Use the singular form here.

44. A comma belongs after the introductory phrase.

45. Homophone error: to and too (see #15).

46. Word usage: contact and contract.

47. Word usage: "further" rather than "farther."

48. Homophone error: your and you're— "your" is possessive; "you're" is the contracted form of "you are."

49. Unnecessary verbiage.

CASE 28: LETTER TO A PRIVATE FOUNDATION

The following letter comes from a non-profit organization, asking a private foundation for $165,000. There are 60 writing errors in this letter.

ORIGINAL VERSION

June 16, 2011   (212)
The Fredonia Cares Foundation
1 We Love FA Lane
Fenwick, FA, 00050

ATTN: Joda Mann, Executive Director

Dear Mrs. Mann:

By this letter, the Fredonia Parent Resource Network, Inc. ("FAPRN") seeks a Twenty-two Thousand Dollar grant from The Fredonia Cares Foundation for FAPRN's Fantasy State Kids Coalition Technology Access Project (" FS Kids Tech Access Project") targeted too families with kids with disabilities. A copy of FAPRNs' letter of tax exempt status, and project budget, is attached for you're records.

FAPRN is Fredonia's designated statewide Parent Information and Training Center on Disabilities. FAPRN's mission is to assist parents to be "there children's first and best teacher and advocate." The information, education and support delivered to families' each day is intended to empower parents' to seek the best possible outcomes for their child(ren). For families who are largely housebound due to the chronic illness or the significant physical disability of their child, the Internet is a vital connection to the outside world.

Thru our pilot technology access project, FAPRN has identified the   (213)
Computer as a tool to foster family's knowledge of their childrens' abilities and special health and educational needs and too enable them to better advocate for their children. Through FSKids families with kids with disabilities can receive computers and computer training, thereby, giving them access to educational and medical information and resources, assisting them to better communicate with educational and health professionals; and allowing them to participate in web-based support networks which may otherwise be unavailable or inaccessible due to the rarity of a child's condition or the geographic or socio-economic limitations on the family.

Why not seek donations of used equipment? Previously owned computer equipment is a mixed blessing. While it seems easy to receive used equipment to pass along to families who could not otherwise afford a computer, the reality of this transfer becomes burdensome when current software does not run with existing operating systems, or they're exists a RAM deficiency or modem equipment is incompatible for some reason. The expense of diagnostics and upgrades quickly becomes a liability that our agency and the family cannot afford to support. To solve this problem, FAPRN located a supplier of reconditioned computer equipment in New York City that can easily provide our FSKids' families with affordable PC's that work, right out of the box. Parents' come to training sessions to receive there computers and to learn how to operate the equipment and access the internet. Respite care is provided during training sessions, as many parents would otherwise not be able to leave home.

(214)

Already, FAPRN has been able to purchase and distribute 15 computers to families in Fredonia. One mother with two sons, one of whom spends 22 hours a day in traction, received a computer threw FAPRN's FSKids project. She attributes the following benefits to her family as result of having a computer and access to the internet:

- The mother has become a true partner with her son's medical team as the information she has searched and downloaded from the web has increased her knowledge about her son's rare condition.
- The mother has developed new email contacts with individuals and organizations that provide her with information and support specifically around her son's condition.
- Both of her son's have improved their computer skills attracting praise from their teachers.
- And the mother has developed her computer skills to an extent that will be attractive to a future employer when she is able to return to work.

The goals for the project and the direct benefits to families are confirmed by this feedback. We intend that all families participating in this program to be empowered in this way.

The projected first year total budget for the OSKids Tech Access Project is One Hundred Sixty-five Thousand Dollars; of this, approximately Seventy-one Thousand Dollars will support the efforts targeted to families with kids with disabilities.

(215)

The Fredonia Department of Health (DOH) is funding the FSKids Project through September 30, 2011. DOH has offered approximately $20,000–25,000 of continued support through June 30, 2012, so long as matching funds are identified. Two local foundations have commited to supporting the Project. Grant applications are pending before 3 other foundations. Additional grant applications will be submitted over the next 6 months. The requested amount of Twenty-two Thousand Dollars from Fredonia

Care Foundation will provide computers and 2 levels of computer training; including respite care for the children during training sessions, to 30 families from October 2011– June 2012.

On behalf of FAPRN and the Fantasy State Kids Coalition Technology Access Project, we thank you for your consideration of this request and urge you to support the Project. For additional information or to communicate about the request, please contact Justin Caise, Associate Director.

Justin Caise
Associate Director

CASE 28: CORRECTED VERSION

Each number in the corrected version refers to an explanation below.

June 16, 2011
The Fredonia Cares Foundation
1 We Love FA Lane
Fenwick, FA, 00050

ATTN: Joda Mann, Executive Director

Dear Ms. ① Mann:

② The Fredonia Parent Resource Network, Inc. ("FAPRN") seeks a ③ grant from The Fredonia Cares Foundation for FAPRN's Fantasy State Kids Coalition Technology Access Project ("FS Kids Tech Access Project"), ④ targeted to ⑤ families with kids with disabilities. Copies ⑥ of FAPRNs' letter of tax exempt status ⑦ and project budget ⑧ are ⑨ attached for your ⑩ records.

FAPRN is Fredonia's designated statewide Parent Information and Training Center on Disabilities. FAPRN's mission is to assist parents to be "their ⑪ children's first and best teacher and advocate." The information, education and support delivered to families ⑫ each day is intended to empower parents ⑬ to seek the best possible outcomes for their child(ren). For families that ⑭ are largely housebound due to the chronic illness or the significant physical disability of their child, the Internet is a vital connection to the outside world.

cont.

EXPLANATIONS OF CORRECTIONS

1. Avoid Mrs. and Miss. Use Ms.
2. Unnecessary verbiage.
3. The amount of the grant is not the title of the grant.
4. Use a comma between an independent clause and a phrase.
5. Homophone error: to and too—"too" means also or excessive.
6. Use the plural form consistently here—there are copies of two items.
7. We deleted the comma because there is no reason for it.
8. We deleted the comma because there is no reason for it.

9. Verb and noun agreement: We used the plural verb form "are" because the noun is plural.
10. Homophone error: your and you're—"your" is possessive; "you're" is the contracted form of you are.
11. Homophone error: their and there—"their" is possessive; "there" refers to place.
12. No apostrophe because the possessive is unnecessary.
13. No apostrophe because the possessive is unnecessary.
14. "Family" is an object, not a person; use "that" as the pronoun for referring to things.

cont.

Through ⑮ our pilot technology access project, FAPRN has identified the computer ⑯ as a tool to foster families' ⑰ knowledge of their children's ⑱ abilities and special health and educational needs, ⑲ and to ⑳ enable them to advocate effectively ㉑ for their children. Through FSKids, ㉒ families with kids with disabilities can receive computers and computer training, thereby ㉓ giving them access to educational and medical information and resources, assisting them to communicate better ㉔ with educational and health professionals, ㉕ and allowing them to participate in web-based support networks which may otherwise be unavailable or inaccessible due to the rarity of a child's condition or the geographic or socio-economic limitations on the family.

Why not seek donations of used equipment? Previously-owned ㉖ computer equipment is a mixed blessing. While it seems easy to receive used equipment to pass along to families that ㉗ could not otherwise afford a computer, the reality ㉘ becomes evident ㉙ when contributed ㉚ software does not run with existing operating systems, or there ㉛ exists a RAM deficiency, ㉜ or modem equipment is incompatible ㉝. The expense of diagnostics and upgrades is ㉞ a prohibitive liability for our agency and the family ㉟. To solve this problem, FAPRN located a supplier of reconditioned computer equipment in New York City that can easily provide our FSKids' families with affordable PCs ㊱ that work, right out of the box. Parents ㊱ come to training sessions to receive their ㊲ computers

cont.

EXPLANATIONS OF CORRECTIONS

15. "Thru" is not a word.
16. "Computer" is not a proper noun. Do not capitalize the word.
17. We used the plural possessive for consistency and clarity.
18. We used the plural possessive for consistency and clarity.
19. Always use a comma between an independent clause and dependent phrase.
20. Homophone error: to and too (see #5).
21. The word "better" split the infinitive of the verb, "to advocate"; "effectively" is more appropriate language in this case.
22. Usually a two-word introductory phrase would not need a comma, but a pause is needed for clarity in this case.
23. We deleted the comma because the sentence does not require it.
24. Again we relocated "better" because it split the infinitive, "to communicate."
25. This is a long sentence, and though it is grammatically correct, it may be advisable to split it into two or three simpler sentences.
26. Use hyphenation when two words are combined to form a one-idea modifier.
27. "Family" is an object, not a person; use "that" as the pronoun for referring to things.
28. Unnecessary verbiage.
29. Word choice is off here. We used a more appropriate word. #29–31 and 33–34 are all vocabulary issues.
30. Word choice is off here. We used a more appropriate word.
31. Word choice is off here. We used a more appropriate word.
32. Use a comma to separate phrases.
33. Unnecessary verbiage.
34. Unnecessary verbiage.
35. We simplified the language for brief, more direct wording.
36. No apostrophe because no possessive necessary here.
37. Homophone error: their and there (see #11).

cont.

and ㊳ learn how to operate the equipment and access the Internet ㊴. Respite care is provided during training sessions, as many parents otherwise ㊵ would not be able to leave home.

Already ㊶ FAPRN has been able to purchase and distribute 15 computers to families in Fredonia. One mother with two sons, one of whom spends 22 hours a day in traction, received a computer through ㊷ FAPRN's FSKids project. She attributes the following benefits to her family as result of having a computer and access to the internet:

- The mother has become a true partner with her son's medical team, as the information she has searched and downloaded from the web has increased her knowledge about her son's rare condition; ㊸
- she ㊹ has developed new email contacts with individuals and organizations that provide her with information and support specifically around her son's condition;
- both ㊺ of her sons ㊻ have improved their computer skills, ㊼ attracting praise from their teachers;
- and ㊽ the mother has developed her computer skills to an extent that will be attractive to a future employer when she is able to return to work.

This feedback confirms the goals for the project and the direct benefits to families ㊾. We intend ㊿ all families participating in this program to be empowered (51) this way.

cont.

EXPLANATIONS OF CORRECTIONS

38. We deleted "to" because it is not necessary.
39. "Internet" is a proper noun in this case.
40. Avoid misplacing modifiers: I moved "otherwise" to modify 'would not be able' for clarity.
41. Comma is unnecessary after a one-word introduction.
42. Homophone error: through and threw—"threw" is hurled or propelled; "through" is over or transgressed.
43. Semicolons are appropriate here and with all the bulleted items because each is an independent clause within one sentence that extends an introductory independent clause: "She attributes the following benefits to her family as result of having a computer and access to the internet."
44. No capital letters because each clause is a continuation of the sentence; "she" is a pronoun for "the mother."
45. No capital letter because each clause is a continuation of the sentence.
46. No apostrophe because no possessive is required.
47. Always use a comma between an independent clause and dependent phrase.
48. No capital letter because each clause is a continuation of the sentence.
49. We corrected the passive voice and made it active: now the "feedback confirms."
50. We deleted the "that" because it is not necessary.
51. "In" is not necessary.

cont.

The projected first year total budget for the OSKids Tech Access Project is $165,000 ⑤②. ⑤③ Of this, approximately $71,000 ⑤④ will support the efforts targeted to families with kids with disabilities.

The Fredonia Department of Health (DOH) is funding the FSKids Project through September 30, 2011. DOH has offered approximately $20,000–25,000 of continued support through June 30, 2012, so long as matching funds are identified. Two local foundations have committed ⑤⑤ to supporting the Project. Grant applications are pending before three ⑤⑥ other foundations. Additional grant applications will be submitted over the next six ⑤⑦ months. The requested amount of $22,000 ⑤⑧ from Fredonia Care Foundation will provide computers and two ⑤⑨ levels of computer training, ⑥⓪ including respite care for the children during training sessions, to 30 families from October 2011– June 2012.

On behalf of FAPRN and the Fantasy State Kids Coalition Technology Access Project, we thank you for your consideration of this request and urge you to support the Project. For additional information or to communicate about the request, please contact Justin Caise, Associate Director.

Justin Caise
Associate Director

EXPLANATIONS OF CORRECTIONS

52. Use numerals to indicate numbers larger than ten.

53. We separated sentences for simplicity and clarity.

54. Use numerals to indicate numbers larger than ten.

55. Spelling error.

56. Always spell out numbers from one through ten.

57. Always spell out numbers from one through ten.

58. Use numerals to indicate numbers larger than ten.

59. Always spell out numbers from one through ten.

60. Use a comma between an independent clause and a dependent phrase.

CASE 29: LETTER SOLICITING A GRANT FROM A FOR-PROFIT CORPORATION

*This is an unsolicited letter to a locally-based corporation with a
philanthropic tradition. There are 42 writing errors in this letter.*

ORIGINAL VERSION

July 25, 2011   (218)
Miss Inda Mand
Director of Community Relations
Ron-En Manufacturing, Inc.
1 Ron-En Way
West Fenwick, FA 00001

Dear Miss Mand:

I am writing this letter is to express interest in being considered for one of
Ron-En's annual grants to non-profit agency's which do not receive public
funding, but who work to benefit woman in Fredonia.

The Fredonia Parent Resource Network (FAPRN) is a statewide 501 (c)
(3) organization that was started in 1990 by parents and professionals
eager to provide information, training and support to families of children
with disabilities and chronic health problems. Today it is our mission to
empower *all* families in Fredonia to become there childs' best advocate.
Our philosophy is that when parent's have the knowledge, contacts
and communication skills necessary to put the appropriate health and
educational services in place for their child, not only does the child's
situation improve, but the whole family benefits. As you might expect, the
majority of parents seeking assistance from our agency are women.

FAPRN relies on state and federal grants and the donations of individuals   (219)
and corporations like Ron-En to offer a myriad of programs and
information services to all families with children in Fredonia.
Currently we have a very limited source of unrestricted funding and as part
of a strategic planning process have created a long-term development
plan to address this issue. At this time, your generous donation would help
us to expand our outreach efforts and ultimately reach more women and
children in underserved communities in Fredonia.

Each year, FAPRN offers dozens of free workshops and training sessions
to families and professionals at various locations throughout the state. We
strive to make our workshops and training sessions culturally sensitive,
inclusive and accessible. Topics include but are not limited to: literacy,
school readiness, successful home-school partnerships, early intervention,
coping with disabilities, transition planning, special education, effective

parenting, positive discipline, communication skills, stress management, and violence prevention.

We also have a toll-free line in Fredonia so that families can reach a knowledgeable FAPRN staff during the week to ask questions, and receive guidance, information, referrals and their children can benefit. FAPRN Program Directors' and Training Coordinators' teach schoolteachers, medical professionals and social service personal how to work more affectively with families' of children with disabilities and health issues regularly. To date we have twelve FAPRN Parent Consultants located at social service agencies and family health centers thru-out the state were they assist parents' with advocating for their child's special needs. Our staffs also sit on many regional, state and national health, education and child welfare committee's to represent and voice the needs and interests of the families we serve so they can achieve their full potential. Our mission is to help Fredonia parents best advocate for their children, and influence family-centered systems change at the state and national level.

(220)

In behalf of the Fredonia Parent Resource Network, I wish to thank you very much for considering a donation of any size to our organization. Every little drop helps. By doing so, Ron-En, Inc. and it's employees can feel pride in helping to empower families' in Fredonia to seek the best possible outcomes for *all* children, including those with special needs.

Sincerely,

Justin Caise,
Associate Director

Enclosures: FAPRN Brochure, Newsletter and Workshop Catalog

CASE 29: CORRECTED VERSION

Each number in the corrected version refers to an explanation below.

July 25, 2011
Ms. ① Inda Mand
Director of Community Relations
Ron-En Manufacturing, Inc.
1 Ron-En Way
West Fenwick, FA 00001

Dear Ms. ② Mand:

The Fredonia Parent Resource Network (FAPRN) ③ wishes to be considered for one of Ron-En's annual grants to non-profit agencies ④ that ⑤ do not receive public funding, but ⑥ work to benefit women ⑦ in Fredonia.

The Fredonia Parent Resource Network (FAPRN) is a statewide 501 (c) (3) organization that was started in 1990 by parents and professionals eager to provide information, training and support to families of children with disabilities and chronic health problems. Our ⑧ mission is to empower *all* families in Fredonia to become their ⑨ children's ⑩ best advocates ⑪. Our philosophy is that when parents ⑫ have the knowledge, contacts and communication skills necessary to put the appropriate health and educational services in place for their children ⑬, the child's situation improves and the whole family benefits ⑭. As you might expect, the majority of parents seeking assistance from our agency are [see corrections note 13] women.

cont.

EXPLANATIONS OF CORRECTIONS

1. Avoid Miss and Mrs.; Ms. is the correct professional address for women.
2. See # 1.
3. Unnecessary verbiage.
4. No apostrophe because no possessive required.
5. That, not which, because "do not receive public funding" is essential for the sentence's meaning.
6. We deleted "who" because the sentence does not require it.
7. Use the plural consistently. The plural in this case is "women."

8. We corrected the passive voice and made it active.
9. Homophone error: their and there—"their" is possessive; "there" refers to place.
10. We used the plural possessive here because the sentence refers to many families, parents, and children.
11. We used the plural for clarity and consistency.
12. No apostrophe because no possessive required.
13. Plural – see #10.
14. Avoid the awkward construction of "not only but." It threatens the clarity of the sentence.

cont.

FAPRN relies on state and federal grants and the donations of
individuals and corporations like Ron-En to offer a myriad of
programs and information services to all families with children in Fredonia.
⑮ Those who provide grant money limit our unrestricted funding; ⑯,
⑰ your generous donation would help us to expand
our outreach efforts and ultimately reach more women and
children in underserved communities in Fredonia.

Each year ⑱ FAPRN offers dozens of free workshops and training sessions
to families and professionals at various locations throughout the state.
We strive to make our workshops and training sessions culturally sensitive,
inclusive and accessible. Topics include but are not limited to: literacy,
school readiness, successful home-school partnerships, early intervention,
coping with disabilities, transition planning, special education, effective
parenting, positive discipline, communication skills, stress management,
and violence prevention.

We also have a toll-free line in Fredonia so that families can reach a
knowledgeable FAPRN staff member ⑲ during the week to ask questions,
and receive guidance, information, and referrals ⑳. FAPRN
program directors ㉑ and training coordinators ㉒ regularly ㉓ teach
schoolteachers, medical professionals and social service personnel ㉔ how to work more
effectively ㉕ with families ㉖ of children with disabilities and health issues. ㉗
Twelve FAPRN Parent Consultants are located at social service agencies
and family health centers throughout ㉘ the state, where ㉙ they assist parents

cont.

EXPLANATIONS OF CORRECTIONS

15. We deleted "currently" because it is unnecessary.
16. We corrected the passive voice so it is clear who limits the funding.
17. We simplified the language to avoid unnecessary verbiage and information; we used a semicolon to connect two related independent clauses.
18. The comma was unnecessary.
19. An individual is a staff member, not a staff; a group of workers comprise the collective group known as "staff."
20. We deleted "and their children can benefit" because it is not parallel construction with the other phrases in the list; it also adds no important information.
21. We deleted the capital letters because they are not proper nouns; also, no apostrophe because no possessive required.

22. See #21.
23. Avoid misplacing the modifier. Relocate so the modifier is close the noun it modifies, for clarity.
24. Word usage: personnel and personal—"personnel" usually refers to employees; "personal" is usually a privacy or individual issue.
25. Word usage: effectively and affectively—"effectively" refers to influence of one factor on another; "affectively" refers to direct influence.
26. No apostrophe because no possessive required.
27. We simplified the language to avoid unnecessary verbiage and for clarity.
28. "Thru-out" is not a word.
29. Word choice is off here: where and were—"where" refers to place; "were" is the past of to be.

cont.

(30) with advocating for their children's (31) special needs. Our staff
members (32) also sit on many regional, state and national health, education and
child welfare committees (33) to represent and voice the needs and interests
of the families we serve (34). Our mission is to help Fredonia parents
best advocate for their children, and influence family-centered systems
change at the state and national levels (35).

On (36) behalf of the Fredonia Parent Resource Network, (37) thank you (38)
for considering a donation (39) to our organization. (40)
By doing so, Ron-En, Inc. and its (41) employees can feel pride in
helping to empower families (42) in Fredonia to seek the best possible
outcomes for *all* children, including those with special needs.

Sincerely,

Justin Caise,
Associate Director

Enclosures: FAPRN Brochure, Newsletter and Workshop Catalog

EXPLANATIONS OF CORRECTIONS

30. No apostrophe because no possessive required.

31. We used the plural consistently for clarity.

32. Use "staff members" and "are" for plural, or "staff" and "is" for singular, but not never use "staffs."

33. No apostrophe because no possessive required.

34. We simplified the language to avoid unnecessary verbiage.

35. We used the plural consistently for clarity–use "state and national levels."

36. Word choice is off here: "on behalf," not "in behalf."

37. Unnecessary verbiage.

38. See #37.

39. See #37.

40. See #37

41. Homophone error: use "its" to indicate possession. Use "it's" as the contraction of "it is."

42. No apostrophe because no possessive required.

CASE 30: APPLICATION FOR A NEW GRANT FROM A STATE DEPARTMENT ($120,000)

In the following case, the state mental health department director invited the Mental Health Association of Fredonia to submit a proposal for a grant to provide communications and public information about mental health and substance abuse. No other agency has the expertise or structure to provide the services in question. The state department director does not require a logic model because the state department director has a positive history with the agency, and already knows that the agency has the expertise to deliver the program. The agency has an "inside track" on the grant process. This situation happens occasionally, especially if discretionary monies are involved, which require a less formal and sometimes a more personal process. There are 86 writing errors in this proposal and letter.

ORIGINAL VERSION

Mental Health Association of Fredonia (MHAFA)   (225)
1732 Route 2
Fenwick, FA 00055
April 13, 2009

Dr. Grant Givins, M.D., Director
Fredonia Department of Mental Health
31428 Pine St.
Fenwick, Fredonia 00227

Dear Dr. Director Givins,

Unfortunately, I am sorry I was still in transit from a conference in California when you met with the MHAFA staffs about a joint communication program; and requested a proposal for a Constituencies Enrichment project. In behalf of my board and staffs, we all appreciate the opportunity to apply for this knew initiative.

I'd appreciate it if you would please consider this enclosed draft document and give me a feedback on this version of a proposal.

I look foward to your feedback and thank you again for considering us.

Sincerely,

Shirley Hope
Executive Director

Strategies for Constituencies Understanding of the Continuums of Mental Health and Illness and the Roles of Recovery and Stigma Reduction therein

(226)

The many systemic changes eminating from the recent reorganization of state mental health services provide opportunities not only for public education about preserving mental health, but also early detection, diagnosis and treatment of mental illness and substance abuse, and our agency is perfectly qualified.

Such education would include: the concerns about cormorbidity with chronic physical illness and decreased life expectancy, related to this and delayed treatment. Biologic and environmental contributions to the causes of mental illness will be explained including the role of trauma. While their is widespread belief that mental illness is chronic, symptom relief is possible for many and, according to the National Institute of Mental Heath (NIMH), overall 60% of the severely mentally ill can get better. Preventative measures such as stress reduction have a role in helping those in recovery as well as individuals at risk for developing illnesses.

(227)

The Mental Heath Association of Fredonia (MHAFA) is in a very unique position to bring education programs to individuals' and there families' thru community settings, such as community action centers and health centers, organizations organizing and promoting the well-being of FA's minority populations, and labor business/organizations. We would also pay particular attention to homeless populations and coordinate our outpatient and crises intervention programs to help expedite SSI and thus Medicaid eligibility for this population. This broad outreach will provide information about access and reduce stigma thru normalizing mental health services in relation to primary healthcare.

We would utilize our status as the state's designated "Wellness Campaign" and our role as the Outreach Partner sharing latest research findings from the National Institute of Mental Health too develop up to date resources that appeal to and are comprehendible to a broad public. This will require special attention and material for linguistic minorities.

To maximize the impact of presentations; their will be collateral print and web materials as well as a radio and local print media campaign. Workplace and other community settings are ideal for short talks and presentations. Follow up in efficient low cost communication should reinforce new learning about mental health and recovery. MHAFA has access too the research data and can develop a statewide plan for this outreach and education strategically. These presentations would combine the general material about mental health and primary care with information about community mental health programs. This will improve access into the mental health system not only for those with medical insurance, but those without insurance too. Information about changes in Medicaid funded services will be included. (228)

Work Plan

July – August 2009
>
> Higher staffs and mete with providers.
> Develope presentations and evaluation format's.
> Schedule Fall groups.

September – December
>
> Minimum of 35 in person presentations. Settings to include an average of 15 persons per presentation targeting all counties, at least 2 presentations in Spanish speaking community and at least 1 each in Southeast Asian and Liberian community settings. Also include range of audiences to include youth, elderly, caretakers, primary care physicians as well as individuals currently receiving services and there families.

December
>
> Review evaluations and "tweak" presentations. Schedule Spring presentations.

January – June 2010
>
> Minimum of 60 in person presentations. Sea above description.
> Staffs will review progress with designated MHRH representatives monthly.

The Evaluation Plan (229)

We will develop and evaluation plan with outside evaluator to help us determine whether our educative goals' are met or not; and to inform revisions in this plan of course. We are looking not only for both concrete learning about the mental health-mental illness continuum but also access services, and stigma reduction.

In June 2010, presentation and scheduling targets will be established, based on year 1 experience.

Annual Budget

1. Education/Communications Specialist to develop materials and present in person on radio/cable and TV news.	1 FTE*	$ 65,000
2. Communications Assistant Scheduling, E-list, updates, Web materials, E-newsletter	.5FTE*	$ 25,000
3. Postage, telephone, office supplies		$ 4,500
4. Printing		$ 1,400
5. Equipment		$ 1,700
6. In-state mileage		$ 2,400
7. Evaluation		$ 10,000
8. Admin Fee		$ 10,000
		$120,000

*FTE: full-time equivalent staff position

CASE 30: CORRECTED VERSION

Each number in the corrected version refers to an explanation below.

Mental Health Association of Fredonia (MHAFA)
1732 Route 2
Fenwick, FA 00055
April 13, 2009

① Grant Givins, M.D., Director
Fredonia Department of Mental Health
31428 Pine St.
Fenwick, Fredonia 00227

Dear ② Director Givins,

③ I am sorry I was still in transit from a conference in California when you met with the MHAFA staff ④ about a joint communication program, ⑤ and requested a proposal for a Constituencies Enrichment project. On ⑥ behalf of my board and staff ⑦, we ⑧ appreciate the opportunity to apply for this new ⑨ initiative.

⑩ Please consider the ⑪ enclosed draft document and share your feedback with me ⑫.

I look forward ⑬ to your feedback and thank you again for considering us.

Sincerely,

Shirley Hope
Executive Director

cont.

EXPLANATIONS OF CORRECTIONS

1. Avoid double honorifics: either "Dr." or "M.D.," but not both.
2. See #1.
3. Avoid unnecessary verbosity.
4. "Staff" is singular. The verb should be singular for verb and noun agreement.
5. Use a comma, not a semicolon, between an independent clause and a dependent phrase.
6. Word choice is off here: use "on" behalf.
7. "Staff" is singular. See #4.
8. "All" is redundant with "on behalf" and the following list.
9. Homophone error: new and knew—"new" is unused; "knew" is the past of know.
10. Unnecessary verbiage.
11. Word usage: use "the" as a general article, rather than "this."
12. We avoided unnecessary verbiage and used more direct language for clarity.
13. Spelling error.

cont.

Strategies for Constituencies' ⑭ Understanding of the Continuums of Mental Health and Illness and the Roles of Recovery and Stigma Reduction Therein ⑮

The many systemic changes emanating ⑯ from the recent reorganization of state mental health services provide opportunities for public education about preserving mental health, early detection, diagnosis, and treatment of mental illness and substance abuse ⑰. Our agency is perfectly qualified ⑱.

Such education would include ⑲ the concerns about comorbidity ⑳ with chronic physical illness and decreased life expectancy, related to ㉑ delayed treatment. The program will provide information about trauma and biologic and environmental contributions to the causes of mental illness ㉒.

㉓ By normalizing mental health services in relation to primary healthcare, our outpatient and crises intervention programs will help expedite SSI and thus Medicaid eligibility for the state's homeless population. This approach provides information about access and reduces stigma.

There ㉔ ㉕ is widespread belief that mental illness is chronic, symptom relief is possible ㉖ and, according to the National Institute of Mental Health ㉗ (NIMH), ㉘ 60% of the severely mentally ill can

cont.

EXPLANATIONS OF CORRECTIONS

14. We inserted an apostrophe to indicate the possessive: the constituencies possess their *understandings—use constituencies' as the plural possessive form.*

15. "Therein" should be capitalized as part of the title of the grant.

16. Spelling error.

17. Unnecessary verbiage.

18. We created a separate sentence in order to avoid a parallelism error: "Our agency is qualified" is not parallel with the objectives of the grant as they are listed in the original version.

19. No colon because no list follows and the subsequent information is not an elaboration or explanation of the previous statement.

20. Spelling error.

21. "This and" confuses the sentence and adds no information; the main point of the sentence is delayed treatment because of limited knowledge.

22. We corrected the passive voice and misplaced modifier; also, the word "biologic" is acceptable, but some prefer "biological."

23. We repositioned this paragraph because it was misplaced. It describes the work under the grant, but was placed in a discussion about MHAPA's credentials. It belongs with information about the work covered by the grant. We also simplified the language to avoid unnecessary verbiage and corrected a misplaced modifier—*normalizing mental health services. . . .*

24. "While" creates an incomplete sentence and convolutes the meaning; we delete "while" and suggest a clearer resolution of the sentence: *according to mental health professionals, mental illness is chronic, symptom relief is possible and, according to the National Institute of Mental Health (NIMH), 60% of the severely mentally ill can improve.*

25. Homophone error: there and their—"there" refers to place; "their" is possessive.

26. "For many" is unnecessary.

27. Spelling error.

28. "Overall" is redundant with "60%."

cont.

achieve recovery ㉙. Individuals in recovery and who are at risk for developing illnesses can benefit from preventative measures such as stress reduction ㉚.

The Mental Health ㉛ Association of Fredonia (MHAFA) is in a ㉜ unique position to bring education programs to individuals ㉝ and their ㉞ families ㉟ through ㊱ community settings, such as community action centers and health centers, organizations serving ㊲ FA's minority populations, and labor business/organizations.

We would utilize our status as the state's designated "Wellness Campaign" and our role as the Outreach Partner, sharing latest research findings from the National Institute of Mental Health, ㊳ to ㊴ develop up-to-date ㊵ resources that appeal to and are comprehensible ㊶ to a broad public. This will require special attention and material for linguistic minorities.

To maximize the impact of presentations, ㊷ there ㊸ will be collateral print and web materials, ㊹ as well as a radio and local print media campaign. Workplace and other community settings are ideal for short talks and presentations. Follow-up ㊺ in efficient low-cost ㊻ communication should reinforce new learning about mental health and recovery. MHAFA has access to ㊼ the research data and can develop ㊽ a strategic ㊾ statewide plan for this outreach and education. These presentations would combine the general material about mental health and primary care with information about community mental health programs. This will improve access into the mental health system both for those with medical insurance ㊿ and

cont.

EXPLANATIONS OF CORRECTIONS

29. Use more formal language in this sort of writing. Clients "achieve recovery" rather than "get better."
30. We corrected the passive voice.
31. Spelling error.
32. "Very" is redundant with "unique." Never write *"very unique." Unique is a superlative that needs no modification or extension.*
33. No apostrophe because the sentence does not require the possessive.
34. Homophone error: their and there (see #25).
35. No apostrophe because the sentence does not require the possessive.
36. "Thru" is not a word.
37. We simplified the language in this sentence for parallel construction and clarity.
38. The phrase, "sharing latest research findings from the National Institute of Mental Health," should be set off with commas because the sentence remains a complete sentence even without it.
39. Homophone error: to and too—"too" means also or excessive.
40. "Up-to-date" should be hyphenated because the three words form one modifier.
41. Spelling error.
42. Always use a comma to separate a dependent phrase from an independent clause.
43. Homophone error: there and their (see #25).
44. Always use a comma to separate a dependent phrase from an independent clause.
45. Use a hyphen when two words form one idea.
46. See #45.
47. Homophone error: to and too (see #39).
48. Spelling error.
49. We relocated a misplaced modifier for clarity.
50. Avoid the phrase "not only but." It is inappropriate in professional writing.

cont.

those without insurance ⑤①. Information about changes in Medicaid-funded ⑤② services will be included.

Work Plan

July – August 2009
>   Hire ⑤③ staff ⑤④ and meet ⑤⑤ with providers.
>   Develop ⑤⑥ presentations and evaluation formats ⑤⑦.
>   Schedule fall ⑤⑧ groups.

September – December
>   Minimum of 35 in-person ⑤⑨ presentations. Settings to include an average of 15 persons per presentation targeting all counties, at least two ⑥⓪ presentations in Spanish-speaking ⑥① communities ⑥② and at least one ⑥③ each in Southeast Asian and Liberian community settings. Also include range of audiences to include youth, elderly, caretakers, primary care physicians and ⑥④ individuals currently receiving services and their ⑥⑤ families.

December
>   Review evaluations and "tweak" presentations. Schedule spring ⑥⑥ presentations.

January – June 2010
>   Minimum of 60 in-person ⑥⑦ presentations. See ⑥⑧ above description. Staff ⑥⑨ will review progress monthly ⑦⓪, with designated MHRH representatives.

cont.

EXPLANATIONS OF CORRECTIONS

51. "Too" is redundant with "and."
52. Use hyphenation because the two words form one idea. Also, we corrected the passive voice: *Information about changes in Medicaid-funded services will be included.* Here is the active voice: *The proposal will include information about changes in Medicaid-funded services.* Use active wording whenever possible because it requires the author to include more information about who is doing what to whom.
53. Homophone error: hire and higher—"hire" means employ; "higher" means more altitude or greater amount.
54. "Staff" is singular.
55. Homophone error: meet and mete—"meet" means encounter; mete means distribute.
56. Spelling error.
57. No apostrophe because no possessive required.
58. Seasons are not capitalized because they are not proper nouns.
59. Use hyphenation because the two words form one idea.
60. Always spell out numbers from one through ten.
61. Use hyphenation because the two words form one idea.
62. Because the phrase is "multiple communities" use the plural form.
63. Always spell out numbers from one through ten.
64. Unnecessary verbiage.
65. Homophone error: their and there (see #25).
66. Do not capitalize the word "spring" because it is not a proper noun.
67. Use hyphenation because the two words form one idea.
68. Homophone error: see and sea—"see" refers to vision; "sea" is a body of water.
69. "Staff" is singular.
70. We relocated a misplaced modifier.

cont.

The Evaluation Plan

We will develop an ⑦¹ evaluation plan with an ⑦² outside evaluator
to help us determine whether our educative goals ⑦³ are met,
⑦⁴ ⑦⁵ and to inform revisions in this plan ⑦⁶. We hope to learn
about the mental health-mental illness continuum, access to services,
and stigma reduction ⑦⁷–⑧⁰.

In June 2010, presentation and scheduling targets will be established,
based on Year One ⑧¹ experiences ⑧².

Annual Budget

1. Education/Communications Specialist Develop materials and present in-person ⑧³ on radio/cable and TV news ⑧⁴	1 FTE*	$ 65,000
2. Communications Assistant Scheduling, E-list, updates, web ⑧⁵ materials, E-newsletter	.5FTE*	$ 25,000
3. Postage, telephone, office supplies		$ 4,500
4. Printing		$ 1,400
5. Equipment		$ 1,700
6. In-state mileage		$ 2,400
7. Evaluation		$ 10,000
8. Administrative overhead ⑧⁶		$ 10,000
		$120,000

*FTE: full-time equivalent staff position

EXPLANATIONS OF CORRECTIONS

71. Word usage: "an" and "and"; or perhaps a typo.
72. The sentence requires the article "an" for clarity.
73. No apostrophe because no possessive required.
74. "And not" is redundant with "whether."
75. Always use a comma, not a semicolon, to separate an independent clause from a dependent phrase.
76. Beware of and avoid including authorial bias.
77. The phrase: "We are looking for" is too informal. Find more appropriate vocabulary to describe the process.
78. There are three items listed, not two, so "both" is inappropriate because it refers to two items.

79. Avoid the phrase "not only but". . .
80. The word "to" is needed between "access" and "services."
81. Spell out numbers from one through ten; also, capitalize Year One if it is a formal title.
82. When used in the singular, "experience" should have an article before it, e.g., "a" or "the." If you choose to use "experiences," no article is required.
83. Use hyphenation because the two words form one idea.
84. We corrected for parallel construction. Numbers one and two lacked parallelism in job descriptions.
85. The word "web" is not capitalized.
86. We corrected to include professional vocabulary.

7

Letters

Social workers write many kinds of letters as part of their professional responsibilities. They write to clients, to other agencies, to government departments, to institutions who fund social services, and to accreditation bodies who oversee social work practice. These letters often include agency reports, professional requests, thank-you notes, professional endorsements, and so on. The following chapter contains examples of several kinds of letters written by social workers on behalf of their agencies.

This chapter includes seven letters. Case 31 is an example of an agency letter to a client. Cases 32 and 37 are thank-you letters. Case 33 is an agency letter to constituents, calling for immediate action to influence an imminent public policy decision. Cases 34–36 are letters sent between and among agencies for specific professional purposes. Numbers on the right side of the original documents note the page locations of the corresponding content in the corrected documents.

31 – Agency Letter to a Client
32 – Thank You Letter to a State Department
33 – E-mail List Call to Action
34 – Letter of Agreement
35 – Letter From a Private Agency to a State Agency
36 – Letter of Support for a Grant Application
37 – Thank-You Letter to a Politician

CASE 31: AGENCY LETTER TO A CLIENT

The following letter is to a client who has missed several appointments and been non-compliant with treatment regimens. The letter is brief, firm, and very clear. At times, such a style is necessary, especially when a client has been nonresponsive to calls and friendlier letters. Based on the client's mental health issues, the agency chose this direct approach as a way of cutting through resistance. There are 21 writing errors in this letter.

The goal of such a letter is to be brief, clear, and logical. Letters like these must be worded in language the client will understand. For typical adult populations you should consider an eighth-grade reading level appropriate. The letter is respectful but direct, and leaves the door open for the client to resume contact with the agency. Letters like these should always be printed on official agency letterhead.

ORIGINAL VERSION

January 4, 2011

Susie Smith
555 Fifth St. Apt. 5
Fenwick, Fredonia 00065

Dear Ms. Smith: (234)

According to our records, you have not seen Dr. Ficks since 12/2/10 and prior to this appointment you had missed your 10/15/10 and 9/8/10 appointments with Dr. Ficks and seem to be receiving services elsewhere or nowhere at all. In addition, you also have not been compliant with your Person-Centered Treatment Plan and have not been available to staff for visits, medication management, ect. In accordance to Fenwick Community Counseling Center, Inc. and the Department of Mental Health regulations, consumers must be seen by the staff psychiatrist no less then one time per each month. In order for FCCC to keep providing you mental health services (including proscribing psychiatric medication), you will have to comply by this regulation. If you chose not to or you are not able to comply, we will consider that you are no longer interested in participating in our program and start the discharge process, which may cause you to loose some other benefits as well. In addition, we will also assist you in finding other mental health services within the community, unless you are receiving

your psychiatric medications through your Primary Care Physician.   (235)
Therefore, if you do not met with Dr. Ficks on your next scheduled
appointment date, 2/9/11 @ 10:00 am, and comply each month after; you
will be given a list of prospective mental health providers and discharged
from the respective FCCC Program. If you have any questions in regards
to this situation, please feel free to contact me at (555) 555-5555, Ext. 555.
Thank-you for your time and consideration reguarding this matter.

Sincerely,

Kindly Helper, MSW

CASE 31: CORRECTED VERSION

Each number in the corrected version refers to an explanation below.

Dear Ms. Smith:

According to our records, you have not seen Dr. Ficks since 12/2/10. ①
Prior to this appointment you had missed your 10/15/10 and 9/8/10
appointments with Dr. Ficks. ② It appears that you may be receiving services elsewhere
or nowhere at all. ③ In addition, you ④ have not been compliant with your
Person-Centered Treatment Plan and have not been available to staff for
visits, medication management, etc. ⑤. In accordance with ⑥ regulations of both Fenwick
Community Counseling Center, Inc. and the Department of Mental Health ⑦,
consumers must be seen by the staff psychiatrist no less than ⑧ one time
per ⑨ month. In order for FCCC to keep providing you mental health
services, including prescribing ⑩ psychiatric medication, you will have to
comply with ⑪ this regulation. If you choose ⑫ not to (or you are not able to) ⑬ comply,
we will consider that you are no longer interested in participating in our
program, ⑭ and start the discharge process, which may cause you to lose ⑮
some other benefits ⑯. In addition, we will ⑰ assist you in finding
other mental health services within the community, unless you are receiving

cont.

EXPLANATIONS OF CORRECTIONS

1. To avoid a run-on sentence we divided it into three separate declarative sentences using periods instead of commas.
2. Separate sentence. See #1
3. Separate sentence. See #1
4. "In addition" and "also" are redundant.
5. "Etc." is correct, while "ect" is not a word or abbreviation. It is best to avoid such abbreviations when possible.
6. "With" is the appropriate preposition, e.g., "in accordance with."
7. "Regulations" is the noun modified by both phrases: "Fenwick CCC" and "the Department of Mental Health Services"; by moving "regulations" to the beginning of the sentence and including "both" in the explanation, we clarified the sentence's meaning.
8. Homophone error: than and then—"than" is for comparisons; "then" refers to time.
9. "Each" and "per" are redundant.
10. Word usage: prescribe and proscribe—prescribe means to recommend; proscribe means to forbid.
11. "With" is the appropriate preposition, e.g., "comply with."
12. Use the present tense consistently: choose rather than chose.
13. "Or are not able to" is an important phrase to include because it acknowledges the potential complexity of a situation. We put it in parentheses to set it off from the main thought. Commas at either end would be okay too.
14. Sentence clarity: without the comma, the sentence is saying that Ms. Smith will begin discharge process. Commas change meaning. Compare: "It's time to eat Grandma" with "It's time to eat, Grandma."
15. Word usage: lose and loose—to "lose" means to misplace or fail; "loose" means unrestrained.
16. "Other" and "as well" are redundant.
17. "In addition" and "also" are redundant.

cont.

your psychiatric medications through your Primary Care Physician. Therefore, if you do not meet with Dr. Ficks on your next scheduled appointment date, 2/9/11 at ⑱ 10:00 am, and comply each month after that, ⑲ you will be given a list of prospective mental health providers and discharged from the respective FCCC Program. If you have any questions in regards to this situation, please ⑳ contact me at (555) 555-5555, Ext. 555. Thank you for your time and consideration regarding ㉑ this matter.

Sincerely,

Kindly Helper, MSW

EXPLANATIONS OF CORRECTIONS

18. "@" is not an acceptable abbreviation. Spell out your words whenever possible in professional writing.

19. "After <u>that</u>" is more complete than "after" for clarity's sake; we used a comma instead of semicolon because the next phrase is not a complete sentence.

20. "Feel free to" is unnecessary verbiage.

21. Spelling error.

CASE 32: THANK-YOU LETTER TO A STATE DEPARTMENT

Thank-you letters should be brief, uncomplicated, and generally avoid mentioning any aspect of business. Recipients appreciate these acknowledgements. There are 16 writing errors in this letter.

ORIGINAL VERSION

Ms. Annee Golden   (237)
Director, Fredonia Department of Elderly Affairs
1 FDEA Street
Fenwick, FA 00077

Dear Annee,

On behalf of the Board of Directors of the National Ass'n of Social Workers - Fredonia Chapter, I would like to Thank-you for taking time out of your very busy schedule to participate in the "Guiding Principal for Social Workers: Assisting Families' in Navigating the Long-Term Care Continuum" workshop; on April 7, 2006. We were very glad you were their to answer questions regarding the Department of Elderly Affairs, but much more importantly four showing support for events such as this one it was a pleasure to see you again.

You're presents do make a hugh difference! Thank you.

Sincerely,

Your friend,
Moe Larry, LICSW
Executive Director
NASW-FA

CASE 32: CORRECTED VERSION

Each number in the corrected version refers to an explanation below.

Ms. Annee Golden
Director, Fredonia Department of Elderly Affairs
1 FDEA Street
Fenwick, FA 00077

Dear Annee,

On behalf of the Board of Directors of the National Association ① of Social
Workers - Fredonia Chapter, thank you ② ③ for taking time
out of your very busy schedule to participate in the "Guiding Principal
for Social Workers: Assisting Families ④ in Navigating the Long-Term Care
Continuum" workshop, ⑤ on April 7, 2006. We were very glad you were there ⑥
to answer questions regarding the Department of Elderly Affairs, and ⑦,
more importantly, ⑧ ⑨ to show support for events such as this.
⑩ ⑪

Your ⑫ presence ⑬ makes ⑭ a huge ⑮ difference! Thank you.

Sincerely,

⑯
Moe Larry, LICSW
Executive Director
NASW-FA

EXPLANATIONS OF CORRECTIONS

1. Spell out most abbreviations in professional writing.
2. "I would like to" is redundant with sending the letter, which is a thank you.
3. "Thank you" should not be capitalized, as it is not a proper noun.
4. No apostrophe because this is a simple plural and requires no possessive.
5. We used a comma and not semicolon to link a complete sentence with a phrase.
6. Homophone error: there and their—"their" is possessive; "there" refers to place.
7. "And" is more appropriate than "but" because there is no contradiction in the meaning of the sentence to suggest using a "but."

8. We deleted "much" because it is not necessary.
9. Parallel construction: "to answer questions should parallel "to show support."
10. We corrected the run-on sentence; "one" is unnecessary and so we deleted it.
11. The final personal comment does not belong in a formal letter between agencies.
12. Homophone error: your and you're—"your" is possessive; "you're" means you are.
13. Homophone error: presence and presents—"presence" is attendance or availability; "presents" are gifts.
14. "Does" is not necessary, so we deleted it.
15. Spelling error.
16. Unnecessary sign-off line. It is too informal for professional writing.

CASE 33: E-MAIL LIST CALL TO ACTION

The Internet offers opportunities for social service agencies to mobilize action in short time frames. Many social welfare organizations have their own websites, containing announcements, pictures, messages from the Executive Director, and often links to their own newsletters, and (of course) instructions for making donations to the agency. Web-sites share information in a fairly passive way and, as a result, they require interested people to find their own way to the website and click their way to posted information. Or not.

Agencies also keep e-mail lists, organized by category of individual participation: categories include donors, board members, volunteers, clients, and so on. Social workers send e-mails on behalf of their agencies to specific recipients, depending on the issue and action needed. All kinds of information can be disseminated this way: professional meeting notices, the minutes of those meetings, requests for information, request for support, or the general dissemination of relevant news items. Large groups of people can be reached via email to facilitate a call to action.

The following example came from The Compassion Center (CC), an agency that primarily undertakes advocacy activities on behalf of low-income people. The announcement was sent to the agency's list of volunteers, donors, and other agencies interested in the issue. The state legislature had passed a bill called "Alvin's Law," named after a man who had frozen to death a few years earlier because his home heating had been cut off. The bill required utility companies to offer customers the option of payment plans, rather than cutting gas and electricity service. It took years for this bill to pass, and then after the legislature passed the bill, the governor expressed some hesitance about signing the bill into law, because he feared it would be overturned in the courts. CC sent the following e-message to its e-mail "action list." Within an hour, the governor's office was besieged with phone calls; only four hours after the CC e-mail called for action, the governor announced he would sign the bill. Such strategies do not always work so well as this example, but, even so, the CC call for action illustrates that a well-written announcement to a specific list of recipients can be effective.

Notice that the e-mail is brief, informal, to the point, and very clear, because the e-mail recipients are knowledgeable and sympathetic—the writer knows their audience to be like-minded. As a result, the message is direct. Even though you may be writing to a sympathetic audience, the quality of the writing remains very important. Recipients of your letter or message must feel confident that you are a well-informed and responsible professional, because they are being asked to take high-visibility action, which always represents some amount of professional risk. There are 17 writing errors and one optional correction in this e-mail.

ORIGINAL VERSION

Hi all:

(240)

Last evening it was brought to my attention that Governor Dullard, in his "infinite wisdom", is seriously considering vetoing "Alvin's Law" (S-412). The Law would generate up to seventeen point five million dollars per year thru a charge of up to $10/year for electric and gas customers, for additional Low Income Home Energy Assistance Program (LIHEAP) assistance. In addition, it also implements the "percentage of income plan" (PIPP) which the Compassion Center has been advocating for for years. This would allow low income Fredonians' to avoid gas and electric shut-offs or too have service restored by paying a percentage of they're bill with an agreement to payoff the balance in reasonable amounts.

Please call the Governors office RIGHT NOW, 555-0000, with the simple message: I'm calling to urge the Governor to sign Alvin's Law. (You can add whatever other statement you want, of course. It's important for him to know that folks are concerned)

(241)

Feel free to pass this along...

Thanks

Marge
Compassion Center
Fenwick, FA 00060

CASE 33: CORRECTED VERSION

Each number in the corrected version refers to an explanation below.

Hi All:

Last evening I learned ① that Governor Dullard ② is ③ considering vetoing "Alvin's Law" (S-412). The Law would generate up to $17.5 million ④ per year through ⑤ a charge of up to $10 per ⑥ year for electricity ⑦ and gas utility customers, for additional Low Income Home Energy Assistance Program (LIHEAP) assistance. It ⑧ also implements the "percentage of income plan" (PIPP), for which ⑨ the Compassion Center has been advocating for years. This would allow low-income Fredonians ⑩ to avoid gas and electric utility shut-offs, ⑪ or to ⑫ have service restored by paying a percentage of their ⑬ bill with an agreement to pay ⑭ the balance in reasonable installments.

cont.

EXPLANATIONS OF CORRECTIONS

1. We changed the passive voice to the active voice—"I learned."
2. Avoid opinion and especially sarcasm—sarcasm does not travel well over the Internet and may alienate some of your supporters.
3. Unnecessary verbiage—"seriously" splits the verb form, "is considering." Splitting the infinitive verb form is not necessarily incorrect depending on who you ask, but be sure the adjective adds necessary information otherwise delete it.
4. Use numerals and dollar signs for amounts above ten—numerals are correct when indicated amounts of money.
5. "Thru" is not a word.
6. The slash (/) is very informal and may be misunderstood. Avoid it.
7. Word choice is off here: "electric" is an adjective and "electricity" is a noun.

8. "In addition" and "also" are redundant.
9. We inserted a comma after PIPP in order to separate independent and subordinate clauses, and we eliminated the double "for" by inserting "for which."
10. No apostrophe because the sentence does not require the possessive.
11. We inserted a comma in order to separate the independent clause and the subordinate phrase.
12. Homophone error: to and too—"too" means also or excessive.
13. Homophone error: their and they're—"their" is possessive and "they're" is a contraction of they are.
14. "Payoff" is a noun; pay is a verb. When in doubt, keep it simple.

cont.

Please call the Governor's ⑮ office RIGHT NOW, 555-0000, with the simple message: I'm calling to urge the Governor to sign Alvin's Law. Please feel free to add whatever other statement you want, of course. It is important for the governor to know that we are concerned. ⑯

Please pass this along to anyone else you think might be interested in helping. ⑰

Thanks,

Marge
Compassion Center
Fenwick, FA 00060

EXPLANATIONS OF CORRECTIONS

15. The apostrophe here is necessary to indicate the possessive: the governor possesses the office.

16. We revised this sentence for the sake of simple clarity. Avoid parenthetical asides. They distract from the flow of the sentence's thought.

17. Though an e-mail may be informal, be specific and clear about what you want your recipients to do with the information.

CASE 34: LETTER OF AGREEMENT

Agencies frequently enter into task-oriented partnerships, cooperating with other agencies on goals that are mutually beneficial. What follows is a letter to an agency attempting to organize a parent education program with another agency in the community. As you will see, the letter writer responding to the invitation agrees to participate on behalf of his agency. The letter identifies the cooperating agency's expertise, a program that participants may utilize, actions the agency will take, and a sense of enthusiasm. It is one page in length. Typically, a letter committing an agency's support, or any other official commitment, would be signed by the executive director and addressed to another executive director. There are 22 writing errors.

ORIGINAL VERSION

Hy Wranker
Executive Director
Fenwick Senior Center
1 Senior Center Drive
Fenwick, FA 00077

Dear Mr. Wranker: (244)

Please except this letter of agreement to participate in the family education program that Fenwick Senior Center is proposing to the Fenwick Community Trust Fund. The Metropolitan Family Care Community Partnership (MFCCP) has identified an ongoing need for the type of family education program that is being proposed. We will participate in the program gladly.

As a state-designated "family support center", we are charged with supporting family's to help prevent there involvement with the state department of elderly affairs (DEA). We are keenly aware of the literature base that identifies' families which struggle with there own functioning issues, in combination with mental health needs and stress, as particularly vulnerable to involvement with DEA.

For your information, MFCCP has developed a program that teaches stress reduction techniques, provides an opportunity for family members' to learn an evidenced based support program and allows for families to practice and self evaluate their progress in a positive and supportive manor.

My staff are excited about participating in this program and pledge to (245)
work collaboratively with FSC. We will identify and support families who
meet the program criterias for the program. Some of our efforts will
include identifying ways for family members to use there natural supports
to help them affectively participate and continue to utilize the skills that
they will learn throughout this program.

We look foward to this new initiative.

Sincerely,

Will B. Thayer
Execute Director
MFCCP

CASE 34: CORRECTED VERSION

Each number in the corrected version refers to an explanation below.

Dear Mr. Wranker:

Please accept ① this letter of agreement to participate in the family education program that Fenwick Senior Center is proposing to the Fenwick Community Trust Fund. The Metropolitan Family Care Community Partnership (MFCCP) has identified an ongoing need for the type of family education program that you are proposing. We will gladly participate in the program ②.

As a state-designated "family support center," ③ the law charges us with supporting families ④ to help prevent their ⑤ involvement with the state Department of Elderly Affairs ⑥ (DEA). We are keenly aware of the literature ⑦ that identifies ⑧ families who ⑨ struggle with their ⑩ own functioning issues, in combination with mental health needs and stress, as particularly vulnerable to involvement with DEA.

For your information, MFCCP has developed a program that teaches stress reduction techniques, provides an opportunity for family members ⑪ to learn an evidence-based ⑫ support program and allows for families to practice and self-evaluate ⑬ their progress in a positive and supportive manner ⑭.

cont.

EXPLANATIONS OF CORRECTIONS

1. Word usage: accept and except—"accept" means agree to; "except" means preclude.
2. We corrected the passive voice. We also corrected the misplaced modifier: "gladly" should be as close as possible to the word it modifies, "participate." This is a case in which splitting the verb form, "we will participate," is preferable to any other placement of "gladly" in the sentence.
3. Comma belongs before the close-quote mark.
4. This is a simple plural noun and no apostrophe indicating possessive required. We also corrected the passive voice into active voice.
5. Homophone error: their and there—"their" indicates the possessive.
6. Capitalize the title of a state department because it is a proper noun.
7. There is no need for the word "base."
8. No apostrophe because the sentence does not require the possessive.
9. "Which" introduces a non-essential phrase. In this case, "who" or "that" are more appropriate than which because "struggle with their own functioning issues" is essential information.
10. Homophone error: their and there (see #5).
11. See #8.
12. We hyphenated these two words to form one compound adjective, and removed the "d" from "evidence," an adjective, not a verb.
13. See #12.
14. Homophone error: manner and manor—"manner" means self-comportment or style; "manor" is a castle or mansion.

cont.

My staff is ⑮ excited about participating in this program and pledge to work collaboratively with FSC. We will identify and support families who ⑯ meet the program criteria ⑰ for the program. ⑱ Our efforts will include identifying ways for family members to use their ⑲ natural supports to help them effectively participate and continue to utilize the skills ⑳ they will learn through ㉑ this program.

We look forward ㉒ to this new initiative.

Sincerely,

Will B. Thayer
Execute Director
MFCCP

EXPLANATIONS OF CORRECTIONS

15. "Staff" is a collective noun and should be treated as singular; an alternative is "my staff members are. . ." and the refer to "members" in the plural.

16. See #9.

17. Use "criteria" as the plural of criterion.

18. "Some of our efforts include" promises more than one effort, but the sentence lists only one effort: be clear and consistent.

19. Homophone error: their and there (see #5).

20. We deleted "that" because it is not needed. Homophone error: "affectively" corrected to "effectively".

21. "Throughout" means "in every phase"; the corrected sentence now says that the program will teach participants to "utilize their skills."

22. Spelling error.

CASE 35: LETTER FROM A PRIVATE AGENCY TO A STATE AGENCY

The following example is a letter from a private non-profit agency to state regional directors, announcing the letter-writing agency will no longer be able to provide psychological evaluations for the state. The author writes the letter in professional language, which is both collegial and respectful. The author indicates that recent budget cuts necessitate reallocation of staff resources. The letter also leaves the door open for restitution of psychological evaluations for state-funded clients in the future. We inserted 42 writing errors.

Abbreviations
DCPS: (State) Department of Child Protective Services
LICSW: Licensed Social Worker
DHS: (State) Department of Human Services

ORIGINAL VERSION

To: Regional Directors, DCPS

From: Mai King-Goode, LICSW
        Director, Fenwick Family Support Center, Parent Education Program

Date: August 12, 2011

Re: Program Changes

I am writing to let you know that we have had to make a change in   (248)
our programming. Recently our agency has sustained significant cuts
in reimbursement from DHS following the General Assembly decision
to farther reduce the Governor's budget. This change has required
restructuring and reduction in our staffing.

We were so pleased to be able to offer you an option for Psychological
Evaluations, but now find that we need to utilize the staff and time that was
allocated for these evaluations to provide psychology services to our adult
residential clients. If we are able, in the future, to expand our staffing and can
offer these evaluations again I will contact you. I will let DCPS workers, who
have clients on our Psychological Evaluation referral list, know that we will not
be able to due the evaluations so that they can look for services elsewhere.

In addition, due to the large size of our referral list for Parent Education   (249)
services it has also become increasingly important too utilize our services to
clients when they are at the highest level of need. This typically means that
they are using <u>at least four hours</u> of staff contact weekly. In the passed, when
requested by yore staff, we have continued our work with families as they

required less hours of services per week. Given the significant need for our specialized parent education services throughout the State, we can no longer keep servicing families when they need and are ready for a lesser intensive program. Our staff will identify to your staff when we feel that it is appropriate to begin the termination process and look for other programming.
They are always willing to discuss individual families that the Department feels may require a lengthier transition period.
Please feel free to call.

I truly am sorry to have to pull back services that are needed by your staff so badly; but the budget cuts that our agency has sustained give us no other choice. It's always a pleasure to work with each of you and I look forward to the day when I am writing to again expand services!

CASE 35: CORRECTED VERSION

Each number in the corrected version refers to an explanation below.

I am writing to inform you ① that significant ② cuts
in reimbursement from DHS, ③ following the General Assembly's ④ decision
to further ⑤ reduce the Governor's budget, has required us ⑥ to
restructure and reduce ⑦ our staffing.

Prior to the cuts ⑧, we were ⑨ pleased to ⑩ offer you a programming option for **psychological
evaluations** ⑪, but now find that we need to utilize the staff and time that we previously
allocated for these evaluations to other priorities, namely to provide psychological ⑫ services to our adult
residential clients. In the future, ⑬ if we are able to expand our staffing and can
offer these evaluations again, ⑭ I will contact you. I will inform ⑮ DCPS workers with ⑯
clients on our **psychological evaluation referral list** ⑰, that we will not
be able to do ⑱ the evaluations, ⑲ so ⑳ they can look for services elsewhere.

cont.

EXPLANATIONS OF CORRECTIONS

1. We used more direct language for clarity.
2. Portions of the first and second sentences were redundant.
3. "Following the General Assembly's decision to further reduce the Governor's budget" should be bracketed with commas because it can be removed without changing the meaning of the sentence.
4. We inserted an apostrophe to indicate the possessive.
5. Word choice is off here: further and farther— "further" is used for concepts; "farther" for measurable items.
6. We simplified the language for style.
7. Parallelism: restructure and reduce should use the same verb form.
8. "Prior to the cuts" added for clarity. "Formerly" or "until now" would be okay too.
9. "So" is unnecessary and informal.
10. "To be able to" is wordy and unnecessary; the meaning is conveyed in these sentences.
11. "Psychological evaluations" is not a proper noun, so it should not be capitalized. we used bold font to set it off from the

rest of the sentence in order to call attention to it.
12. The adjective form of the noun "psychology" is "psychological," which modifies the noun, "services."
13. We relocated a misplaced introductory phrase, "in the future."
14. Use commas on both sides of a phrase that can be removed without changing a sentence's meaning.
15. "Let know" is unprofessional; "inform" is shorter, more appropriate, and clearer.
16. We used "with" to replace "who have" in order to make the sentence clearer.
17. Do not capitalize a common noun. We used bold for emphasis.
18. Homophone error: do and due—"do" is a verb; "due" refers to deadline.
19. Always use a comma in front of a connecting conjunction that links two independent clauses.
20. "That" is unnecessary. "So" is necessary here, unlike correction #9.

cont.

In addition, due to the large size of our referral list for **parent education** ㉑ services, ㉒ it has ㉓ become increasingly important to ㉔ offer our services to ㉕ clients when they are at the highest level of need. Typically ㉖ this means ㉗ clients use <u>at least four hours </u>of staff contact time every week. In the past ㉘, when requested by your ㉙ staff, we have continued our work with families when they required fewer ㉚ hours of services per week. However, given the significant need for our specialized parent education services throughout the state ㉛, we can no longer maintain services to families who need—and are ready for—a less ㉜ intensive program. We will inform ㉝ you when ㉞ it is appropriate to begin the termination process and for your clients to look for other programming services. My staff is always willing to discuss individual families who ㉟ the Department feels may require a lengthier transition period and we will work to accommodate such a situation. Please feel free to call.

I apologize for reducing essential services ㊱ ㊲ but our ㊳ budget cuts ㊴ give us no other choice. It is ㊵ always a pleasure to work with ㊶ you, ㊷ and I look forward to the day when I am writing again to expand our services!

EXPLANATIONS OF CORRECTIONS

21. See #17.
22. See #19.
23. "Also" is redundant with "in addition."
24. Homophone error: to and too—"too" means also or excessive.
25. Word usage: "offer" is more appropriate than "utilize."
26. We relocated "typically" for clarity.
27. "That" is unnecessary.
28. Homophone error: past and passed—"past" means ago; "passed" means went by.
29. Homophone error: your and yore—"your" is possessive; "yore" refers to the distant past.
30. Writing style: fewer and less—"fewer" is for countable items; use "less" when discussing concepts.
31. "State" should not be capitalized if it is used as a common noun.
32. Word choice is off here: less and lesser—use "lesser" when comparing.

33. Use "inform" here because it is more direct than "identify to."
34. Unnecessary verbiage.
35. The pronoun for people is <u>who</u> or <u>whom</u>; in this case, <u>who</u> because it takes the verb, <u>may require</u>.
36. We deleted the passive voice and reduced wordiness.
37. We used a comma because the semicolon is redundant with the conjunction, "but." An alternative: keep the semicolon and delete "but" between the independent clauses.
38. "Our" instead of "the" helps reduce the verbiage.
39. See #36.
40. Avoid contractions in professional writing.
41. "Each of" is unnecessary, as they are all listed as recipients of the letter.
42. Always use a comma before connecting conjunction between two independent clauses.

CASE 36: LETTER OF SUPPORT FOR A GRANT APPLICATION

Some grant applications require letters of support from individuals and their organizations who can attest to the grant proposal's merits, as well as to the service provider's credentials and competency. This is a letter of support for a grant application. The letter contains 29 writing errors.

ORIGINAL VERSION

July 16, 2011   (252)

Mrs. Lee Ward
Safe Communities Specialist
U.S. Department of Urban Education
Federal Office Complex
Fenwick, FA 00010

Dear Mrs. Ward:

The Fredonia Parent Resource Network (FAPRN) wishes to go on record as offering it's support for the Fredonia Department of Human Services' proposal to DUE for "Community-integration Personal Assistance Services and Supports with Maximum Consumer Control (Community PASS).

As a statewide agency serving *all* families with children, FAPRN strongly supports community initiatives such as the one being proposed by Department of Human Services. We receive requests each week from families' trying to arrange inhome medical treatment, respite care and special transportation services for there children with special needs. The Community PASS program would help to address this important need. With appropriate information, resources and support from the DHS Community PASS program, and the agencies with whom it collaborates, families with children with disabilities and chronic illnesses in Fredonia could assume greater responsibility and control over there lives.

FAPRN regularly collaborates with the Department of Human Services to provide families with the information, skills and resources they need to act as effective and independent advocates' for there child's well being. With planning, management and monitoring of a community-integrated reimbursible personnel assistance system, Medicaid eligible families in Fredonia could learn how to best select and arrange the personnel care services they need for there children.

FAPRN is a statewide non-profit agency who's mission it is to encourage,   (253)
educate and empower parents to seek the help they need for their child's social, emotional and physical well-being. Like the Department of Human

Services, our agency's philosophy is that parents are their child's best advocate and as such need and deserve to be both knowledgeable and in charge of procuring appropriate medical care, education and supplementary services for their child or children with chronic illnesses and/or disabilities.

Our agency applauds the Department of Human Services and it's efforts to implement family-centered systems change.

We know that many families' of children with disabilities and chronic illnesses have long-awaited the opportunity to become more independent and responsible for their child's care. The Community PASS program, as proposed by DHS, promises to deliver a cost-effective approach to meeting these needs.

Sincerely,

Justin Caise
Associate Director

CASE 36: CORRECTED VERSION

Each number in the corrected version refers to an explanation below.

Letter of Support for a Grant Application

July 16, 2011

Ms. ① Lee Ward
Safe Communities Specialist
U.S. Department of Urban Education
Federal Office Complex
Fenwick, FA 00010

Dear Ms. ② Ward:

The Fredonia Parent Resource Network (FAPRN) supports ③
the Fredonia Department of Human Services' proposal to DUE
for "Community-integration Personal Assistance Services
and Supports with Maximum Consumer Control (Community PASS)." ④

As a statewide agency serving *all* families with children, FAPRN strongly
supports community initiatives such as the one being proposed by
the Fredonia ⑤ Department of Human Services. We receive requests each week from
families ⑥ trying to arrange in-home ⑦ medical treatment, respite care and
special transportation services for their ⑧ children with special needs.
The Community PASS program would help to address this important
need. With appropriate information, resources and support from the DHS
Community PASS program, and the agencies with which ⑨ it collaborates,
families with children with disabilities and chronic illnesses in Fredonia
could assume greater responsibility and control over their ⑩ lives.

cont.

EXPLANATIONS OF CORRECTIONS

1. Avoid Mrs. and Miss. Use Ms.
2. See #1.
3. Unnecessary verbiage.
4. We inserted a quotation mark in order to close the quote.
5. Article (the) and "Fredonia" specify the Department of Human Services.
6. No apostrophe because the sentence did not require the possessive.
7. We hyphenated because the two words combine to form one idea.
8. Homophone error: their and there—"their" is possessive.
9. "With which" when referring to things; "with whom" when referring to people.
10. Homophone error: their and there—see #8.

cont.

FAPRN regularly collaborates with the Department of Human Services to provide families with the information, skills and resources they need to act as effective and independent advocates ⑪ for their ⑫ children's ⑬ well-being ⑭. With planning, management and monitoring of a community-integrated reimbursable ⑮ personal ⑯ assistance system, Medicaid-eligible ⑰ families in Fredonia could learn how best ⑱ to select and arrange the personal ⑲ care services they need for their ⑳ children.

FAPRN is a statewide non-profit agency whose ㉑ mission ㉒ is to encourage, educate and empower parents to seek the help they need for their children's ㉓ social, emotional and physical well-being. Like the Department of Human Services, we believe ㉔ parents are their children's ㉕ best advocates, and as such need and deserve to be both knowledgeable and in charge of procuring appropriate medical care, education and supplementary services for their child or children with chronic illnesses and/or disabilities.

Our agency applauds the Department of Human Services and its ㉖ efforts to implement family-centered systems change.

We know that many families ㉗ of children with disabilities and chronic illnesses have long awaited ㉘ the opportunity to become more independent and responsible for their children's ㉙ care. The Community PASS program, as proposed by DHS, promises to deliver a cost-effective approach to meeting these needs.

Sincerely,

Justin Caise
Associate Director

EXPLANATIONS OF CORRECTIONS

11. See #6.
12. Homophone error: their and there—see #8.
13. Use the plural "children's" for parallel construction.
14. "Well-being" is a two-word hyphenated noun—two words combine to create one idea.
15. Spelling error.
16. Word usage: personal and personnel— "personal" means private or individual; "personnel" refers to employees.
17. We hyphenated because the two words combine to form one idea.
18. Writing style: avoid splitting the infinitive form of the verb, in this case, "to select" was split by "best."
19. Word usage: personal and personnel. (see #16)

20. Homophone error: their and there. (see #8)
21. Homophone error: whose and who's— "whose" is possessive; "who's" is the contraction of "who is."
22. "It" is unnecessary.
23. We used plural for consistency.
24. Unnecessary verbiage.
25. See #23.
26. Homophone error: its and it's—"its" is possessive; "it's" is the conjunction of "it is."
27. No apostrophe because the sentence does not require the possessive.
28. No hyphen because "long" is an adverb and it modifies "awaited," a verb.
29. See #23.

CASE 37: THANK-YOU LETTER TO A POLITICIAN

*The following letter comes from a housing coalition that consists of
20 social agencies, consumer groups and advocacy organizations.
The coalition sent the letter to the president of the state senate and
asks her to reinstate a housing subsidy program in the state budget.
Fredonia has a serious homelessness problem. The Neighborhood
Progress Program (NPP) combines state funds with matching federal
dollars to create new housing for people with low and moderate incomes.
The original state budget did not include funding for NPP. The coalition
lobbied the senate president, who then reinstated funding for the NPP.*

*Thank-you letters to politicians should be short and focus strictly on the
politician's support. There may be other issues you would like to raise
when thanking a politician, but they do not belong in a thank-you letter.*

This thank-you letter has 17 writing errors.

ORIGINAL VERSION

June 14, 2011   (256)

Dear Senate President Welda Gavell:

THANK YOU!

Because of you're support, 1 of Fredonia's most successful programs' will continue: the Neighborhood Progress Program!

We know we speak not only for our Board of Directors and our staffs, but our constituencies' when we convey our feelings' of appreciation for you're work to restore funding for the Neighborhood Progress Program. Moreover, we thank you for listening to the rank and file legislators, and taking action to save NPP by urging leadership to reinstate the only state funded affordable housing program in the fiscal year 2012 budget.

As you know, NPP already provides 1188 units of very low-income and supportive housing, in all cities and towns, to individuals and families who have experienced homelessness or are at-risk of homelessness. An integral part of a comprehensive housing strategy in our state.

Because of you're support, we are one-step closer to a State of Fredonia   (257)
that provides Housing options for all our citizens. Refusing to let any man, woman, or child be homeless.

Sincerely,

May Knoyz	P. Pooles Voyse	Howsers Forall
FA Coalition for	Housing Action	Housing Network of FA
the Homeless	Coalition of FA	

CASE 37: CORRECTED VERSION

Each number in the corrected version refers to an explanation below.

June 14, 2011

Dear Senate President Welda Gavell:

THANK YOU!

Because of your ① support, one ② of Fredonia's most successful programs ③ will continue: the Neighborhood Progress Program!

We speak ④ on behalf of ⑤ our Board of Directors, our staff members ⑥, and our constituencies ⑦ when we convey our ⑧ appreciation for your ⑨ work to restore funding for the Neighborhood Progress Program. Moreover, we thank you for listening to the rank-and-file ⑩ legislators, and taking action to save NPP by urging leadership to reinstate the only state-funded ⑪ affordable housing program in the fiscal year 2012 budget.

As you know, NPP ⑫ provides 1,188 units of very low-income and supportive housing, in all cities and towns, to individuals and families who have experienced homelessness or are at-risk of homelessness. NPP is an ⑬ integral part of a comprehensive housing strategy in our state.

cont.

EXPLANATIONS OF CORRECTIONS

1. Homophone error: "your" indicates the possessive; "you're" is the contracted form of "you are."
2. Always spell out numbers one through ten.
3. No apostrophe because the sentence does not require the possessive.
4. Avoid unnecessary verbiage.
5. Avoid "not only . . . but."
6. "Staffs" means many sticks; use "staff members" when referring to employees or workers in the plural.
7. See #3.
8. Avoid unnecessary verbiage. Also, see #3.
9. Homophone error: "your" indicates possessive and "you're" is the contracted form of "you are." Or, here is a better way to write this sentence: "On behalf of our constituent members, thank you for your work to restore funding for the Neighborhood Progress Program." This is active language with minimal verbiage.
10. Hyphenate "rank-and-file" because the three words become one modifier—an adjective—of "legislators."
11. Hyphenate "state-funded" to create a single modifier for "affordable housing program."
12. We deleted the unnecessary word "already."
13. This was an incomplete sentence; we added a subject and verb.

cont.

Because of your ⑭ support, we are one step ⑮ closer to a State of Fredonia that provides housing ⑯ options for all our citizens. NPP helps us prevent any man, woman, or child from becoming ⑰ homeless.

Sincerely,

May Knoyz
FA Coalition for
the Homeless

P. Pooles Voyse
Housing Action
Coalition of FA

Howsers Forall
Housing Network of FA

EXPLANATIONS OF CORRECTIONS

14. See #9.

15. "One step" should not be hyphenated because the two words do not form a single-idea in this case; rather, "one" as an adjective modifies "step" as a noun.

16. Do not capitalize "housing" because it is not a proper noun.

17. This was a sentence fragment. We completed the thought and formed a complete sentence.

Appendix A

Glossary of Writing and Writing Errors

In an op-ed article in the *Austin* [Texas] *American-Statesman*, a University of Texas professor identified six categories of common writing errors, and made the following suggestions (Dorn, 2007):

1. Use the active voice, not the passive voice. Here is an example of the passive voice: "The ball was thrown into the crowd." Revising the passive voice into active voice requires that the writer knows who is doing what to whom. Here is the previous sentence revised into active voice: "The accused threw the ball into the crowd." In this case, the active voice "activates" the main verb—to throw—and deletes the weak, "was thrown." Further, the active voice provides more information to the reader—we now know who it was who threw the ball. In many cases the passive voice is a way of concealing the fact that the writer does not know who threw the ball, yet the entire sentence, paragraph, or larger argument may depend upon that information. Passive voice is more than a grammatical or syntactical error. It often masks the fact that the writer is not on top of the information required to make his or her case.
2. Depending on the kind of writing you are doing, it is almost always preferable that the writer makes clear their intentions, usually within the first paragraph. Traditionally this is the time to announce your thesis, or the main point of your writing. The writer should know what their point is by the final draft. Early drafts are the place to search and explore. The final draft is the place to be clear and on point. After the introduction, the writer should then use supporting evidence, perhaps introduce an alternative view through a citation of a secondary source, along with analysis of both the evidence and the alternative view, all toward making the writer's point.
3. Avoid contractions in a formal paper. Contractions are informal, colloquial, and may undermine the author's authority.

4. Precision! The English language is a subtle web-work of interrelated meanings. It is up to the writer to know and observe the differences between words that sound alike or are commonly confused, like affect and effect, among and between, their and there, and so on.

5. Avoid unnecessary wordiness and trite modifiers. Keep your prose simple, spare, and precise. Simple is not simplistic, so be lean and mean in how you construct your sentences. Examples:
   a. Please do not hesitate to contact me could be: please contact me.
   b. I am appreciative of .... Just write, "I appreciate ...."
   c. Very (or totally) unique. Unique is just that. No need to modify it.
   d. Truly, really, actually, literally. Unnecessary adjectives.
   e. Could be possible. Either something is possible, or it is not.

6. Limit the use of "and." The connective "and" is used for words, phrases, or clauses that are of equal value. Thus, when you use "and," you are making a list, not developing an argument. Words that advance an argument include "therefore" and "however."

7. Be mindful of how often you employ the "to be" verb. "Is" and "was" drain a sentence of its energy and focus. Find stronger, more precise verbs. Overusing "is" and "was" is often a sign of the passive voice, and suggests that the writer is not sure of the point of their argument.

Perhaps the most important piece of advice: Think before you write. Writers make choices. Writing is not simply transcribing your thoughts word for word like some sort of court stenographer keeping track of the dialogue in your head. Effective writing takes time, and multiple drafts. As you work out what you want to communicate, drafting your work allows you to figure out precisely what you want your principal message to communicate. Dorn's advice is on the right track: "Crafting those opening paragraphs can be the biggest challenge in writing. Seldom does a writer get them right the first time." What this means is this: Writers have to write and rewrite because through writing we discover what we want to say. Writing is a process of discovery along with a multi-draft process of figuring out how best to communicate what we have to say about what we have discovered as we write.

Unfortunately, in social service settings, writers seldom get the luxury of second and third drafts, so you have to tailor your writing to each specific context. Writers who write in social service settings need to work to develop professional writing habits that communicate events directly, clearly, and as completely as possible without spending too much time doing so. Good writers need to be good readers as well. When doing service work writing the writer needs to know and largely understand the situation, the relevant, specific details and how all of it fits together. Then, the writer must "translate" this understanding into words and get into the client's record the information required so that a stranger could read that record and understand the situation. This way the reader will understand the reported information and respect the reporter for her/his reporting. Once the writer understands the type of writing required in a professional situation, *how* you say it is almost as important as *what* you are saying. Writers would do well to avoid phrases like "sort of," "it seems to me," "it felt like (as if)" when endeavoring to describe basic facts about a situation. Get the facts down clearly. Be mindful of the difference between when your opinion is necessary and when your opinion is irrelevant. It all depends on the nature of the writing task.

The English language is difficult in several ways, beginning with the sheer number of words (between 250,000 and 750,000, depending on the definition of "word"), some of which have correct usage (http://oxforddictionaries.com/page/93) while nearly all lend themselves to misreadings and misapplications in one way or another. With all these words and just so many different ways to use them, it is often difficult to be as clear and precise as we need to be. Yet when we pay attention to what we do when we write, clarity and precision of a sort suddenly become quite possible. No matter how busy your job, when it requires writing, strive to do your best work. Know what the job entails. Effective writing is a sign of a well-developed mind, and when the reader trusts the writer, all things are possible.

With so many words vying for attention and use, some young writers use the same words over and over, which is a mistake. Grow your vocabulary. But beware, because some young writers overreach and employ words that are spectacularly out of place. Keep it simple, but not simplistic. Find clear, precise, varied language that helps you make your point. When you read, note how other writers use verbs, transition phrases, secondary sources, and let us not forget: punctuation. Punctuation is often corrupted by misuse. Learn how it works so your reader does not lose faith in your credibility as a writer. Proper punctuation adorns writing and organizes it clearly and smoothly, like a pair of earrings or how a tie finishes an outfit, adding coherence and style to all the rest. If you get it wrong, you look bad, you sound bad, and your reader may give up on you.

A complete guide to correct writing may require almost as many words as the language has, and would be beyond the scope of this book. If you need a general-purpose guide to the basic rules of writing, I suggest *A Writer's Reference*, by Diana Hacker and Nancy Sommers (www.bedfordstmartins.com). Our purpose here is to present and explain the writing needs of social workers in practice settings. With that in mind, let's proceed to the writing topics that create the most challenges for social work documentation, reporting, and advocacy.

CATEGORIES OF COMMON WRITING ERRORS

Sentences

The essentials of the sentence: noun and pronoun and verb:
Noun: A person (e.g., the client); or a place (e.g., my office); or a thing (e.g., my computer).

Pronoun: A word that stands in for a noun as a kind of shorthand reference. Pronouns can be in the first, second, or third person. For example, the following are pronouns: I, you, us, it. Pronouns can be the subject or object of a sentence and change when used as either the subject or the object.

	Singular		Plural	
	Subject	Object	Subject	Object
First person	I	Me	We	Us
Second person	You	You	You	You
Third person	He, she, it	Him, her, it	They	Them

<u>Subject and object</u>: All sentences have subjects, and without a subject your words do not add up to a sentence. Most sentences also have objects (discussed in detail below). Briefly, the subject is the main topic of the sentence (it could be a noun or a pronoun), and the subject must take or do some action. Action words are verbs. The subject does something, and the object of a sentence receives the action, or is affected by it.

<u>Verb</u>: Word that gives action to the noun or pronoun. The "home base," or "root" of verbs, is the unconjugated form of the action: to eat, to see, to write, to run, to swim, to think, and so on.

Most people conjugate verbs automatically. But thinking about English as we might about a second language helps the writer of English understand the way verbs get *conjugated* into six categories, just as they would in other languages. Here are a few examples in the present tense:

Example, using the verb **to write**:

	Singular	Plural
First person	I write	We write
Second person	You write	You write
Third person	He, she, or it writes	They write

Note that the formula for the conjugated word endings (additions to the to-form [the root] of "to write"), is just to add an s in the third person singular; the other forms just use the root word, "write." Many other languages change the verb's last letter for each conjugation, but in English we add "s" to the third person singular form and use the root word for the other five conjugations. The verbs **to be** and **to have** are basic for building more complex verb forms, and are *irregular*, meaning they are conjugated unusually:

	To Be		To Have	
	Singular	Plural	Singular	Plural
First person	I am	We are	I have	We have
Second person	You are	You are	You have	You have
Third person	He, she, it is	They are	He, she, it has	They have

The words that make up the unconjugated form of "to be" appear nowhere in its singular or plural conjugations. For example, "to be" in the first person is "I am." In the case of the verb "to have," the third-person singular conjugated form is "irregular," but the other five forms follow the formula of regular verb conjugation.

Let us consider verb conjugation in the *past tense*: compare the regular verbs, "to write" and "to smile", with the irregular verbs, "to be" and "to have," in the following examples of past tense conjugation.

	Regular Verb: To Write		Regular Verb: To Smile	
	Singular	Plural	Singular	Plural
First person	I wrote	We wrote	I smiled	We smiled
Second person	You wrote	You wrote	You smiled	You smiled
Third person	He, she or it wrote	They wrote	He, she, it smiled	They smiled

	Irregular Verb: To Be		Irregular Verb: To Have	
	Singular	Plural	Singular	Plural
First person	I was	We were	I had	We had
Second person	You were	You were	You had	You had
Third person	He, she, it was	They were	He, she, it had	They had

For past-tense conjugation of regular verbs (and some irregular verbs like "to have"), the root word changes its spelling, and so "write" becomes "wrote" in the past tense, and the writer then must use it for all six conjugations in the past tense. In this example, write changes to wrote in the past tense ("i" became "o"). Note, however, that in the case of "smile" the past tense requires that smile add a "d" to the end of the word, while verbs that end in consonants like "bark" gain an "ed" at the end when in the past tense (e.g., "barked"). And another important example is that the past tense of the verb "to be" follows yet a different pattern from those already mentioned.

If English is your second language, you should memorize the various English verb forms for the most commonly used verbs. This will make your writing more precise and more effective. Unfortunately, grammarians have long noted that English is notoriously difficult to learn because there are more exceptions to the rules than there are rules! Many other languages have much more consistent conjugation rules—once you know those rules, you can conjugate almost any verb accurately. This is not the case in English.

Sentence Structure

As we move forward into sentence structure, occasionally in our examples we will refer to first-, or second-, or third-person verb forms, as well as to whether the verb is singular or plural. We will also refer to pronouns and whether they function as the subject or object in the sentence. We want to concentrate on these particular issues because they tend to create problems for writers of social work documentation. Let us consider a bit more about pronouns.

Possessive Pronouns, Subject and Object of a Sentence:

	Singular		Plural	
	Subject	Object	Subject	Object
First person	My	Mine	Our	Ours
Second person	Your	Yours	Your	Yours
Third person	His, her, its	His, hers, its	Their	Theirs

Pronouns substitute for names of people, places, or things. When a noun possesses the object, the noun takes on an apostrophe to indicate ownership. For example, "Maria's bike does not work." Marie is the noun and takes the apostrophe. But if you were to use a sentence with a pronoun, the pronoun does not take an apostrophe to indicate possession. For example, "her bike is broken" or "the broken bike is hers."

Here are a few examples of nouns, pronouns, and the uses of apostrophes:
Noun and apostrophe: Steve's bank account is down to single digits.
Pronoun without apostrophe: His bank account is down to single digits.
Noun with apostrophe: The social service agency's case load grew by 15% last year.
Pronoun without apostrophe: Its case load grew by 15% last year.
The agency's expanded hours are convenient for my clients' schedules.
The agency's expanded hours are convenient for their schedules.
Its expanded hours are convenient for their schedules.
The benefits of our expanded hours are theirs.

Note that there are no apostrophes in any of the pronouns in the last four examples, including the last example, in which "theirs" seems to require an apostrophe. Nevertheless, to use one would be incorrect. (For more information on the apostrophe, go to the Punctuation section on page 275.)

Sentences need at least one noun or pronoun, plus at least one verb. Anything less is an incomplete sentence. But let us move from nouns, verbs and pronouns to other parts of speech you can include in a sentence.

<u>Adjective</u>: An adjective is a word that modifies a noun.
Example: "You, my brown-eyed girl." A color like brown, modifies a noun (e.g., *brown* eyes). All colors are adjectives. For example, "Look at the *green* grass," or, "I miss the *blue* and *yellow* houses of my old neighborhood."

<u>Adverb</u>: An adverb is a word that modifies a verb, adjective, or another adverb. In social work writing, use adjectives and adverbs sparingly, because they tend to add unnecessary detail and/or opinion, and/or wordy and unclear sentences.

Example: *Bright* brown eyes (here the adverb "bright" modifies the adjective, "brown"); *extremely bright* brown eyes (an adverb modifying another adverb); or, she *furtively* eyed me with those *bright* brown eyes (furtively modifying the verb, *eyed*).

<u>Conjunction</u>: a conjunction is a word that connects words or phrases together. The most common conjunctions are: *and, or, but*, and *however.*

Article—direct and indirect: *A, an,* and *the* are used to introduce nouns. In some cases no article is needed.

If a common noun is a specific unnamed person (the woman in red), place (the subway platform) or thing (the marble), the is the proper lead-in because you are referring to a specific thing. Of course, most proper nouns do not get an article, because those nouns stand on their own: For example: "Paris," "Shirley," "Fredonia University School of Social Work." But some proper nouns need "the," including proper nouns like: "the Atlantic Ocean," "the Silk Route," or "the Republic of Fredonia." Most singular proper nouns do not need a lead-in, like "Mt. Everest," but a few do, especially noteworthy places, "the Gobi Desert" or "the Taj Mahal." If the sentence refers to a complete category, usually no article is needed: "Fish usually swim into the current." In this sentence "fish" captures a complete category (all the fish on Earth), but "current" does not. There are other currents besides the ones in rivers and streams, so "current" receives an article.

The spell check function on most word processers will usually indicate errors of omission or inclusion involving articles. The issue for human service documentation is not *which* article to use, but *when* to use it. Basic rules of English dictate situations that call for articles or other lead-ins. A lead-in is a word that introduces a noun (e.g., "all," "some," "any," "this," "that"). But human service agencies usually have their own rules for whether and when an article is used. For example, often "client" does not get the expected direct article "the": "Client arrived at 3 PM, as scheduled." Sometimes, the agency will have a printed set of guidelines; other times you need to figure it out on your own. A good orientation activity when you begin a new field placement or job is to read some client files, to learn both about the work the agency is doing and how the agency documents information. This applies to the way the agency prefers to have their documents formatted. (We will discuss formatting further in the human behavior and practice case study sections.)

Basic Components of Sentences: Subject, Verb, and Predicate

We write in sentences. In order to understand proper word usage (managing all those thousands of words correctly), it is essential to understand the sentence: its components, its requirements, and its possible structures. Many of the errors that appear in students' and practitioners' writing are due to mangled sentences.

In social work narratives, we rely most frequently on the simple declarative sentence, requiring a subject (the person or thing the sentence is about), a verb (what the subject does, says, or has), and usually a *predicate* (the object of the verb—the receiver of the action).

For example, "my agency [subject] lost [verb] 15% of its funding [predicate: object of the verb]."

Although the order of these three basic parts of a sentence can be altered, it is a good idea to use this formula (subject, verb and predicate) until you are ready to get more adventurous. Simple clarity is preferable in documentation such as clients' files and reports to funders. When you write for public consumption, like letters to newspapers or testimony about legislation, you can vary the writing style and make it your own by varying the basic declarative sentence model, and by adding to it.

Subjects, verbs, and predicates can be elaborate, yet still use the declarative structure. One way is to use more than one predicate: "My agency [subject] lost [verb] 15% of its funding [predicate] and cut the Saturday programs [second predicate]." Notice that the second predicate ("cut the Saturday program") is not a complete sentence by itself. Instead, it is a subordinate clause (or a sentence fragment) because it is missing a subject (one of the two essentials for a sentence—the other is a verb). There is a verb in the sentence, "cut," and a predicate, "the Saturday program," but no subject. This means the phrase does not say who or what cut the Saturday program. We know "the agency"—the sentence's subject—did the cutting, but "the agency" is not mentioned in the phrase, "and cut the Saturday programs," which is why it is only a fragment of a sentence.

The thought can be written correctly several additional ways:
- Make it a separate sentence by adding a subject—"My agency lost 15% of its funding. The director cut the Saturday program."
- Write it as one sentence with two complete thoughts and use a semicolon to link both parts of the sentence—"My agency lost 15% of its funding; the director cut the Saturday program."
- Insert a conjunction—like, and, but, consequently, or therefore—between the two complete thoughts, sometimes with a comma: "My agency lost 15% of its funding, therefore the director cut the Saturday program."
- Write it as one sentence with a second predicate. Rather than simply stringing simple declarative sentences together, you can alter these forms to make your writing more interesting.

Here is another example of a more complex sentence that includes a compound predicate: "The family arrived ten minutes early for our appointment, eager to get started."

Subject: The family
Verb: arrived
Predicate: ten minutes early
Second predicate: for our appointment

But what do we do with "eager to get started"?

In this example, "eager to get started" can be a third predicate, or a modifier of the other predicates. If "eager to get started" is equal in importance and message to "ten minutes early" and "for our appointment," it is a third predicate. But if "eager to get started" explains "ten minutes early" and "for our appointment," it is an *adverb phrase* (modifying the verb "arrived"). Either way, the sentence is correct, but there is a degree of ambiguity about what the phrase "eager to get started" is referring to, meaning the writer may want to clarify the meaning of "eager to get started."

Here are some alternatives:
- The family arrived ten minutes early for our appointment because they were eager to get started.
- The family arrived ten minutes early for our appointment; they were eager to get started.
- The family arrived ten minutes early for our appointment. They were eager to get started.

Modifiers are words or phrases that add meaning to other words or phrases. For social work documentation, the rule is to use modifiers that clarify and specify, but do not add unneeded information.

Example of modifiers: The three-person family arrived ten minutes early for our appointment, very eager to get started.

The addition of "three-person" tells us the components (three members) of the family and not its composition – adults, children, and their relationships. The phrase "three person" modifies the noun, "family." "Very" tells us the family was more than just eager. In some documentation, "very" is avoided because it is imprecise and subjective: what may be "very" to me may be routine to you. Instead, the writer might cite evidence of "very."

For example, "the mother and the two daughters [composition of the family] arrived ten minutes early for our appointment, eager to get started. The girls fidgeted and the mother kept looking at the clock." When describing how clients handle themselves, actual direct reporting of their behavior is preferred to ambiguous adjectives.

Notice in the example above that we avoided the two-predicate structure. Instead, there are two stand-alone sentences joined into one sentence with the conjunction "and." We did this because there are two separate subjects ("the girls" and "the mother"), each doing different things. As an alternative, we could have used a colon instead of the conjunction. That would be fine. It would be difficult to combine these two bits of information in the same sentence with two predicates because there are two unrelated actions. Predicates receive the action of verbs; this means that the two predicates in the sentence receive different actions from two different verbs. Thus, the correct ways to write the sentence include: two separate sentences; one sentence with two clauses joined by a conjunction; or one sentence formed from two complete sentences joined by a colon.

Compound and Complex Sentences

The basic idea here is when and if a phrase can stand alone as a complete sentence.

Compare these two sentences again:
The family arrived ten minutes early for our appointment because they were eager to get started.
The family arrived ten minutes early for our appointment, eager to get started.

The first is a compound sentence. It consists of two complete sentences joined by a conjunction—in this case, "because." A colon instead of "because" would also work. The second example is a complex sentence. It consists of one complete sentence and a phrase—or clause—that cannot stand alone. "Eager to get started" is a sentence fragment because there is no subject – no one is identified as "eager to get started."

Both the compound and the complex sentence forms are grammatically correct, but as you write, here are a few key ideas to keep in mind:

- Avoid sentence fragments! These are incomplete sentences missing either a subject or a verb. More on this below.
- Avoid using the semicolon to connect a complete sentence with a sentence fragment (see the discussion of semicolons, in the punctuation section).
- The semicolon can substitute for a coordinating conjunction, but the two cannot be used together.
  - This is correct: The family arrived ten minutes early for our appointment; they were eager to get started.
  - This is incorrect: The family arrived ten minutes early for our appointment; so they were eager to get started.

- Avoid stringing together more than two stand-alone sentences into one long sentence and joining them with a comma. This kind of writing, called *comma splice*, is incorrect and difficult to understand.
- Avoid the problem of *misplaced modifiers*. This problem occurs when the modifier ("ten minutes early") is placed too far from the word(s) it modifies and so the sentence becomes difficult to understand. The rule is to place the modifier as close as possible to the word or phrase it modifies.

In addition to declarative sentences, consisting of a subject, a verb, and usually a predicate (or multiples of each), there are three other kinds of sentences in common usage:

- Imperative sentences order the reader to do something—"Read all your assigned homework."
- Interrogative sentences are questions—"When will I see you again?"
- Exclamatory sentences exclaim—"I am so excited!!"

In agency and client narratives, these three sentence formats generally are avoided. In writing for public audiences, imperative, interrogative, and exclamatory sentences should be used judiciously because they can detract as much as emphasize important messages. Like all tools, they have productive uses, but there are more opportunities to misuse or overuse them than to apply them effectively.

Incomplete Sentences

A complete sentence contains a subject and a verb. There can be more components, but a subject and a verb are necessary. The subject is the person or thing the sentence is about; the verb is the action undertaken by the subject. Incomplete sentences—sentence fragments—are missing either a subject or a verb.

The "ing" form of verbs can create confusion for writers. Verbs like: being, eating, reading, practicing, and any verb ending in "ing" means that these are not stand-alone verbs, and if used as the main verb in a sentence they will lead to an incomplete sentence. Verbs ending in "ing" become compound verbs when a form of the *to be* verb comes before them. For example, I *was* being entertained; they *were* eating, we are swimming, and so on. Verbs ending in "ing" can be used as nouns called "gerunds." Consider the following sentence and how the gerund functions as a noun: "Eating a balanced diet is essential for good health."

> Eating [gerund/noun/sentence subject] a balanced diet [adjective modifying "eating"] is essential [verb] for good health [predicate/object of sentence].

Examples of incomplete sentences:

1. "Research, including single-subject design, my favorite class in the entire program." There is no verb for the subject of the sentence, "research." In other words, the subject "research" is not taking any action from a verb. Here is a corrected version: "Research, including single-subject design, *is* my favorite class in the entire program." "Is" is a verb (to be). Now the subject is taking action.
2. "Research, being my favorite class, including single subject design, but there is a lot of reading."

Using "being" in this way is a common error but it is still incorrect because "being" does not function as a verb in this sentence. Here is a corrected version: "Research is my favorite class, but there is a lot of reading." Note that we deleted the phrase, "including single-subject design" because it adds nothing to the sentence's meaning.

3. "Although, research is my favorite class in the entire program. There is a lot of reading." There are two easy corrections: remove the "although" and add a coordinating conjunction between the remaining stand-alone sentences. "Research is my favorite class, but there is a lot of reading." Or keep "Although," change the period to a comma, and combine the two thoughts into one sentence: "Although research is my favorite class in the entire program, there is a lot of reading." We can also combine both sentences and avoid a run-on sentence by using a semicolon: "Research is my favorite class in the entire program; however, there is a lot of reading." Both statements are complete sentences, but the semicolon allows us to combine them into one sentence with the conjunctive adverb "however."

Clauses, Phrases and Incomplete Sentences

A sentence may contain clauses, which are groups of words that have a subject and verb. Some clauses can stand as complete sentences on their own, but others cannot, usually because they are introduced by a conjunction (see Case 2: subordinate clauses, on following page).

<u>Case 1: An independent clause</u> is a clause within a sentence that *can stand alone as a separate sentence.* Independent clauses are joined to other independent clauses by a colon, a semicolon, or a conjunction preceded by a comma.

Example: *My brother is younger than I am,* <u>but</u> *he finished college before I did.*
"But" is a coordinating conjunction that connects two stand-alone sentences—My brother is younger than I am. He finished college before I did. The result is one complete sentence.

You can use a semicolon with a conjunctive adverb instead of a coordinating conjunction, for the same effect:
My brother is younger than I am; however, he finished college before I did.

Or, you can just use two sentences:
My brother is younger than I am. He finished college before I did.

Sometimes you can collapse the two sentences into one simple sentence:
My younger brother finished college before I did.

Notice that the sentence with the fewest words has no internal punctuation or conjunctions, yet it retains the same meaning. That is because both sentences are about "my brother," and "is younger than I am" can be replaced by one adjective ("younger").

We advise our students to begin writing with separate sentences and move to combining simple sentences with coordinating conjunctions and semicolons when they are sure they understand how to use them. We are interested in striving for saying as much as we can with as few words as possible, but that may take some practice.

For a colon to be appropriate, the second sentence would need to be an elaboration of the first, and not present totally new information:
My younger brother was an excellent student: he finished college before I did.

All of these cases involve stand-alone sentences that can be united into one sentence by coordinating conjunctions, appropriate punctuation, and, sometimes, elimination of redundant information. Beware: Commas cannot be used to connect two stand-alone sentences. Connecting two stand-alone sentences with a comma is called a ***comma-splice***. This is to be avoided.

In the strict grammatically correct world, the only coordinating or "connecting" conjunctions that can combine two independent clauses into one sentence are ***and, but, or, nor, for, so*** and ***yet***, and all *must be preceded by a comma* (Hacker, 2009, p. 58).

Case 2: subordinate clauses: Sometimes a sentence contains a subordinate clause: a group of words with a subject and verb that cannot stand on their own, because they are preceded by an introductory word like a **subordinate conjunction** or **introductory pronoun** that interferes with the complete thought, for example, who, whom, whose, which, that, when, where, although, because, if, unless, when (Hacker, 2009, p. 242). When used alone, a subordinate clause is an incomplete sentence because the subordinate conjunction is added, requiring additional information. For example, if you add the conjunction "when" to an independent clause (*my brother graduated from college*), you get "When my brother graduated from college," which promises a new piece of information: something related to the "when." So a perfectly fine sentence—"My brother graduated from college"—becomes a subordinate clause with the addition of the conjunction, "when."

One common writing error is beginning a sentence with a subordinate conjunction but not finishing the thought in that sentence: *Although, my brother is younger than I am. He finished college before I did.* You can avoid this error by remembering that subordinate conjunctions are never set off by commas unless directly followed by a *nonrestrictive* (parenthetical or nonessential) clause or phrase. Without the comma, subordinate conjunctions imply a thought that needs to be completed.

Subordinate clauses must be combined with independent clauses to create complete sentences.

Example: "Although my brother is younger than I am [subordinate clause] he finished college before I did [independent clause]."
The subordinate clause cannot stand as a complete sentence because "although" (subordinate conjunction) requires more information. Note that both clauses have nouns and verbs. As we noted earlier, the subordinate clause loses its status as a complete thought when the subordinate conjunction is added. But if you remove "although" from the subordinate clause, it becomes a complete sentence or an *independent* clause. The use of a comma between subordinate and independent clauses depends on a number of factors, which we will discuss later in the punctuation section. If you are not sure, use the comma.

Run-on Sentences

Run-on sentences contain too much information for one complete thought. Convoluted sentences may be grammatically correct but are difficult to understand, as there is too much information for the reader to connect a verb with a subject and understand that connection along with other information in the sentence. Commas cannot repair run-on sentences—in fact, they are often the cause of run-on sentences—but colons, semicolons and conjunctions can solve the problem.

Here is a run-on sentence: "Research is my favorite class, all the topics are interesting." This example is also known as a "comma-splice" because two complete sentences are "spliced" together with a comma when a stronger form of punctuation is needed to link or separate the two independent clauses.

Here are three ways to fix the problem:
- Use a colon: "Research is my favorite class: all the topics are interesting."
- Use a semicolon: "Research is my favorite class; all the topics are interesting."
- Use a conjunction: "Research is my favorite class because all the topics are interesting."

Of course, two separate complete sentences are always an option: "Research is my favorite class. All the topics are interesting."

When in doubt, use simple sentences. (See the Punctuation section for more information about commas, colons, semicolons, and conjunctions.)

Misplaced and Dangling Modifiers

What is a modifier and when is it dangling? As a rule, words or phrases that modify or add meaning to other words in a sentence should be placed as close as possible to the ideas being modified. For example, note how the adjectives modify their nouns: "the speedy horse," "the lengthy meeting," "the motivated student." Adverbs modify as well. They modify adjectives or verbs: "The very speedy horse," "the extremely lengthy meeting," "the highly motivated student."

More Examples of Modifiers:
"The highly motivated student studied hard for her mid-term exam."
"Highly" is an adverb and it modifies "motivated," an adjective; "hard" is an adverb and it modifies "studied," a verb.

"The long meeting slowly covered its lengthy agenda." "Long" and "lengthy" are both adjectives, modifying the nouns "meeting" and "agenda," respectively. "Slowly" is an adverb, modifying the verb "covered." Without modifiers, the sentence would read, "The meeting covered its agenda." "Long," "lengthy," and "slowly" add meaning.

But beware of too many modifiers. They can lead to a "wordy" writing style rather than clarify; they can make things more difficult to understand when overused.

Other problems arise when the writer includes modifiers (adjectives or adverbs) at the end of a sentence or far away from the action, objects, or people they are modifying: "The long meeting covered its lengthy agenda slowly." Here, "slowly" is a misplaced modifier. In addition, it is a "dangling" modifier because it "dangles" at the end of a sentence.

Another Example:
Research, my favorite class, meets Mondays 9–12, with very interesting topics. "Very interesting topics" modifies Research, not Mondays, so it should go as close as possible to Research: "Research, with very interesting topics, meets Mondays 9–12."

Sometimes misplaced modifiers have no explicitly-identified nouns or verbs to modify. The information may be important, but it is not applied directly to anyone or anything in the sentence.

Examples:
- Diligently following his medical regimen for two weeks, the clinician congratulated the client.
- Beginning right on time, the chairperson was able to cover all the items on the agenda.
- Having recently received her MSW, the homeless shelter was quick to hire Mandy.

Each of these three sentences begins with phrases that appear to modify nouns at the opposite end of the sentence: the client was diligent; the agenda began on time; Mandy received her MSW. But the modifiers are so far removed and indirectly worded that it is not entirely clear what they are modifying.

Correct wording:
- The clinician congratulated the client for diligently following his medical regimen for two weeks.
- The chairperson covered all the items on the agenda because she began the meeting on time.
- Mandy received her MSW and was quickly hired by the homeless shelter.

For us, the distinction between misplaced and dangling modifiers is less important than knowing to place modifiers close to the words they modify, and making sure the modifiers are adding necessary information to the nouns or verbs intended to be modified.

Syntax

Sometimes writing instructors may tell you that you have *syntax* errors. This is another way of saying your writing style is difficult to follow. Syntax refers to the ways words are ordered to form a sentence, and so syntax is closely related to the placement of modifiers, among other things.

Forms of syntax errors

Verb-Noun Agreement:
Verbs and subjects should agree in tense and case. The common problem for most young writers is consistency in verb tense in a sentence, especially present and future tenses. Once a case is selected, meaning that the writer chooses to present a narrative in the future, present or past tense, that case should be used throughout the narrative, unless the information itself occurs in a different tense (or is permanent).

A Correct Example of Verb Tense:
"We arrived at the nursing home at 9:30 AM and met with the director, who took us on a tour of the facility. The building is clean and bright. The staff is friendly. There is artwork on almost every wall, some of it the products of the residents. The social work director said there is no waiting list."

Can you find the different tenses in this example? Note the events in the story occurred in the past: the arrival at the nursing home, the meeting with the director, that we took a tour, and the social worker saying there is no waiting list. All of these events occurred in the past, and so are written in the past tense because they happened in the past. However, the conditions of the environment—not the events—described in this story are "always happening," even now. These conditions include: the openness and brightness of the building, the friendliness of the staff, the artwork, and the absence of a waiting list. These conditions take on the present tense because they are conditions, not events; still, if we think these conditions are not likely to be permanent, we can use the past tense to describe them.

Here is an incorrect example:
"We arrived and met with the director, who gives us a tour of the facility. It rains while we visit. The tour took an hour." In this example, events that occurred in approximately the same time frame are reported in two different tenses, a verb agreement error.

A good rule of thumb: if it happened in the past, tell it in the past tense. Switch to the present tense when describing a permanent condition: "I met with my client, who suffers from diabetes."

Active and Passive Voice
Consider these two sentences:

- Cognitive-behavioral therapy is easily understood by practitioners who work with truant teenagers.
- Practitioners who work with truant teenagers easily understand cognitive-behavioral therapy.

Which statement do you prefer? The first is written in the passive voice. Typically, in passive statements people do not take action; the action happens to them. Thus people are passive. In the active version, people take action. Both statements are grammatically correct, but the active voice is clearer. Passive voice often leaves unstated who is doing the action—hence, the action just "happens" and it is not clear who is doing it. The active voice demands that the writer knows who is doing what to whom. Also, the active voice uses fewer verbs, so you can say more with less. For example, "the ball was thrown" is the passive voice. Who threw the ball? We do not know. Solution: "Jack threw the ball." In this solution, it becomes clear that Jack threw the ball, and more, the verb "threw" is activated and not sharing space with a "to be" verb. "Jack threw" is clearer and contains more information than "the ball *was* thrown."

Unless it is important to convey the idea that the action came to the person, or if knowing who is doing the action is impossible to discover, we typically prefer the active voice.

Forms of the verb "to be," (am, are, is, be, being, were, was, would be) can be warning signs of passive sentences. So can introductory phrases with forms of "to be."

Examples:
1) The budget cuts were testified against.
2) My client testified against the budget cuts.

1) It was decided to stand up and fight the budget cuts.
2) My agency decided that it was time to stand up and fight the budget cuts.

1) The budget cuts were felt by the residents of the homeless shelter.
2) The residents of the homeless shelter felt the budget cuts.

1) The community garden was worked on.
2) Many community residents worked on the community garden.

In each pairing, #1 is in the passive voice, and #2 is the active voice.

When a writer feels uncertain or ambivalent or simply lacks necessary information, this can often take the form of wordy, passive sentence structure.

1) It felt as though there was tension in the room.
2) I felt the tension in the room.

In #1, the writer conveys an unnecessary element of uncertainty, when a declarative sentence could express the situation more actively.

Keep it Lean and Mean. Avoid Repeating Yourself. Say More With Less.
For example, words like "also," "and," "as well," "in addition," and "too" should be used carefully and sparingly. The rule is one of these words per sentence. Here is an example of an incorrect sentence: "Also, the client came in with many questions about her medications as well." Here is a corrected version: "The client came in with many questions about her medications as well."

For brevity, equity among elements in a sentence, and professional clarity, replace the words "not only" with "and" or another conjunction. Incorrect: "The client came in with *not only* her son, but his friend as well." Correct: "The client came in with her son and his friend."

Here is a sentence that needs pruning: "What I saw was a very satisfied client."
Corrected version: "I saw a very satisfied client." Alternative corrected version: "The client was very satisfied."

Capital Letters
Capital letters are reserved for proper nouns, like people and place names, initials, titles, and for the beginnings of sentences and quotes. Regions and places get capitalized when they are in the form of proper nouns: the South, Europe, East Fredonia, the Sahara, the USA, North America. When they are descriptors rather than proper nouns, regions do not get capitalized: the northern hemisphere; an arctic cold front; southern Spain. Common nouns do not get capitalized: for example, bus, street, continent, coffee. Directions are not capitalized: drive south; northerly wind; eastern exposure. But "Northern Lights" is capitalized because it is the name of a natural effect.

A common error in social work writing is erroneous capitalization of some terms, like social work itself. Your agency's name (proper noun) should be capitalized: the Fredonia Mental Health Center. But the common noun, "the agency," should not. On the other hand, the Center, when it is used as a substitute for the agency's title, is capitalized. Since "agency" does not appear in Fredonia Mental Health Center's title, it is a descriptor, and does not get capitalized.

Your client's name or initials, of course, should be capitalized, but not the common noun, "client." Months of the year and days of the week should be capitalized, but not the words "month" and "year." The President (of the United States) and the (U.S.) Congress are always capitalized, regardless of whether the titles are fully spelled out, but the mayor of Fredonia City (the state capital) is not, unless her name directly follows: Mayor Morra Meyer. The state legislature (unlike Congress) is not capitalized, unless written formally: the Fredonia State Legislature. State House is capitalized. When used as adjectives, proper nouns usually are not capitalized: congressional investigation; legislative hearing. "President" or "Presidential," when referring to the U.S. chief executive, is usually capitalized. Note that "chief executive," a descriptor rather than a title, is not.

Latin abbreviations (i.e., e.g., etc., et al.) do not get capitalized unless they begin a sentence, a very rare occurrence, but abbreviated organizational names and titles do get capitalized: NAACP, NASW, Dr., Ms. Abbreviations that describe title after a name or in the body of a sentence (MD, PhD, MSW) get capitalized; "she received her MSW from Fredonia State University." But when written out as descriptors, credentials or degrees do not get capitalized: He has a master's degree in social work; she is a physician (or medical doctor); they are clinical psychologists. Lawyers get "Esq.," short for Esquire, after their names; public officials get "Hon.," short for Honorary, before their names. Public officials who are also lawyers get Hon. but not Esq. A rule of thumb: when a person carries two titles, refer to the highest title, not both.

The term "social work" is often mistakenly capitalized. It is not a proper noun: The social worker arrived at the scheduled time. However, if you write it as a proper title, as in the Fredonia State University School of Social Work, it becomes a proper noun and gets capitalized.

Opinions

The writer's personal opinion—editorializing—should be avoided in most social work narratives. This is not to say that your professional judgment is unimportant. If you can connect your opinion to human behavior theory or to practice knowledge relevant to the issue you are describing, then include it judiciously. If you are writing about social policy and it is your intent to change minds, then so you should, in fact, include your opinion and professional judgment, but be careful to present a persuasive explanation so that the reader can appreciate the validity of your views. In other words, your rationale along with your credentials should be used so the reader is treated with respect.

Punctuation

The semicolon has only two correct uses. First, it connects two complete and equally-important sentences that are closely related to each other. When a semicolon is used in this way, each clause is independent and can stand on its own, but the writer uses a semicolon in order to indicate that the two independent clauses belong together as a more complete thought than presenting them separately. This is an optional but effective way to tell the reader that the second complete sentence is connected to the first. For example, "The president's report made several important points; she emphasized punctuality, thrift, staff recruitment, and morale."

Note again that the first independent clause, "the president's report made several important points," and the second independent clause, "she emphasized punctuality, thrift, staff recruitment, and morale," are complete sentences on their own. Both clauses have subjects and verbs.

Second, semicolons are used to separate items (usually multiple words) in a long list, and usually after a colon. For example, "The president's report made several important points: the need to arrive to work on time; the cash-flow crisis affecting the company; vacancies in staff positions; morale at all levels of the organization."

The colon indicates something important is coming next. It also may follow the phrases "for example", or "as follows", or a summary, an explanation, or a list. A colon may introduce a quote. The items that follow a colon do not have to be full sentences or even a list. And beware: Neither colons nor semicolons substitute for commas. Each of the three punctuation marks has its own specific purpose.

The comma should be used to make sentences clear by eliminating ambiguity, but it can do quite the opposite. Here are a few amusing examples:

In her book about punctuation, Truss (2003) writes the panda "eats, shoots, and leaves." This is also the book's title. On the cover there is a drawing of a panda with a handgun. Without commas, the meaning of the sentence should read, "The panda eats shoots and leaves," meaning that the panda's diet consists of "shoots and leaves." The absence, presence, and placement of commas make a total difference in the sentence's meaning. With the commas included, it sounds as if the panda eats, then shoots something, then leaves. The meaning of the sentence then is completely dependent on the use of commas. If the panda were your client, it would be essential to be clear about the different scenario—eating versus shooting—you intend to describe in your narrative.

Here is another example where proper comma usage makes all the difference: My client "walked on her head, a little higher than usual." It should be: My client "walked on, her head a little higher than usual" (Truss, 2003, p. 97). Which would you write in the client's file?

For social workers—as for all writers—when properly used, commas clarify how one word or phrase relates to another word or phrase in a sentence. Think of commas as a type of signpost telling the reader when to slow down, pause, and then to proceed again. When a comma indicates a pause, it often means the writer is expanding on or clarifying the main idea of the sentence, even if very subtly. A comma indicates to the reader that a shift is occurring, or, in the case of the panda and his diet, when there are no commas, it means that there is no shift occurring and the sentence should be read as one single thought, and in the following example, one single activity: "The panda eats shoots and leaves."

Commas are brief rest points, separating information in ways the reader can follow. Do not interrupt coherent statements with commas. Use commas to indicate where pieces of information begin and end. In addition to these general rules of thumb, here are a few more specific rules for the correct use of commas in social work narratives.

- If you have a sentence with multiple clauses, look to see if any one clause or phrase can be removed without changing a sentence's meaning. If so, and if the clause you have removed subtracts valuable information, put the clause back in and bracket the clause with commas. For example: "My client, *who just completed her GED*, was thinking about enrolling in a college course." If the phrase between the commas adds no useful information, consider dropping it as excess verbiage: "My client was thinking about enrolling in a college course." If the phrase, "who just completed her GED," adds important information, leave it in but use a comma before and after.

- If you begin a sentence with a conjunction, be sure to use a comma after the opening phrase: "Although she just finished her GED, she wanted to continue her education." This is especially true with "although" and "however" because these words require a counterpoint in order to complete a thought. When this is done incorrectly, it often looks like this: "Although, she just finished her GED. She wanted to continue her education." There's a period where the comma should be. Be sure to add the comma after the introductory conjunctive phrase if the rest of the sentence can stand on its own as a complete sentence. Otherwise, the sentence may be difficult to understand: "Although she just finished her GED, she wanted to continue her education." The comma after GED (the end of the introductory phrase) tells the reader the main idea of the sentence will be developed in the next phrase. When a conjunction occurs inside a sentence, a comma goes before, but not after, the conjunction. Here is an example that is incorrect: "She was interested in taking a summer research course, but, she could not afford the tuition." Correct: "She was interested in taking a summer research course, but she could not afford the tuition."

  Note: "However" and "therefore" are exceptions to this last rule and get different treatment. For example: "She was tired of school, however, she decided to go on for her bachelor's degree" (Sidell, 2011, p. 37).

- Commas cannot be used to separate two otherwise complete sentences. If you do, you have created a *comma-splice*. In this case the pause needs to be longer, and that is the job for either a coordinating conjunction, or another form of punctuation like the period, the semicolon, or the colon (depending on the sentence and what you think works best).

  Incorrect: "She was interested in taking a summer research course, she could not afford the tuition." This is a run-on sentence, or a "comma-splice." Correct: "She was interested in taking a summer research course, but she could not afford the tuition." The sentences are joined by a conjunction and so it is now correct.

  Correct: "She was interested in taking a summer research course; she could not afford the tuition." The semicolon connects two complete, related sentences.

  Correct: "She did not register for the summer research course: she could not afford the tuition." The colon is used when the second sentence or phrase is an elaboration or explanation of the first.

- When two adjectives modify the same noun, they should be separated by a comma.

  Example: "She was not interested in taking a research course during the *long, hot* summer."

  Exception: if they comprise a compound adjective, they should be connected with a hyphen: "She was not interested in taking a research course during the *two-month* summer session."

<u>Periods, Question Marks, and Exclamation Points</u> indicate the end of a sentence. The next letter should begin a new sentence and be capitalized. The punctuation marks indicate that the information in the sentence comprises one complete thought.

Apostrophe

Perhaps one of most commonly misused punctuation marks (along with the comma) is the apostrophe. An apostrophe should appear only in a very specific situation:

1. to indicate possession. When a noun (person or thing) possesses something in the sentence, the apostrophe should appear before the "s" if the noun is singular, after the "s" if the noun is plural. Here is an example: one client's strengths; many clients' strengths.

2. in a contraction of two words. For example: was not contracts to *wasn't*. But it is a good idea to avoid contractions in professional writing.

Common errors with apostrophes:

Incorrect: childrens', peoples', womens' and mens'. Each is already plural, so placing the apostrophe after the "s" is redundant. Instead, because the pronoun begins as plural, just add an apostrophe and "s," indicating possession: children's, people's, women's, and men's.

We suggest memorizing the following chart:

Possessive pronouns, subject and object of a sentence:

Singular Possessive	Plural Possessive – Subject	Plural Possessive – Object
My	Our	Ours
Your	Your	Yours
Her, his, its	Their	Theirs
Family's	Families'	Families
Child's	Children's	Children's
Person's	People's	Peoples
Woman's	Women's	Women's
Man's	Men's	Men's

Examples of Apostrophes to Indicate Possession:

The child's books; the children's books; the books are the children's; children's books are colorful. A man's hairstyle; men's hairstyle; men's hairstyles are boring. Her room; their room; rooms are theirs; theirs are small rooms. The family's appointment; the families' appointments; the 5 PM appointment includes three families.

Also note that the possessive pronoun is not sensitive to the number of items being owned: For example: "The family's neighborhood" and "the families' neighborhood." Here the phrase refers to one neighborhood, but different numbers of families. As the chart above shows, some plural possessive pronouns get apostrophes before the "s" in direct statements: people's choice; men's/women's room(s); but not in indirect statements or objective portion of sentences: the pencils are theirs; the cake is yours. As discussed under pronouns, the conjugation pronouns—I, you, he, she, it, we, you, they—do not take apostrophes in the singular or plural.

Names and apostrophes indicate possession: This is Mary Wilson's home. This is the Wilsons' home. The Wilsons live here.

Names ending in "s" require a slightly different treatment to indicate possession. This is John Stevens' home. Note that the apostrophe goes after the "s" to indicate possession. The Stevens family lives here. No apostrophe needed because the sentence does not indicate possession.

Quotation Marks

Quotation marks indicate that the words within them belong to somebody else, and not the writer. Quotation marks indicate, in other words, another speaker you have included in your narrative. Perhaps the clients exact words are necessary, and so you quote them and use quotation marks. Or, for policy issues in social work, perhaps you are quoting your supervisor in order to demonstrate that you understand the situation in whatever you are writing.

Quotation marks serve a second, more unusual purpose. Sometimes writers use them in order to highlight words for special attention, sometimes sarcastically, or sometimes to set the word off for special attention.

A common error with quote marks comes from confusing the British and American systems of quoting: In the British system, the quotation mark belongs inside the comma or period at the end of a clause or sentence. For example: According to the Code of Ethics, "do no harm". In the American system, however, the quotation marks go outside the comma or period at the end of a sentence or clause. For example: According to the Code of Ethics, "do no harm."

When using a quotation inside of a quotation, the inside quote is offset by single quotation marks (use the apostrophe on your keyboard) rather than regular or double quotation marks.

Example: My client described the tension between the two children: "Joey was angry at his sister, accusing Martha of 'contradicting everything I say.'" In this example, the parent's quote includes another quote, so the two quotes are separated by different types of quotation marks: the first quotation is set off with double-apostrophe quotation marks ("), but the second quote within the quote is set off with single-apostrophe quotation marks. We have to remember to close both quotes as appropriate. As shown, if both quotes conclude the sentence, they go outside the period. For example: "She complained about her sister saying that she was 'contradicting everything I say.'"

Dashes and Hyphens; Parentheses and Brackets

The hyphen (-) is used in cases when two words are combined to create a single, hyphenated word. In the English language, there is no rule or formula for all the correct uses. Check online or print references if you have a question. Here are some basic guidelines:

- Use a hyphen if you join two words together to form an adjective and you place it before a noun. For example: yellow-colored folder; long-suffering servant; glad-handing politician; self-cleaning oven.

- Use a hyphen when two or more words belong together, regardless of placement in a sentence: the author is world-renowned; the solution is tried-and-true; her date-of-birth is Oct 17th.
- Use a hyphen before and after some specific words: pre-tax dollars; president-elect.
- Hyphens are also used when two-digit numbers are spelled out: Thirty-Third Street,three-quarters.

Em Dashes (often typed or represented by double hyphens) are used to set off some words or phrases from the rest of a sentence, usually for emphasis or illustration, to introduce a new thought, or to indicate the writer's own thinking.

Examples:
- The staff meeting—called for Tuesday morning—was scheduled for us to discuss the agency's budget. (Commas, rather than the dashes, work here just as well.)
- The meeting was scheduled for Tuesday morning—first item on the agenda was the budget. (A colon would work just as well as the dash.)
- The chairperson—confused?—skipped the first item on the agenda.

Overall, use hyphens, em dashes, and parentheses sparingly because they interrupt thoughts and can be disruptive to the flow of a sentence.

Parentheses

As is the case with dashes, parentheses can be used to set aside some words from the rest of the sentence. Example: The community treatment team (a social worker, psychologist, and nurse) arrived on the scene ten minutes after the emergency was phoned in. Alternative: The community treatment team, consisting of a social worker, psychologist, and nurse, arrived on the scene ten minutes after the emergency was phoned in. Both versions are acceptable.

Parentheses also indicate documentation: The police report (page 2) indicates that a pothole in the road caused the accident.

In student papers and formal reports, parentheses are used in some citation styles. The American Psychological Association (APA) citation rules, for example, require the author and year of publication in parentheses: "Correct writing is very important for effective social work practice (Weisman and Zornado, 2012)."

Note: if a full sentence is written inside parentheses, the period goes inside the closing parenthesis mark; otherwise the period goes outside.

Brackets

Brackets are used to separate a comment inside parentheses.

Example: "The budget for last fiscal year (ending in red [the director under-estimated fuel costs]) included no funds for program growth."

Brackets are also used to insert commentary inside quotes.

Example: According to the client's record, "The family experienced many challenges [for example, the father lost his job] last year." The brackets indicate words that did not appear in the quoted sentence, but add an explanation.

Another example: As the patriot, Patrick Henry, said: "Give me liberty [e.g., freedom of speech] or give me death." We all learned in grade school that the quote was, "Give me liberty or give me death." In the above sentence, the writer who quoted Henry may have been making the point that freedom of speech was one of the freedoms Patrick Henry cared about.

Parentheses and Brackets With Punctuation Marks

When words or phrases are placed in parentheses or brackets inside a sentence, there should not be any punctuation before the first bracket or parenthesis. Instead, commas, semicolons, colons, periods, question marks, exclamation points, dashes, and hyphens, if needed, should come after the end of the bracketed or parenthesized material.

Examples:
- The community group scheduled a meeting with the city council person (a social worker), who was on the record as supporting the group's program.
- The Head Start program has an enrollment of 75 children (about 60% girls), most of whom are reading at or above their age level.
- In social work research classes (often students' least favorite), math phobia is challenged head-on.

HOMOPHONES, ALMOST HOMOPHONES, AND OTHER CONFUSING WORDS

In English there are many words that sound alike, or almost alike, but are spelled differently, and mean different things. An extensive list of such combinations can be found at http://fivejs.com/homeschool-downloads/homophones-list/. *Homonyms* are words that sound alike, are spelled alike, but have different meanings. *Homophones* are words that sound alike, but have different spellings and different meanings. The difference between homophones and homonyms is largely irrelevant for this discussion. The challenge is to know which word you need. There are no shortcuts; you need to learn the meanings of the words you use. Here are some examples of homonyms that may appear in social work writing:

Words that sound alike but have different spellings and different meanings:
Accept: to agree to receive or take
Except: to exclude
Aid: assistance
Aide: an assistant
Ade: a fruit drink

Air: a gas
Heir: offspring; inheritor

Aisle: corridor between rows of seats
I'll: I will
Isle: island

Allude: to hint at
Elude: to evade or avoid

A lot: many; an empty field
Allot: to mete out, to allocate
Alot: this is not a word

Altar: a place of worship
Alter: to change, to modify

Apart: separated
A part: a component of

Assent: agreement
Ascent: to rise, take off

Ashore: on land
Assure: to put someone at ease
Ensure: to make certain
Insure: to guarantee, to buy insurance

Bare: unclothed
Bear: to carry (verb) or a large animal (noun)

Base: location
Bass: musical voice, or instrument, or fish

Beat: defeat, pound, or flap (wings)
Beet: vegetable

Board: panel (board of directors) or plank (piece of wood)
Bored: tired, disengaged

Brake: to stop (as a car)
Break: destroy or to take relief (rest)

Bread: wheat product
Bred: raised

Buy: to purchase
By: authored, beside
Bye: "see you later"

Censor: silence
Sensor: receiver of impulses

Coarse: rough, uneven, or vulgar
Course: path or class

Counsel: to advise
Council: committee or deliberative body

Do: to act (verb); hairdo (noun)
Due: scheduled to occur
Dew: morning moisture

Capital: Upper case letter (e.g., capital A), money, or city in which the seat of government is located
Capitol: State House, Legislative building, Congress

Cite: quote or identify a source of information as a reference
Sight: vision, view
Site: a place or location

Complement: to add to, to augment
Compliment: to say something nice about something or someone
Complimentary: no cost; flattering

Cease: to stop
Seize: to grab or take

Dual: two, a pair
Duel: contest, as with swords; a debate is a duel of ideas

Device: an object, often a machine or appliance
Devise: to make, to create, to think up

Decent: trustworthy, well-mannered, good-natured, fair, nice
Descent: to fall, to descend in altitude, also indicates ethnic heritage
Dissent: to disagree, to oppose a decision or the majority view

Faint: to lose consciousness; to pass out
Feint: to make-believe, pretend; also to be timid

Fair: equitable, a good outcome for all involved
Fare: price, cost of admission

Feat: an accomplishment
Feet: what you walk on; or, units of measurement

Find: locate or discover
Fined: penalized with a required cash payment

Flair: style, charm
Flare: sudden fire or outburst

Forth: to go ahead
Fourth: number four in line

Genes: genetic components of biological inheritance
Jeans: a type of pants

Groan: a low vocalization
Grown: full size

Guessed: to form an opinion with no evidence
Guest: visitor

Hardy and hearty: hearty is the correct word except in idioms (e.g., hale and hardy)

Hear: to perceive sound
Here: this place

Heard: past tense of to hear
Herd: a large group, usually animals

Higher: loftier, greater in altitude or magnitude
Hire: to employ

Idle: inactive
Idol: an item of worship or a person of high regard

Incite: to initiate, set in motion
Insight: awareness

Intense: existing in an extreme degree
Intents: goals, plans, or aspirations

Know: to be aware of and to understand
No: a negative reply

It's: a contraction for "it is"
Its: an impersonal possessive, e.g., my car needs its battery replaced

Leased: rented, not owned
Least: lowest

Lessen: to reduce
Lesson: source of information, training

Loose: unrestrained
Lose: fail to win; to misplace

Manner: how one behaves
Manor: castle or mansion

Medal: an award
Metal: any ductile, fusible, lustrous material
Meddle: to interfere
Mettle: fortitude, strength

Mind: to care, to pay attention (verb), brain (noun)
Mined: took from the ground, as in coal

Miner: a person who digs in the ground
Minor: a person under the legal age of adulthood

Missed: did not catch or make contact with
Mist: water vapor

Mode: method or largest category
Mowed: cut down

Morn: the time before noon
Mourn: to feel the effects of loss

Naval: about the Navy
Navel: belly button

Pail: bucket
Pale: colorless

Pain: discomfort
Pane: a sheet of glass

Pair: two
Pare: to cut or trim
Pear: a tasty fruit

Passed: went by
Past: what came before

Patience: ability to wait
Patients: people served by healers

Peak: the tip top
Peek: to steal a look
Pique: to spark one's interest, curiosity, or anger

Peace: tranquility, absence of conflict
Piece: a portion
Peas: green vegetables

Peal: to ring, as a bell
Peel: the rind of a fruit (noun); to remove the exterior of a fruit (verb)

Pedal: to propel a bicycle
Peddle: to sell something

Pole: northern or southern ends of the Earth; or, a long rod
Poll: to take measure of, sample

Poor: to lack the means of support
Pore: an opening in the skin
Pour: to cause to flow

Pray: beseech a deity
Prey: to seize animals for food

Principal: main, most important, ranking person
Principle: guiding idea, tenet, or value

Precedents: events that legitimize occurrences that come after
Precedence: single event that legitimizes subsequent events
Presidents: chief executives

Presence: to occupy a place
Presents: gifts

Rain: precipitation
Reign: monarch's term of office
Rein: to tether or restrain

Raise: to increase or elevate
Rays: beams of light
Raze: to tear down

Residents: occupants
Residence: a home

Rack: storage shelf
Wrack: ruin, wreck, revenge

Rapped: knocked or criticized
Rapt: under a spell
Wrapped: enclosed or encased

Real: true, actual
Reel: dance or fishing apparatus

Review: summarize or assess
Revue: a musical show

Right: correct or specific direction; to east when facing north
Write: to form words on a surface with an instrument

Ring: finger adornment or the sound a bell makes
Wring: to squeeze and twist

Raw: not cooked
Roar: to bellow

Road: paved path
Rode: traveled
Rowed: to propel a boat with an oar

Roil: agitate
Royal: having to do with monarchy

Role: activities related to a specific position
Roll: a small bread; or, to tumble

Root: to cheer for; or, underground portion of a plant
Route: path

Rye: a type of grain
Wry: a kind of humor; disappointment

Sail: travel by water; a part of a boat
Sale: transaction; lowered price

Seam: place where separate pieces meet and are joined
Seem: to appear

Serf: landless peasant
Surf: to ride waves on a board; breakers on the beach

Scene: vista or view; or, a part of a movie, or play
Seen: what one has viewed

Scent: aroma
Sent: mailed
Cent: penny

Sea: body of water
See: to view, observe

Shear: to remove, as wool from a lamb
Sheer: nothing but, totally

Shone: glowed
Shown: put on display

Shore: where water meets land
Sure: certain

Slay: to kill
Sleigh: a form of transportation over snow

Sore: achy, angry
Soar: fly
Saw: viewed; or, a tool to cut wood

Stair: set of steps
Stare: to look intently

Stake: pointy stick; or an investment
Steak: a piece of meat

Stationary: fancy paper
Stationery: unmoving

Steal: to obtain illegally
Steel: hard metal

Straight: unbending
Strait: a narrow channel of water

Suite: group of offices or rooms
Sweet: tasty

Succeed: to achieve your goals
Secede: separate from

Team: group working together
Teem: to be full to overflowing

Tear: water emanating from an eye; or, a rip in fabric
Tier: section of a stadium
Tare: fee

Tern: a bird
Turn: to twist; opportunity

Threw: hurled or propelled
Through: done with, went by
Thru: not a word

Than: introduces the second element in a comparison
Then: a point in time

There: refers to a place, person, or thing
Their: the third person plural possessive pronoun
They're: a contraction of "they are"

Tied: tethered; or, an even score in a contest
Tide: the ocean's rising and falling action

To: a preposition; to go in the direction of
Two: a number
Too: also or excessive

Toad: large frog
Towed: dragged

Vain: unsuccessful; conceited
Vane: a wind direction indicator
Vein: blood vessel

Vice: assistant; or, a bad habit
Vise: instrument in a wood shop

Vial: medicine bottle
Vile: evil, loathsome

Waver: to vacillate
Waiver: to relax the rules

Way: route
Weigh: to measure
Whey: protein from milk

Weather: atmospheric conditions
Whether: if it be the case that

While: during
Wile: cunning, trickery

Whine: to complain
Wine: alcoholic drink from grapes

Would: intended action
Wood: hard, fibrous substance from trees

Yoke: Apparatus for managing a team of work animals, e.g., oxen
Yolk: the yellow part of an egg

Your: the second person singular possessive pronoun
You're: a contraction of "you are"
Yore: the past

Words That Sound Almost Alike
Adapt: adjust to
Adept: capable
Adopt: take custody of, or to take on the attributes of

Adverse: to act in opposition
Averse: opposed or reluctant

Advice: recommendations
advise: to offer recommendations

Affect: usually a verb – one person or thing affects another; or, a person's appearance or demeanor
Effect: usually a noun – something or someone has an effect on something or someone else

Affective: refers to emotional states
Effective: the ability to bring about an outcome

Appraise: assess value
Apprise: to inform others

Continual: repeated actions that do not happen all the time
Continuous: uninterrupted actions

Desert: an arid, waterless place; also, to vacate one's job, position, or responsibility
Dessert: an after-meal sweet

Eminent: Lofty, accomplished, highly respected
Imminent: Coming very soon; about to happen; inevitable

Emigrant: one who leaves from
Immigrant: one who comes to

Facility: a place, usually a building, or space in a building; it also means competence
Faculty: intellectual ability; or, the teaching staff of a school

Father: another name for dad (noun); also, to contribute to a birth (verb)
Farther: a greater distance measured in unites of distance
Further: refers to the depth of a situation or a concept, like a dilemma, debate, or an idea

Former: previous; formerly; the way it was in the past
Formal: officious, official; formally; officially

Gecko: very small tree frog
Get-go: the beginning

Legislator: an individual member of the legislature (House or Senate)
Legislature: the State House, Congress, House or Senate
Legislation: the bills that the legislature try to make into law

Personal: private or individual
Personnel: employees

Precede: come before
Proceed: go ahead

Predominate: to have or gain controlling power
Predominant: having superior strength

Prescribe: to recommend
Proscribe: to forbid

Respectful: to treat with courtesy
Respectively: to handle things in proper order

Wary: careful or nervous
Weary: tired

Other Misused Words and Rules of Thumb

About Contractions:
It is a good idea to avoid them unless your agency requires them.

"A" and "an"
Both "A" and "an" function as articles that come before nouns; "an" is used before nouns beginning with vowels, for example, "an ax is an indispensible tool for splitting wood."

Among and amongst:
Both are correct; amongst is an older and somewhat outdated version. I suggest using among.

Apart and a part
My model plane came apart when I dropped it.
I was glad to get a part in the school play.

Alot:
Alot is not a word, but it is misused—a lot.

Downfall:
This word is used frequently to indicate a disadvantage or negative consequence of an action, situation, or decision. "The client takes the bus to her job. The downfall is it takes an hour to get there." Downfall means loss of status, standing, privilege, or power, not negative consequence. Correct: "The client takes the bus to her job. Unfortunately, it takes an hour to get there."

Fewer and Less
Use "fewer" when you are discussing things that can be counted individually.
Use "less" when you are discussing things that are counted as categories or collectively.

Good and Well
Good is an adjective and should modify a noun. Good work, good meal.
Well is an adverb and should modify a verb or adjective, as in well done; it is also a noun and is a source of water or oil.

Graduate from
Students graduate *from* college.

Irregardless:
This is not a word. *Regardless* is the correct word.

Lay: to recline or to place something
Lie: to tell an untruth, to deceive

Imply: to suggest, or to hint at
Infer: reach a conclusion on the basis of evidence; to figure out something

I and E

Here's an old grammar school rhyme to help you remember this spelling rule: "I before E, except after C, and when sounding like "A," as in neighbor and weigh." Some of us forget the second part of the saying: when the sound is like a long A (ay), E comes before I, examples: "weigh" and "neighbor" in the saying. Add sleigh, rein, vein, and several others. But there are still exceptions in words social workers use: either, foreign, leisure (E before I, no C and no AY sound). It is best to commit common words to memory.

I and me

As Dorn (2007) said emphatically, "Never, never write 'him and I.'" You should not say it either. Why? The answer is rooted in sentence structure. Remember the subject and predicate in sentences? When the first person (I or me) is the subject of a sentence, "I" is used. We am writing a book about writing. "We" is the subjective form of the second person. "Us" is the objective form (receives the action described by the verb). I wouldn't say "We is writing a book," and I should not say "the book is written by we." Rather, in the passive voice or predicate part of a sentence, I would use me: "The book was written by us."

Confusion arises when you are talking about two or more people. For example, "he and I are writing a book together" is correct. So is "the book is written by him and me." It is either "he and I" (subject) or "him and me" (object). It is never, ever *him and I*.

This rule (I vs. me), applies to *he* and *him*, *she* and *her*, and *they* and *them*. If it is the subject of the sentence, use *I, you, he, she, it, we,* or *they*; if it is the object, *use me, him, her, us,* or *them*. Do this in speech as well as writing, and it will begin to feel natural. Note that *you* and *it* are correct in both the subjective and objective parts of a sentence.

Examples:
I look good in this shirt. In this example "I" is the subject.
This shirt looks good on me. In this example "me" is the object.
You and I look good in these shirts.
These shirts look good on you and me.
We look good in these shirts. "We" is the subjective form.
These shirts look good on us. "Us" is the objective form.

You look good in that shirt.
That shirt looks good on you.
Note that "you" is correct in both the subjective and objective parts of the sentence.

Raise: to move to a higher position
Rise: to get up from a lying, sitting, or kneeling posture

Reason is because: redundant. Reason means because.
        My client was late for our appointment because.....

Set: to put something or someone in a particular place
Sit: to be located or situated in a particular place; to be seated

That and *Which*—What's the Difference?
Choosing between the use of *that* or *which* depends on the phrase that follows its use. Both words introduce phrases. If the phrase can be removed from the sentence without changing the sentence's meaning, making it a non-essential phrase, use the term "which," usually preceded by a comma; if the phrase introduced by the term is essential for the sentence's meaning, making it an essential phrase, then use the term "that," usually without a preceding comma.

Examples:
* Statistical software, *which* came loaded on the hard drive when I bought the computer, makes my job easier.
* Statistical software *that* came with my computer when I bought it makes my job easier.

In the first example, the additional information between the commas does not change the sentence's meaning: the software helps me do my job. The second sentence reorganizes the information and makes it all essential: and so it is not just "statistical software" that makes the job easier as it is in the first example. According to the second example, the *software that came with my computer* makes my job easier.

Toward and Towards:
Both are correct. In American English, *toward* is used more often and generally strongly preferred by style books; in the British system *towards* is the preferred usage.

Unique:
One of a kind. Like no other. "Very unique" is redundant; "somewhat unique" is confusing. No modifiers are necessary.

Who, Whom, and *That*:
To choose between "who" and "' whom" follow the same criteria as the rules that govern the choice between "I" and "me." So, use "who" in the subjective case; use "whom" in the objective case.

Examples:
* "Who left this book in my office?" ("Who" is the subject; "left" is the verb; "book" is the object/predicate; "in my office" is a modifier of "left.")
* "To whom should I return this book?" ("I" is the subject; "should return" is the verb; "whom" and "this book" are the objects.)

No form of whom can be the subject of a sentence. Whom or whomever can only be used in the objective portion (predicate) of a sentence if they do not take verbs of their own.

Examples:
* Incorrect: Whomever wants to attend is welcome. Correct: Whoever wants to attend is welcome.
* Incorrect: The meeting is open to whoever we invite. Correct: The meeting is open to whomever we invite.

In the first example, "whoever" is correct because it is the subject of the sentence and takes the verb "wants."

In the second example, "whomever" is correct because it is part of the predicate, "to whomever we invite." If "whomever" did the inviting (making it a subject), it would change to whoever. But in the second example, "we" did the inviting, not "whoever."

Another Example:
The meeting is open to whoever brings a pot-luck dish. In this case, although "whoever" is in the predicate of the sentence (object of the verb "is open"), it takes a verb ("brings"). So it gets worded in the subjective form.

That and Who
Besides who and whom, *that* can be a pronoun for things in the third person case, but not for people. Incorrect: "I was worried about my client, *that* was late for his appointment." Correct: "I was worried about my client, *who* was late for his appointment."

Abbreviations
Earlier, we suggested that you avoid contractions (I'll, we'd, you're, it's) in social work writing, and that you should spell out words unless your agency follows a different convention. What about abbreviations? Should we spell out everything? What about mister?

Some commonly used abbreviations are acceptable in human service writing. Here are the basic rules:

Well-known organizations (e.g., USA, NASW) can be abbreviated without periods. Titles (Mr., Ms., Dr., Prof., Rev.) should be abbreviated with periods, as shown. Do not give anyone two titles (Dr. Martin Luther King, Ph.D). Pick one "honorific" and use it consistently. Use Mr. for men and Ms. for women, unless a formal honorific applies.

The abbreviations for time (a.m. and p.m.) should only be used with numerals: 4 a.m. But a.m. and p.m. do not substitute for the words morning and evening. Here is what we mean: "I usually wake up early in the a.m." This is not right. Rather than a.m., use "morning." Here's an example that uses a.m. correctly: "I set my alarm for 6:00 a.m. every day." While a.m. and p.m. (lower case with periods) are the proper identifiers of time, AM and PM are widely used and acceptable.

Numbers
The numbers one through ten should be spelled out, except dates, ages, and percentages. For example, "the mother had two children, ages 3 and 5." Sentences should not begin with numerals. Spell out any numbers that begin sentences. For example: "Twenty-four percent of local children attend the Fredonia Pre-School Program."

Latin Abbreviations
Etc. is an abbreviation for "et cetera," meaning "and so on." It is two Latin words combined into etc. In earlier times, it was sometimes written as "et c." (with "cetera" being abbreviated). Eventually, the et and c. got combined to etc. It is not "ect" or "and etc." Etc. cannot be combined with other Latin abbreviations: one per sentence.

<u>e.g</u>. means "for example," and is always followed by a comma (e.g.,), which is followed by an example of the idea or item in question. There is no exception.

<u>ie</u>. means "that is." As with e.g., i.e. is always followed by a comma (i.e.,), which is followed by the required elaboration or definition.

<u>Et al</u>. means "and others." It is used in citations and legal documents. Note there is no period after et (which means "and"). Only the "al" gets a period because it is an abbreviation of the Latin word "alia," others; "et" is not an abbreviation.

Prepositions

The English language contains more than 100 prepositions. One website lists 85 single-word prepositions, and 36 consisting of two words (http://www.listofprepositions.com/). *In, of, at, to, as,* and more join with nouns to modify other words or phrases in sentences and provide contexts. While several prepositions may fit a given situation (<u>in</u> school and <u>at</u> school), most are not interchangeable. Be sure the preposition you use fits the situation in which you are using it.

Examples:
* The kids were playing stickball *at* the park.
* The kids were playing stickball *in* the park.
* The kids were playing stickball *outside* the park.
* The kids were playing stickball *before* the park.
* The kids were playing stickball *with* the park.

Each sentence contains a preposition (italicized word). Clearly, the first two sentences make sense and mean almost the same thing, because "at the park" and "in the park" are nearly interchangeable—though not always! You could play stickball at the park, while waiting for the Red Sox game, but you will not be playing *in* the park during the game. But, *outside* the park means something very different, and *before* and *with* the park are nonsensical.

Spelling Pointers

For better or worse, a computer's spell-check software will indicate most misspellings in a document. Even so, spell-check is not perfect, and neither are most writers. It is a very good idea to know the correct spelling of words that frequently appear misspelled in human service documents. Here are the most common:
Attend<u>a</u>nce
Auth<u>o</u>r
Banned
Banning
Benefi<u>t</u>ed
Cal<u>e</u>nd<u>a</u>r
Commi<u>t</u>ment
Congra<u>t</u>ulate
Contro<u>l</u>led
Controlling
Correspond<u>e</u>nce

Emba<u>rrass</u>
Ha<u>r</u>ass/ha<u>r</u>assment
Int<u>eg</u>ration
L<u>a</u>beled
L<u>ei</u>sure
L<u>ia</u>ison
Occurr<u>e</u>nce
Panicking
Priv<u>i</u>lege
Rec<u>ei</u>ve
Sep<u>a</u>rate

Clichés

Clichés are popular phrases or sentences that are used frequently in routine speech.

There are thousands in popular use, but try to avoid clichés. They are like labels that are easy to use, but often misrepresent the complexities of a situation. Stay present and focused and use language that is appropriate to the situation.

PROFESSIONAL JUDGMENT

Plagiarism

Plagiarism is a complicated issue. The most common form of plagiarism is when writers steal someone else's words and ideas and present them as their own. This is about the most serious intellectual crime one can commit. Plagiarism can be grounds for dismissal from a college or university for students. For researchers, authors, historians, and others whose work involves writing about what they read, plagiarism can destroy one's career and reputation.

Most episodes of plagiarism appear to be inadvertent. In these types of cases, students either forget to put quotation marks around direct quotes or forget to give credit to an author or a website they have used as a source of information. It does happen, however, that students copy language from what they believe to be obscure websites, books, or manuscripts and try to pass it off as their own work. Both situations are violations, but the second is clearly a more serious violation of academic honesty standards. The former usually results in deducted points on a paper; the latter can lead to much more serious consequences.

There are a few simple rules about drawing on the work of others:

- When using others' work, give them credit, regardless of whether you have used their exact words within quotation marks; even if you paraphrase or refer to what you have learned from them in your paper, give the authors credit. When in doubt, give credit.
- Exact quotations require quotation marks.
- Paraphrasing another's words or ideas requires a citation at the end of the paraphrased material.
- More than three consecutive words lifted from another source comprises a quote. Use quotation marks.

- Check the preferred citation format for your field. In general, the social sciences use APA (American Psychological Association) formatting. Other disciplines may use other formats. Be sure to check for the current proper citation styles in use in your field.

Labelling

When describing service recipients, whether you call them clients, consumers, members, or participants, avoid writing about them and defining them in terms of their conditions or diagnoses. The strengths-perspective, as well as basic respect, leads us to view service recipients as people first, and as experiencing difficulties or challenges second. When we define people by their deficits, we dehumanize them and tend to disregard their strengths.

Incorrect: "My schizophrenic client is late again."
Correct: "My client who has schizophrenia is late again."

REFERENCES

Dorn, E. (2007, September 1). Goodbye, good luck and thanks. *Austin American-Statesman*. http://www.utexas.edu/lbj/archive/news/fall2007/dorn_oped.php

Hacker, D., & Sommers, N. (2011). *A writer's reference* (7th Ed.). New York: Bedford St. Martin's.

Sidell, N.L. (2011). *Social work documentation: A guide to strengthening your case recording*. Washington, DC: NASW.

Truss, L. (2003). *Eats, shoots, and leaves: The zero tolerance approach to punctuation*. London: Profile Books.

BIBLIOGRAPHIC WEB RESOURCES

English Forums: http://www.englishforums.com

English Trainer blog: http://englishtrainer.blogspot.com

Five J's, Homseschool Downloads, Homophones List: http://fivejs.com/homeschool-downloads/homophones-list

Future Perfect, Grammar Tips: http://www.future-perfect.co.uk/grammartips

Judy Vorfield's Office Support Services, Editing and Writing Services: http://www.editingandwritingservices.com

List of Prepositions: http://www.listofprepositions.com

Oxford Dictionaries: http://oxforddictionaries.com/?region=us

Steven Morgan Friedman's Cliché Finder: http://www.westegg.com/cliche

Washington State University, Common Errors in English Usage: http://public.wsu.edu/~brians/errors

Appendix B

Resumés and Cover Letters

Hopefully you will find a job after you graduate. Even in a good economic climate, you will need to prepare yourself for the competitive job-seeking process. Most often, as you apply for positions, your writing will represent you in the form of your resumé and cover letter. Whether you submit your job application via e-mail or hard copy, in order to pass the first screening step you will need to prepare these two written documents with care and attention to detail. Your goal is to prepare your resumé and cover letter to get you to the interview phase, at which time you can wow the employer with your persona. It should go without saying that you do not want your resumé and cover letter to cost you the chance of interviewing, particularly if you are well-qualified for the position. Let us take a look at how to prepare your resumé and cover letter in order to get past the first screening process.

An employer of BSWs and MSWs usually separates job applications into three categories: promising, back-up, and not acceptable.

Promising: these applications meet or exceed an agency's basic qualifications in terms of an applicant's education and relevant experience; further, agencies must determine if the applicant appears to be a good fit for the position.

Back-up: these applications meet at least one of the agency's criteria-- usually education-- and they come close on other(s), usually relevant professional experience; they are not obviously a poor match for the agency, but something in the application indicates the applicant may not be a good fit, or may not be adequately prepared. Writing errors in the resumé and/or cover letter are often a warning sign to perspective employers.

Not acceptable: these applications indicate that the job seeker is not qualified because she or he does not meet the position's stated requirements in terms of education and/or lacks the appropriate professional experience for the job. Writing errors in the resumé and/or cover letter are often a warning sign to prospective employers.

You are responsible for preparing your resumé and cover letter so that you present your education and experience clearly and factually. A sloppy resumé or cover letter indicates that you may not be a good fit for an agency. What do we mean by "good fit?" Employers are concerned that new staff members will fit in with an agency and work well with the staff. You should demonstrate that you are capable, knowledgeable, cooperative, flexible, and ready to take on the responsibilities of professional life. Employers cannot confirm that you are a "good fit" solely from your application, but they may rule you out if your materials convey any clue that you would not fit in well. One key piece of evidence about who you are and how you think is your writing. Beware of presenting incomplete or disorganized information, or phrases that may be mistaken for arrogance, for example, "I know I am a perfect candidate." Avoid defensive posturing or padding your resumé or cover letter with unnecessary information just to add length.

Guidelines for Resumés:

- Clarity is key. Be sure your resumé is easy to read. Use a traditional 12-point font like Times New Roman, or Garamond. Avoid italics or specialized fonts that are difficult to read. Resumés for entry-level jobs are usually only one page. If your resumé is longer than one page, be sure it is absolutely necessary.

- Your resumé should be entirely accurate and without errors of any kind.

- Develop and follow a clear outline:
  - College education (omit High School information), your professional experience, your other qualifications, and your contact information.
  - Order your information according to date, most recent first. Include names of places you worked and very brief descriptions of your responsibilities.
  - Be consistent with your formatting, e.g., use one font throughout, and if you choose to use headings, capitals, indentation, margins, or dates, do so consistently throughout.

- Appearance:
  - Avoid clutter. Do not pad your resumé with unnecessary information.
  - Use good business-quality paper but keep it simple. This is not a wedding invitation.
  - Do not overdo: graphics and artwork are not necessary and frequently clutter and get in the way of a quick scan of your resumé.

- Appropriate information:
  - You may include an "Objectives" section at the top of your resumé, though this is optional. "Objectives" briefly state your professional goals.
  - Your age, marital status, and other family information are not appropriate—nor is it legal for prospective employers to ask you about these things.
  - Your life prior to college is irrelevant unless particularly noteworthy.
  - Certificates, awards, and credentials are optional—cite them when they bear directly on the job you are applying for. Use your judgment.
  - Your college GPA is unnecessary information unless particularly impressive; dean's list is acceptable.

Guidelines for Cover Letters: be brief, courteous, and clear. Your letter should have no errors, no personal information, and should be no longer than one page. In your opening address, follow these guidelines:

- If a person's name is given in the job advertisement, for instance, Josephine Shmo, Fredonia Social Work Agency, then address your letter as follows:

Josephine Shmo
Fredonia Social Work Agency
Address

Dear Ms. Shmo:

- If an entity is named in the job advertisement, for example, "Search Committee," then address your letter as follows:

Search Committee,
Fredonia Social Work Agency
Address

Dear Search Committee:

- If the job announcement directs you to Human Resources or another office, address your letter as follows:

Human Resources Director
Fredonia Social Work Agency
Address

Dear Director:

- If no contact information is given, use the following format:

Fredonia Social Work Agency
Address

To Whom it May Concern: (or Dear Search Committee)

CASE 37: COVER LETTER

Stu Dent
555 Fifth Street, Apt. 5
Fenwick, FA 05555
Sdent_5555@fsc.edu
(888) 555-5555 (cell)

Tender Mercies Homeless Shelter
314 Circle Rd.
West Fenwick, FA 00227

To Whom it May Concern:

This is in response to your advertisement in the Sunday Fenwick Gazette of January 10 announcing the position of case manager at the Tender Mercies Homeless Shelter. I would like to be considered for the position.

Enclosed is a copy of my resumé. As you will see, I will graduate this May from Fredonia State College with a Bachelor's Degree in Social Work (BSW). My professional work experiences include a year at Community Resources, Inc., where I was placed for my BSW field practicum, another four years at Youth for Anarchy, where I began as a clerical worker and was promoted to the professional staff, and four additional years in several other work settings. My employment experience has been complemented well by my professional education at FSC. I am enthusiastic about moving into full-time social work employment.

I am very interested in exploring the possibility of joining your agency and I hope you will find me well-qualified and consider me for the advertised position. I would welcome the opportunity for an interview. You can reach me at sdent_5555@fsc.edu, (888) 555-5555.

Thank you in advance for considering me for this position.

Sincerely,

Stu Dent [signed]

Stu Dent [typed]

CASE 38: RESUMÉ

Stu Dent
555 Fifth Street, Apt. 5
Fenwick, FA 05555
Sdent_5555@fsc.edu
(888) 555-5555

Objective: To secure a position in generalist social work practice with
increasing responsibilities.

Education

B.S.W.	2012	Fenwick State College (FSC) Minor: Psychology. Dean's List, four of six semesters Alpha Delta Mu, National Social Work Honor Society Volunteer: Student Crisis Hot Line
A.A.	2010	Community College of Eastern Fredonia (CCEF) Dean's List, all four semesters

Professional Experience

2010 - Present	Community Resources, Inc. Garden City, FA FSC BSW field placement working with attitudinally-challenged "baby boomers"
2006–2008	Youth for Anarchy, Inc. Central Falls, FA Progressive responsibilities, ranging from telephone intake to case management
2009–2010	Bleeding Hearts for Welfare Rights, Inc. Fenwick Heights, FA CCEF field placement: organizing clients for self advocacy and self-help

Other Experience

2010 - Present	Chief Cook and Bottle Washer
	FSC Dining Center. Fenwick, FA
2005–2007	Candy Striper
	Medicaid Mill Hospital
	East Checheepee, FA

Other Information

Proficient in conversational Spanish

Completed In-Service Training Program, Community Resources, Inc.
  Topics: Psycho-social assessments, DSM IV orientation and
        grant writing

CCEF Social Work Student of the Year, 2000

CPR certified

References: Available upon request

Index

"a," "an," "the," 265
abbreviations, 293
active *vs.* passive voice, 259, 273–274
adjectives, 264
adjudicated family with multiple issues
case. *See* family social history,
adjudicated family with multiple
issues
adverbs, 264
advocacy letter, same-sex marriage
corrected version, 127–128
explanations of corrections, 127–128
original version, 126
advocacy writing, 16
agency-, community-level documentation,
15
agency letter to client. *See* letter, agency
letter to client
agency-based research, quantitative data,
135
"and," 260
annual treatment plan, mental health
diagnosis
corrected version, 95–96
explanations of corrections, 95–96
individual treatment plan, 92–94
original version, 92–94
apostrophes, 264, 278–279
articles, direct *vs.* indirect, 265
Austin American-Statesman, 259–260
averages, medians, standard deviations,
137, 139–140

blogs, 112
brackets, 280–281

cable television, 111–112
capital letters, 274–275
case documentation, purposes, 11
Catalog of Federal Domestic Assistance,
201
categories, 261–281
child neglect case. *See* emergency motion,
child neglect
children at risk, Gramme family case
case file, original version, 25–26
corrected version, 27–28
explanations of corrections, 27–28
family background, 25
clauses, phrases, incomplete sentences,
269–270
clichés, 295
client progress notes case. *See* disabilities,
client progress notes
client records, writers rules, 14
colons, 267, 276
comma splicing, 268
commas, 276–277
communication conventions, 1
community needs assessment, deaf and
hard of hearing residents
corrected version, 63–66
explanations of corrections, 63–66
needs assessment summary,
60–62
compound predicates, 266
compound *vs.* complex sentences, 267
conjunctions, 264, 269–271, 277
contact information, 113
content, 112
contractions, 259
court letters, 12–13, 15

crisis planning, psychotic episode
  abbreviations in document, 89
  corrected version, 90–91
  explanations of corrections, 90–91
  family members in document, 89
  original version, 89

daily newspaper giveaways to the rich. *See* let-
    ter to editor, daily newspaper giveaways
    to the rich
dashes, hyphens, 279–280
Data, Assess, Plan (DAP) notes, 14–15
data collection, 139
deaf and hard of hearing assessment. *See* com-
    munity needs assessment, deaf and hard
    of hearing residents
disabilities, client progress notes
  corrected version, 99–100
  explanations of corrections, 99–100
  original version, 97–98
disabilities, status notes, progress notes
  corrected version, 104–107
  explanations of corrections, 104–107
  original version, progress notes, 102–103
  original version, status notes, 101–102
  progress notes, correction, 107
  status notes, correction, 104–106
Dorn, E., 259–260
drafts, 260
Driver family. *See* family assessment, Driver
    family case

email list call to action. *See* letter, email list call
    to action
emergency motion, child neglect
  abbreviations in document, 80
  corrected version, 82–83
  explanations of corrections, 82–83
  original version, 80–81
  participants in document, 80
  summary of facts, 80–81
emergency motion, family court
  abbreviations in document, 84
  corrected version, 86–88
  explanations of corrections, 86–88
  original version, 84–85
  participants in document, 84
English as second language, 263
English language, word usage, 261

executive summary
  corrections, 176–177
  explanation of corrections, 176–177
  original version, 175

family assessment, Driver family case
  abbreviations in document, 18
  corrected version, 20–24
  explanations of corrections, 20–24
  family members in document, 18
family court case. *See* emergency motion,
    family court
family social history, adjudicated family with
    multiple issues
  abbreviations in document, 73
  corrected version, 76–79
  explanations of corrections, 76–79
  family members in document, 73
  original version, 73–75
focus group reports
  data, 178
  process, 178
  surveys *vs.,* 178
focus group reports, parents and teachers program
  corrected version, 184–189
  executive summary, 183
  explanations of corrections, 184–189
  original version, 179–183
frequency distributions, 137–140
frequency distributions, client report
  abbreviations, 142
  explanations of corrections, 151–158
  original version, 142–150

Gramme family case. *See* children at risk,
    Grammer family case
grant application, letter of support
  corrected version, 252–253
  explanations of corrections, 252–253
  original version, 250–251
grant application, letter to for-profit corporation
  corrected version, 218–220
  explanations of corrections, 218–220
  original version, 216–217
grant application, letter to private foundation
  corrected version, 212–215
  explanations of corrections, 212–215
  original version, 209–211
grant application, small religious or family
    foundations

corrected version, 206–208
explanations of corrections, 206–208
original version, 203–205
grant application, state mental health
     department
corrected version, 225–229
explanations of corrections, 225–229
original version, 221–224
grant writing. *See also* press releases, public
     announcement of grant
activities, interventions, 200
available grants, 201–202
collaboration, 201
evidence, 200
funding organizations, 199
government agencies, large foundations, 199
information included, 201
inputs, 200
logic model, 200–201, 203
outcomes, 200
outputs, 200
Requests for Proposals (RFPs), 199
smaller grants, 199–200
"theory of change" and, 201
Grants.gov (website), 201
A Guide to Funding Resources, 201

Hacker, Diana, 261
HBSE. *See* Human Behavior in the Social Envi-
     ronment
HHS Grants Forecast, 202
homophones, homonyms, confusing words,
     281–290
Human Behavior in the Social Environment
     (HBSE), practice and policy
advocacy writing, 16
agency-, community-level documentation, 15
case documentation, 11–15
cases, assessments overview, 17
client records, writers rules, 14
closing cases, 12
content, 13
court letters, 12–13, 15
Data, Assess, Plan (DAP) notes, 14–15
incidents reporting, 12
new cases, opening, 12
professional writing skills, 13–14
progress monitoring, 12
rules to follow, 15
Subjective, Objective description (SOAP), 14
writing format, 13

human service agency
case documentation, 11–12
writing protocols, 3, 11
human service agency protocols, 3

"I" and "E," 291
"I" and "me," 291
incomplete sentences, 268–269
independent clauses, 269–270
individual social history, James mental health
     and substance involvement
abbreviations in document, 68
corrected version, 70–72
explanations of corrections, 70–72
Internet, blogs, social network sites, 112

James mental health, substance involvement
     case. *See* individual social history, James
     mental health and substance involvement
Jones family. *See* self-assessment, Jones family
     case study

labeling, 296
Latin abbreviations, 275, 293–294
letter, agency letter to client
corrected version, 234–235
explanations of corrections, 234–235
letter, email list call to action
corrected version, 240–241
explanations of corrections, 240–241
original version, 238–239
letter of agreement
corrected version, 244–245
explanations of corrections, 244–245
original version, 242–243
letter of support, grant application
corrected version, 252–253
explanations of corrections, 252–253
original version, 250–251
letter, private agency to state agency
corrected version, 248–249
explanations of corrections, 248–249
original version, 245–247
letter to editor, daily newspaper giveaways to
     the rich
corrected version, 120–121
explanations of corrections, 120–121
original version, 118–119
letter to editor, newspaper, 117

letter to editor, weekly newspaper state
constitutional convention
corrected version, 124–125
explanations of corrections, 124–125
original version, 122–123
letter to for-profit corporation. *See* grant
application, letter to for-profit corporation
letter to private foundation. *See* grant
application, letter to private foundation

medical social work intake, hospital setting
health, mental-health, substance abuse
issues
abbreviations in document, 29–30
explanations of corrections, 32–33
intake note, corrected version, 32–33
intake note, original version, 29–31
patient, family members in document, 29
shorthand, deliberate, 29
mental health diagnosis case. *See* annual
treatment plan, mental health diagnosis
mental health, integrated summary of care
corrected version, 42–44
explanations of corrections, 42–44
original version, 40–41
patient, family background, 40–41
Michigan State University Libraries, 202
misused words, rules of thumb, 290–293
modifiers, 266–267
modifiers, misplaced and dangling, 271–272

new cases, opening, 12
nouns, 261
numbers, 293

opening paragraphs, 260
opinions, 275
oral, written testimony at hearings, 129
original assessment, Tender Mercies Homeless
Shelter (TMHS)
corrected version, 57–59
explanations of corrections, 57–59
over-the-air media, 111–112

parentheses, 280
parentheses and brackets, with punctuation
marks, 281

parole-readiness report
abbreviations in document, 34
corrected version, 37–39
explanations of corrections, 37–39
individuals in document, 34
original report, 34–36
past tense, 263
periods, question marks, exclamation points,
277–278
photos, 112
plagiarism, 295–296
possessive pronouns, 264
practice, 1–2
precision, 260
prepositions, 294
press releases, public announcement of grant
corrected version, 115–116
explanations of corrections, 115–116
original version, 114
print, television media. *See also* traditional media
social policy and, 110–113
professional judgment, 295–296
professional writing skills, 13–14
progress monitoring, 12
pronouns, 261–262, 263–264
psychotic episode case. *See* crisis planning,
psychotic episode
public announcement of grant. *See* press
releases, public announcement of grant
publishing platforms, 111
punctuation, 275–281

quantitative *vs.* qualitative data, 140–141
quotation marks, 279

regular *vs.* irregular verbs, 262–263
research reports
averages, medians, standard deviations, 137,
139–140
data collection, 139
frequency distributions, 137–140
quantitative *vs.* qualitative data, 140–141
survey administration, 139
types, 137
research results reporting, public policy
corrected version, 194–197
explanations of corrections, 194–197
original version, 190–193
resumés, cover letters
appearance, 298

appropriate information, 298
back-up applications, 297
clarity, 298
cover letter, opening address guidelines, 299
font selection, 298
guidelines, 298
outlines, 298
promising applications, 297
resumé length, 298
sample cover letter, 300
unacceptable applications, 297
rules to follow, 15
run-on sentences, 270–271
Rural Assistance Center, 202

satisfaction survey, students at social work program report and executive summary
abbreviations, 167
executive summary, explanation of
corrections, 176–177
executive summary, original version, 175
report, explanations of corrections, 170–174
report, original version, 166–169
school social work, social assessment
abbreviations in document, 45
birth, development, mental history, 45–46
birth, development, mental history corrected
version, 50–51
corrected version, 50–54
explanations of corrections, 50–54
participants in document, 45
social assessment summary, 45–49
self-assessment, Jones family case study, 3
abbreviations in document, 3
corrected version, 6–10
explanations of corrections, 6–8
grammar, 10
punctuation, 9
quotation marks, U.S. *vs.* UK, 9
sentence structure, 9
spelling, 10
word usage, professional language, 10
semicolon, 275
sentence fragments, 267
sentence structure, 263–275
sentence types, 268
sentences composition of, 261–263
small grants, 135
small religious or family foundations. *See* grant
application, small religious or family
foundations

social network sites, 112
social policy
policy-changing texts, 109
press releases, news coverage, 110–113
social workers and, 109
traditional media and, 110–113
Sommers, Nancy, 261
special interest print media, 111
spelling pointers, 294–295
state mental health department, grant
application. *See* grant application, state
mental health department
status notes, progress notes. *See* disabilities,
status notes, progress notes
subject, verb, predicate, 265–266
Subjective, Objective description (SOAP), 14
subjects, objects, 262, 264
subordinate clauses, 270
survey administration, 139
survey report to state legislature, gun ownership and domestic violence
corrected version, 162–165
executive summary, 165
explanations of corrections, 162–164
original version, 159–161
syntax, 272–273

Tender Mercies Homeless Shelter (TMHS). *See*
original assessment, Tender Mercies
Homeless Shelter
thank-you letter, politician
corrected version, 256–257
explanations of corrections, 256–257
original version, 254–255
thank-you letter, state department
corrected version, 237
explanations of corrections, 237
original version, 236
"that," "which," 292
thesis development, 259
"to be," 260
"toward," "towards," 292
traditional media
cable television and, 112
competition among, 111–112
contact information and, 113
content and, 112
Facebook and, 112
Internet, blogs, social network sites and, 112
over-the-air, cable media and, 111–112
photos and, 112

traditional media *(continued)*
  publishing platforms, 111
  social policy and, 110–113
  special interest print media, 111
  strategies, 21
Twitter, 112

verb conjugation, 262–263
verb noun agreement, 272
verb tense, 272–273
verbs, 262–263

weekly newspaper state constitutional
     convention. *See* letter to editor, weekly
     newspaper state constitutional convention
"who," "whom," "that," 292–293
wordiness, trite modifiers, 260
A Writer's Reference (Hacker, Sommers), 261
writing format, 13
writing, writing errors
  "a," "an," "the," 265
  abbreviations, 293
  active *vs.* passive voice, 259, 273–274
  adjectives, 264
  adverbs, 264
  apostrophes, 264, 278–279
  articles, direct *vs.* indirect, 265
  brackets, 280–281
  capital letters, 274–275
  categories, 261–281
  clauses, phrases, incomplete sentences, 269–270
  clichés, 295
  colons, 267, 276
  comma splicing, 268
  commas, 276–277
  communication conventions, 1
  compound predicates, 266
  compound *vs.* complex sentences, 267
  conjunctions, 264, 269–271, 277
  contractions, 259
  dashes, hyphens, 279–280
  drafts, 259
  English as second language, 263
  English language, word usage, 261
  formal elements of, 2
  homophones, homonyms, confusing words,
    281–290
  human service agency protocols, 3
  "I" and "E," 291
  "I" and "me," 291
  incomplete sentences, 268–269

independent clauses, 269–270
labeling, 296
Latin abbreviations, 275, 294
misused words, rules of thumb, 290–293
modifiers, 266
modifiers, misplaced and dangling, 271–272
nouns, 261
numbers, 293
opening paragraphs, 260
opinions, 275
parentheses, 280
parentheses and brackets, with punctuation
    marks, 281
past tense, 263
periods, question marks, exclamation points,
    277–278
plagiarism, 295–296
possessive pronouns, 264
practice, 1–2
precision, 260
prepositions, 294
professional judgment, 295–296
pronouns, 261–263, 264
punctuation, 275–281
quotation marks, 279
regular *vs.* irregular verbs, 262–263
run-on sentences, 270–271
semicolon, 275
sentence fragments, 267
sentence structure, 263–275
sentence types, 268
sentences, 261–263
spelling pointers, 294–295
subject, verb, predicate, 265–266
subjects, objects, 262, 264
subordinate clauses, 270
syntax, 272–273
"that," "which," 292
thesis development, 259
"toward," "towards," 292
use of "and," 260
use of "to be," 260
verb conjugation, 262–263
verb noun agreement, 272
verb tense, 262–263
verbs, 262
"who," "whom," "that," 292–293
wordiness, trite modifiers, 260
written, oral testimony at hearings, 129
written testimony, domestic partner benefits
  corrected version, 132–133
  explanations of corrections, 132–133
  original version, 130–131